Sentence Strategies for Canadian Students

Reading *Writing Basics*

Geri Dasgupta
Centennial College

Nell Waldman
Centennial College

Nelson
Thomson Learning

Australia • Canada • Denmark • Japan • Mexico • New Zealand • Philippines
Puerto Rico • Singapore • South Africa • Spain • United Kingdom • United States

1120 Birchmount Road
Scarborough, Ontario M1K 5G4
www.nelson.com
www.thomson.com

Canadian Cataloguing in Publication Data

Dasgupta, Geri, 1949–
Reading writing basics : sentence writing strategies for Canadian students

Includes index.
ISBN 0-17-616716-1

1. Reading. 2. English language – Sentences. 3. English language – Grammar.
I. Waldman, Nell Kozak, 1949– . II. Title.

PE1408.D2342 1999 808'.042 C99-931416-5

Editorial Director	Michael Young
Acquisitions Editor	Nicole Gnutzman
Project Editor	Jenny Anttila
Production Editor	Natalia Denesiuk
Production Coordinator	Helen Jager Locsin
Marketing Manager	Kevin Smulan
Art Director	Angela Cluer
Cover and Interior Design	Sue Peden
Compositor	Janet Zanette
Proofreader	Betty Robinson
Cover Images	DiMaggio/Kalish/First Light (runner); Pieter Folkens/Masterfile (whale)
Printer	Webcom

Printed and bound in Canada
1 2 3 4 03 02 01 00

Contents

Preface

Reading Writing Basics is designed to enable students to improve the writing and reading skills that are essential for college and career success. The book focuses on the interrelated abilities to comprehend the meaning of what one reads and to create meaning in one's own writing. Its approach is a fairly nuts 'n' bolts, part-to-whole one. It provides brief, accessible explanations of the rules that govern our use of English grammar and writing conventions, as well as ample opportunity to apply and practise those rules.

A key feature of *Reading Writing Basics* is the thematically linked readings in each unit that engage students, encourage them to read for comprehension through cloze exercises, direct them to both main ideas and specific details, and stimulate them to respond to the ideas through writing or discussion. The themes are diverse, ranging from language in Unit 1 to heroes in Unit 3 to sports in Unit 5. The readings in Units 1 to 5 range in length from single paragraphs to longer selections of six to nine paragraphs.

The text is versatile. Its organization is carefully sequenced, yet it allows teachers to move between units and skills to accommodate student needs. Unit 1, "Getting It on Paper," invites students to look objectively at their writing, and then takes them through key issues of capitalization, punctuation, spelling, and document presentation. Unit 1 also emphasizes skimming, scanning, and active reading skills.

Unit 2, "Recognizing and Writing Sentences," examines the basic building blocks of English sentence structure, including subject, verb, phrase, and clause. Unit 3, "Working with Nouns and Pronouns," expands the kernel provided in Unit 2 with as much theory as is required, backed up by plenty of practice. Unit 4, "Using Verbs," focuses on the fundamentals of verb structure and provides students with sufficient opportunities to practise occasionally problematic issues such as *ed* and *s* endings. Unit 5, "Combining Sentences," encourages students to learn the coordination and subordination strategies that lend coherence and sophistication to their writing.

Unit 6, "Composing Paragraphs," presents an organized approach to both the writing and the reading of clear paragraphs. It provides many examples (some from the previous units) of the topic sentence/supporting detail pattern that distinguishes competently written paragraphs. This unit also presents the principles of writing good summaries, a process that integrates reading and writing skills. Several longer readings with challenging questions complete Unit 6. Appendixes at the end of the text define parts of speech, list irregular verb forms, give tips on using the dictionary, and provide an answer key.

Acknowledgments

We wish to acknowledge the support of people at Nelson, including Jenny Anttila, Natalia Denesiuk, Nicole Gnutzman, Paul Saundercook, Betty Robinson, and Siobhan Dooley. We would also like to express our gratitude to the reviewers, whose detailed responses to the manuscript at early and later stages have enriched the book by providing the perspective of the teaching professional. Those reviewers include Frank Gavin and Michael S. Hume of Centennial College, Jim Liabotis of Fanshawe College, and Iris Rich-McQuay of University College of the Cariboo.

Geri Dasgupta and Nell Waldman
July 1999

"It is a river, this language."
(Carl Sandberg)

UNIT ONE

Getting It on Paper

Unit 1 explores the nature of written language and then focuses on what your writing looks like when other people read it. The concepts you need to learn are listed below. (After you finish the unit, you can look back at this box to see whether you understand the key ideas.)

1. How We Write English
2. Capitalization
3. Punctuating the End of a Sentence
   - 3.1 The Period
   - 3.2 The Question Mark
   - 3.3 The Exclamation Mark
4. Spelling: Three Strategies for Improvement
   - 4.1 Sort Out the Deadly Sound-Alike Words
   - 4.2 Outsmart the Spell Checker
   - 4.3 Learn to Spell Contractions
5. How Your Finished Document Should Look
6. Skimming, Active Reading, and Scanning

HOW WE WRITE ENGLISH

... for there is so gret diversite
In Englissh and in the writyng of oure tongue

Can you read these lines? They probably require some translation for most of us. Here is what they say:

... for there is great diversity
In English and in the writing of our tongue
("tongue" here means language)

Well, that's true. There are a lot of differences in the way that people communicate in English. Just listen to someone from Scotland speak your language; you'll probably need a translator for that, too! Is the first example above just poorly spelled and odd in terms of its syntax (word order)? *Englissh* with two *s*'s? *Gret* for *great*? An *e* on *oure*?

No; in fact, the first quotation was written by one of the "gret" poets of the English language, Geoffrey Chaucer. Chaucer lived in the fourteenth century, and he wrote *Troilus and Criseyde,* the poem from which these lines are taken, in the 1380s. His spelling and syntax were perfectly correct at that time, but the language has changed dramatically since then.

That's the thing about language generally and English specifically. It is a changing, dynamic means of communication. For instance, words come into style and go out of style. Sometimes they even come back again: think of *cool* meaning *good*. *Cool* (as in a "cool dude") was a slang term in the 1950s and has returned with a vengeance nearly fifty years later. We hear it—and use it—all the time.

It's not just words that change, though. The way we speak, the accents we have, the sentences we put together all reflect the world in which we live. A change of place (from Australia to Jamaica, let's say) or a change in time (e.g., 1850 to 2000) causes many changes in both spoken and written language. The language we speak changes quickly. The language we write changes more slowly, but, as the lines from Chaucer show, it changes significantly over time.

PRACTICE 1

Copy the lines below. Make sure that you spell, space, and punctuate the lines exactly as they are written on the page.

It is more blessed to give than to receive.

To every thing there is a season, and a time to every purpose under heaven.
A time to be born, and a time to die;
A time to sow, and a time to reap;
A time to kill, and a time to heal;
A time to break down, and a time to build up.

—The Bible

It was a Sunday afternoon, wet and cheerless: and a duller spectacle this earth of ours has not to show than a rainy Sunday in London.

—Thomas De Quincey, *Confessions of an English Opium-Eater*

It is a truth universally acknowledged that a single man in possession of a good fortune must be in want of a wife.

—Jane Austen, *Pride and Prejudice*

All happy families resemble one another, but each unhappy family is unhappy in its own way.

—Leo Tolstoy, *Anna Karenina* (translated from Russian)

Now go back and look at what you've written. Is the handwriting readable? Better yet, pass it to someone else and see whether that person can read it. Did you capitalize *Sunday* and *London*? Did you spell *receive* and *season* and *families* correctly?

Even though most of us will use computers with word processing capability at work, the look of our handwriting says something about us. In fact, professional graphologists analyze handwriting to discover the writer's character. There are things about our handwriting we cannot change or disguise.

Nevertheless, forming letters legibly, distinguishing between lower- and uppercase letters, leaving enough white space between words, using correct spelling and punctuation, and thinking about the appearance of our writing are all part of our responsibility when we communicate. If we don't care about what the piece of writing looks like, we won't communicate at all. No matter how well chosen our words are, we cannot get our message across if the reader can't decipher them.

PRACTICE 2

Below you'll find some handwriting samples. Some are clear and legible; others aren't. Pretend you're a graphologist and decide what the writing says about the person who wrote it. Here are some adjectives you might apply. (Use your dictionary if you don't understand some of the words.) Or you can come up with your own adjectives.

creative	careful
messy	thoughtful
intelligent	disorganized
unreadable	dull-witted
bright	incisive
careless	untidy
elegant	aloof
devious	distinguished
sloppy	conscientious

It is more blessed to give than to receive.

It is more Blessed to give than to recieve

It is more blessed to give than to receive.

IT IS MORE BLESSED TO GIVE THAN TO RECIEVE.

To everything there is a season, and a time to every purpose
under heaven.

To everything there is a season, and a time to
every purpose under heaven.

To everything there is a season, and a time
to every purpose under heaven.

To everything there is a season, and a time
to every purpose under heaven.

It was a Sunday afternoon, wet and cheerless; and a duller
spectacle this earth has not to show than a rainy Sunday
in London.

It was a Sunday afternoon, wet and cheerless
and a duller spectacle this earth has not to show
than a rainy Sunday in London.

It was a Sunday afternoon, wet and
cheerless; and a duller spectacle this earth
was not to show than a rainy Sunday in London.

It was a Sunday afternoon,
wet and cheerless: and a duller
spectacle this earth has not to
show than a rainy Sunday in
London.

It is a truth universally acknowledge that a single man in possession of a good fortune must be in want of a wife.

It is a truth universally acknowledged that a single man in possession of a good fortune must be in want of a wife.

It is a truth universally acknowledged that a single man in possession of a good fortune must be in want of a wife.

It is a truth universally acknowledged that a single man in possesion of a good fortune must be in want of a wife.

All happy families resemble each other, but each unhappy family is unhappy in its own way.

All happy families resemble each other, but each unhappy family is unhappy in its own way.

All happy families resemble each other, but each unhappy family is unhappy in it's own way.

All happy families resemble each other, but each unhappy family is unhappy in it's own way.

cApitALiZaTioN

The word above looks strange because it is an incorrect mixture of upper- and lowercase letters. As you know, CAPITAL letters (also known as uppercase letters) look different from lowercase letters. It's not just their size that is different; the actual shape of the letters and their relationship to the line are different, too. Lowercase letters such as *f, g, j, p, q,* and *y* dip below the line on which they're written. Except for *Q*, uppercase letters stay above the line (whether it's a line you can see or one that you can't). Practise distinguishing between uppercase and lowercase letters. It's an important factor in making your writing legible.

A	a	B	b	C	c	D	d
E	e	F	f	G	g	H	h
I	i	J	j	K	k	L	l
M	m	N	n	O	o	P	p
Q	q	R	r	S	s	T	t
U	u	V	v	W	w	X	x
Y	y	Z	z				

Now that we're clear about what capitalization is, what words get the CAPITAL LETTER TREATMENT? There are six rules to remember.

Rule 1: The first word of every sentence and the word *I*

We always take the car to school.
The storm blew in some fresh air.
The boss and I had a huge fight.

Rule 2: Names of particular places or organizations

Nova Scotia	Cedarbrae Collegiate
Baffin Island	Lake Michigan
Toronto-Dominion Bank	Jupiter
Asia	Ottawa
Yonge Street	University of Calgary
United Nations	Vancouver Canucks
Canada	Pacific
the Rockies	the St. Lawrence

Capitalize the term only if it is a *specific* place or organization. Don't capitalize *general* names. (The general names of the specific examples above are listed on the next page.)

province	high school
island	lake
bank	planet
continent	city
street	university
international organization	hockey team
country	ocean
mountains	river

Rule 3: Names of people

Leonardo Di Caprio	Oprah Winfrey
Nancy Lopez	Wayne Gretzky
Will Smith	Gwyneth Paltrow
Homer Simpson	Avril Benoit

Don't capitalize a title unless it is used before a proper name.

Premier Mike Harris	Meet the premier.
Pope John Paul II	She wants to be pope.
Dr. Martin Luther King, Jr.	You should see a doctor.
Prince Charles	He's a prince of a guy.
Uncle Rufus	Do you remember your uncle?
President Mandela	Who will be president?

Rule 4: Days of the week, months of the year, holidays, but *not* seasons

Monday	January
Rosh Hashanah	Thanksgiving
July	Wednesday
winter	spring

Rule 5: Titles of books, magazines, newspapers, articles, stories, movies, TV shows, songs, but not *kinds* of shows or books

All My Children	soap opera
Titanic	movie
Toronto Sun	newspaper
Ally McBeal	television show
War and Peace	novel

Something to note: titles such as those above—books and TV shows, for example—are written in *italic* print, *the typeface that slants to the right.* If you're not using a word processor that is capable of producing italics, make sure that you underline titles.

Rule 6: Names of languages or peoples, historical events, and documents

Spanish (language)
the Chinese (people)
Hebrew
the Renaissance
Europeans
Guyanese
Urdu
the Constitution
World War II
North American Free Trade Agreement

PRACTICE 3

Supply words and capitalize them where needed.

1. David and Winnie will join us on Saturday.
2. _________________ is my favourite _________________ player.
3. _______________ you know how to speak ________________?
4. Roger and _________________ know how to skate.
5. The largest country in the ______________ is ______________.
6. _____________ Aunt Minnie is married to my _____________.
7. _________________ like to ski in the _________________.
8. _________________ favourite movie star is ________________.
9. Thanksgiving comes in the _________________.
10. _______________ you like to have dinner on _______________ evening?

PRACTICE 4

Correct the capitalization where necessary.

1. Seneca college is a good place to study.
2. My uncle Vladimir only speaks russian.
3. Next Summer we hope to take a trip to the Ocean.

4. why do I have to take english?

5. a new Grocery Store is being built on carver street.

6. People of the islamic Faith fast during ramadan.

7. the x-files is a good Television show.

8. Her Family likes to spend the Summer on lake titicaca.

9. I read a good book about chinese families called the joy luck club.

10. did you know that Singer celine dion is from quebec?

PUNCTUATING THE END OF A SENTENCE

The end of a sentence is an important boundary in clear writing and can be marked in three ways. Unit 2 will explain exactly what a sentence is. For now, remember that you can use a period, a question mark, or an exclamation mark to signal to your reader that a sentence has come to an end.

. The Period

The dot known as a period or a "full stop" is the stop sign at the end of most sentences. If you are writing by hand, make sure your periods are dark and legible. If you are writing with a word processor, make sure that you include them.

> Golf is a game of skill and patience.
> A sentence starts with a capital letter and ends with a period.
> I know we will have fun.
> Dogs chase cars.

? The Question Mark

The question mark is placed at the end of a sentence that asks a question. Usually you can tell that a sentence asks a question by looking at the word order. Sometimes the sentence begins with a question word such as *what, why, who,* or *where.*

Do you play golf?
What do you put at the beginning of a sentence?
Will we have fun?
Why do dogs chase cars?

Don't use a question mark if the sentence is really just part of a statement.

I wondered whether you play golf.
The teacher asked what should go at the end of a sentence.
He asked if we would have fun.
The veterinarian asked whether our dog chases cars.

! The Exclamation Mark

The exclamation mark is used to add drama or emphasis to a sentence. The key to using the exclamation mark is to save it for special occasions. Use it sparingly! And never use more than one!!! (As you can see, multiple exclamation marks make your writing look hysterical.)

She got a hole-in-one!
Never forget your end punctuation again!
We had such a wonderful time!
The dog has been squashed by the car!

PRACTICE 5

Insert the correct punctuation at the end of each sentence.

1. Have you ever watched the sun rise
2. I asked whether you like to watch the sun rise
3. There's a grizzly bear behind you
4. Did you hear the announcement
5. The flight attendant asked whether we had heard the announcement

Correct the punctuation where required.

6. I need to ask you a question. Where does this bus stop.
7. Don't touch that dial?

8. Don't you know your own limitations!

9. How many languages does he speak.

10. He speaks seven languages!!!!

PRACTICE 6

Read the paragraph below and correct the capitalization. Include correct end punctuation in the blanks.

Every field of Human endeavour has its stars; for example, babe ruth in Baseball or michael jordan in Basketball____ Even an organization known as the linguistic society of america has its champion. Its champion is francis e. sommer, a Man who was fluent in ninety-four languages______

Mr. Sommer grew up in germany and amused himself as a boy by inventing his own Languages. While he was just a schoolboy, he learned swedish, sanskrit, and persian. He later picked up all the major European Languages______ By the late 1920s, when he immigrated to the united states, he knew nearly eight dozen languages. What did a Man of mr. Sommers's amazing talent do for a living____ A shy man, he worked as a Research Librarian at the cleveland public library. In his spare time he wrote textbooks about learning russian, arabic, chinese, and japanese_______

Toward the end of his life, mr. Sommer, who died in 1978, said he had given up learning new Languages because he was experiencing information overload. He said that he was afraid to cram any more words into his head "or some morning i will wake up speaking babel."

(Condensed from "To Masters of Language, A Long Overdue Toast," by William H. Honan. The *New York Times*, December 31, 1997, C21.)

SPELLING: THREE STRATEGIES FOR IMPROVEMENT

Let's get one thing straight at the beginning of our work on spelling: English spelling can be a nightmare! For many complex linguistic reasons, English spelling has developed in weird and not-so-wonderful ways. Often there is a big difference between the way we say a word and the way we spell it. For example:

Where's the *w* sound in *sword*?

Where's the *k* sound in *knife* or the *b* in *climb*?

Why does *four* have a *u*, yet *forty* leaves it out?

What sound does *gh* make? See *ghost*, *enough*, and *brought*.

Why does the *f* sound come in so many varieties? Compare *phone, fax, enough.*

How come the *o* sound can be spelled so many ways—*go, toe, dough, sew, beau*?

How can *one* and *won* sound the same? Or *would* and *wood*?

It's enough to make your head hurt. Spelling English words with confidence is difficult and frustrating, but it is also necessary for communicating clearly in writing. No one wants to read a report, an essay, a letter, or a long e-mail full of misspelled words. It makes the writing look careless, even if the writer has given it time and attention. It's a little like wearing clothes out of your dirty laundry hamper to a job interview. The same talented, energetic "you" is inside those clothes, but the people you're dealing with will have a hard time getting past your grungy exterior.

There are several strategies you can use to improve spelling. Three important ones are included here. Learning them takes some time and effort, but—like getting to the laundromat—it is worth it in the long run.

Strategy 1: Sort Out the Deadly Sound-Alike Words

Many words in English sound alike, but they have different meanings and different spellings. *Here* and *hear* are examples of deadly sound-alike words. (Their official name is *homonyms.*) Study these tricksters, do the exercises (after Strategy 2) to help yourself remember, and learn to recognize the words that present special problems for you.

Allot/a lot

Allot means to give out or assign:

I will allot you each $100.
I hope they allot me an easy job.

A lot means much, many (note that *a lot* is two separate words):

He made a lot of money.
A lot of people came to the meeting.

Are/our

Are is a linking or a helping verb:

They are ugly.
We are going to work.

Our shows ownership:

Our work is finished.
Our plans have changed.

Buy/by

Buy is a verb that means to pay money for something:

Did you buy a house?
He will buy a car.

By is a preposition that means near, before, or through the action of:

The house is by the sea.
I will finish by tonight.
The poem was written by Geoffrey Chaucer.

Hear/here

Hear is a verb that means to listen to a sound:

I hear the music.

Here means at, to, or in this place:

Can we stay here?
The party was here last night.

Its/it's

Its (without an apostrophe) shows possession or ownership:

The lizard ate its food.
We like to keep everything in its place.

It's (with an apostrophe) is a contracted form of the words *it is* or *it has*:

It's time to go.
It's been nice knowing you.

Know/no; knew/new

Know means to have knowledge or understanding:

I know how to cook.
I don't know him.

No is a negative:

We have no bananas.
He is no friend of hers.
No, you can't go.

Knew is the past tense of *know*:

I knew the police would give him a ticket for speeding.
I knew him when we were in school, but then we lost contact.

New means recently acquired, never used:

I have a new car.
Buy some new clothes.

Passed/past

Passed is the past tense of the verb *pass*:

I passed the course.
The jeep passed me on the right.

Past means previous, something that is over:

My past experience is in banking.
Their past life has been difficult, but now they are happier.

Their/there/they're; theirs/there's

Their shows ownership or possession:

Did you see their house?
Their marriage is very happy.

There shows a direction or introduces a thought:

We will go there after lunch.
There are two boys in the tent.

They're is the contracted form of *they are*:

They're fighting with the police.
They're telling us the truth.

Theirs also shows ownership or possession:

The prize is theirs.
The picnic lunch we ate was theirs.

There's is the contracted form of *there is* or *there has*:

> There's lightning in the sky.
> There's been a complaint about you.

Threw/through

Threw is the past tense of the verb *throw*:

> He threw the ball.
> She threw the pizza crust into the air.

Through means passing from one side to the other; it also means finished:

> We drove through the tunnel.
> Let me know when you are through eating.

To/too/two

To means in the direction of something:

> I go to school.
> Did you go to the concert?

Too means also, as well, very, or excessive:

> I would like to go too.
> They were too tired to stay up late.
> She is too lazy.

Two is the number 2:

> I have two surprises for you.
> They have two cars.

Weather/whether

Weather means the condition of the atmosphere:

> I hope we have good weather.
> The weather was cold last week.

Whether expresses a choice or question:

> I want to know whether you are going.
> He'll go whether you do or not.

Whose/who's

Whose shows ownership or possession:

> Whose car is that?
> They know whose fingerprints are on the gun.

Who's is the contracted form of *who is* or *who has*:

> Who's on first base?
> Who's seen the new movie?

Your/you're

Your shows ownership or possession:

> Your pants are on fire.
> Did you do your homework?

You're is the contracted form of *you are*:

> You're my best friend.
> You're going to learn a lot in the course.

One way to keep homonyms straight is to keep a list of words that you often confuse. Here are some more homonyms you may want to remember:

bare/bear	lessen/lesson	rain/reign/rein
coarse/course	miner/minor	right/rite/write
forth/fourth	peace/piece	weak/week
heard/herd	principal/principle	which/witch

Strategy 2: Outsmart the Spell Checker

The strategy described here is closely related to Strategy 1, the Deadly Sound-Alikes. Spell-check foolers are almost homonyms. They don't sound exactly like their evil twin but are close enough to cause problems for you (e.g., *accept/except*). Does your computer know the difference between homonyms and near-homonyms? Maybe yes, but probably no.

Computers and word processing have made a big difference in the confidence with which people spell. Along with typographical errors (such as typing *teh* instead of *the*), the spell-check feature on your word processor will pick up spelling mistakes such as *writting* for *writing, lonly* for *lonely, decieve* for *deceive, truely* for *truly*, and *buisness* for *business*.

But before you decide that you never have to worry about spelling again, take a look at the paragraph below. Try to fix the spelling mistakes. (There are lots of them!) And it has already been run through a spell-check program! Confusing words, such as the Deadly Sound-Alikes in Strategy 1 and many of the contractions in Strategy 3, will not be caught by a spell checker. If your mistake is actually another word—the wrong word—that is spelled correctly, the spell checker won't catch the error. Writing *grate* when you mean *great* will look like a careless spelling error to the person who reads it, but to your computer they're both correctly spelled.

> Have ewe herd about the women who ran at the site of a bare? Goldie was walking in the woods won sonny day hopping to relax and raze her moral. Four she had being working vary hard all weak an needed to take sum time of. Goldie found the woods quite, and soon she felt at piece. Suddenly a bare appeared rite in front of her. She was rally frightened! The bare, of coarse, growled menacingly wen he saw her. Goldie didn't scream for help, butt she turned, ran passed the bare, and started a sharp dissent down the hill she had been climbing. Latter she said that she had leaned a valuable lessen. Never wonder along in bare county!

Explained below are some of the more frequently confused words that a spell-check program won't identify. Study them carefully. You'll get a chance to review them in the practices that follow.

A/an/and

A is used in front of words that begin with a consonant (or a consonant sound):

> a man, a tree, a sizzling day, a university

An is used in front of words that begin with a vowel (or silent *h*):

> an eagle, an aardvark, an unreasonable person, an honest lawyer

And is used to join words or ideas together:

> a man and an eagle, a tree and an aardvark, a sizzling day and an unreasonable person, a university and an honest lawyer

Accept/except

Accept means to receive something:

> I accept payment with credit cards.
> Please accept my apology.

Except means to leave something out:

> You can pay with any credit card except American Express.
> He apologized to everyone except me.

Ask/axe (or ax)

Ask is a verb meaning to put forth a question:

> She will ask him to marry her.
> Ask the teacher.

Axe (ax) is a tool with a handle and sharp blade for cutting down trees:

> He swung the axe with skill.
> Ask him where the axe is.

The two words sound different when they're pronounced: *a-s-k* for the verb versus *a-k-s* for the tool.

Been/being

Been is the past participle of the verb *be*. It is never used alone and it is preceded by the helping verbs *have, has,* or *had*:

> I have been at home.
> She has been sick.

Being is the *-ing* form of the verb *be*. *Being* is used after *am, is, are, was,* and *were*:

> I am being followed.
> They are being stubborn.

Choose/chose

Choose (rhymes with *booze*) is the present tense of the verb meaning to make a choice:

> You should choose your classes before the semester starts.
> I choose you for the team.

Chose (rhymes with *froze*) is the past tense of the same verb:

> I chose bad courses last semester.
> I chose him for the team, but he wasn't a very good player.

Does/dose

Does (rhymes with *fuzz*) is the singular form of the verb *do*:

> Dave does housework.
> Does your friend like tacos?

Dose (rhymes with *toast* minus the *t*) means an amount of medicine:

> Take a good dose of vitamins every day.
> The dose of penicillin wasn't enough to fight the infection.

Find/fine

Find means to locate something:

> I will find time for the project.
> Did you find him?

Fine means good or well; it can also mean a penalty:

> I feel fine.
> She is a fine person.
> You will have to pay a fine for the speeding ticket.

Loose/lose

Loose (rhymes with *juice*) means not fastened together or not too tight:

> I found a lot of loose change at the bottom of my backpack.
> He wore very loose pants.

Lose (rhymes with *cruise*) is a verb that means to be unable to find something or to not win:

> Did you lose the money?
> The Blue Jays lose a lot of games.

Quiet/quit/quite

Quiet means silent:

> Be quiet so the baby can get to sleep.
> The class was very quiet during the test.

Quit means to stop doing something:

> He quit his job.
> I quit smoking.

Quite means very:

The course is quite demanding.
She is quite beautiful.

Suppose/supposed to

Suppose means to guess or assume something:

I suppose you are going with us.
The teachers suppose you do your work yourself.

Supposed to means ought to or should (notice the *d* at the end of the word):

I'm supposed to finish the project by next week.
He is supposed to be home by tonight.

Than/then

Than is used to compare things:

He is taller than I am.
They are richer than we are.

Then means in the past or in the future:

We were living in Saskatoon then.
We will have soup, and then we'll have salad.

Used/used to

Used is the past tense of the verb *use*:

Someone used all the paper.
We used their apartment while they were away.

Used to expresses a state or condition in the past (note the *d* at the end of the word):

I used to work there.
People used to live in that house.

Were/we're/where

Were (rhymes with *fur*) is the past tense of *are*:

The people were happy with the show.
The teams were tied at half time.

We're (rhymes with *fear*) is the contracted form of *we are:*

> We're glad to have friends.
> We're out of here.

Where (rhymes with *care*) refers to position or place:

> Where did you leave my keys?
> I know where you live.

Woman/women

Woman is the singular form of the word meaning female (opposite of *man*):

> One woman stood in the doorway.
> She is a friendly woman.

Women is the plural form of the word meaning female (opposite of *men*):

> Two women stood in the doorway.
> They are friendly women.

Here are some more spell-check foolers to keep in mind:

allusion/illusion	device/devise	moral/morale
altar/alter	decent/dissent	personal/personnel
ascent/assent	elicit/illicit	proceed/precede
desert/dessert	later/latter	

Become your own spell checker! Know what words present problems for you, and make sure that you learn them.

One other factor with a spell checker is the difference between Canadian and American spelling. Most word processors are set up to identify American spelling conventions (e.g., *labor* for *labour, theater* for *theatre, check* for *cheque*). Change your program to accept Canadian spelling conventions, which are closer to British, or simply add the Canadian spellings when the spell checker queries them.

PRACTICE 7

Choose the correct word for each blank.

1. ______________ (Does, Dose) ______________ (your, you're) family ______________ (know, no) ______________ (your, you're) ______________ (hear, here)?

2. __________ (Ask, Axe) Dave to __________ (accept, except) the trophy.

3. __________ (Were, We're, Where) afraid __________ (are, our) phone conversation is __________ (been, being) taped.

4. __________ (Its, It's) about time he decided to __________ (buy, by) us a meal.

5. The handle of the __________ (ask, axe) came __________ (loose, lose), and the blade sailed right __________ (passed, past) his head.

6. Last year when I got a ticket I __________ (choose, chose) to pay the __________ (find, fine).

7. They __________ (were, we're) __________ (suppose, supposed) to __________ (find, fine) out about the __________ (weather, whether) report.

8. __________ (There, Their, They're) __________ (know, no) longer in charge of looking after the __________ (to, too, two) __________ (woman, women).

9. I __________ (knew, new) the __________ (does, dose) of antibiotic you __________ (are, our) taking is __________ (to, too, two) large.

10. Jessa has __________ (been, being) learning Spanish and has become __________ (quiet, quite, quit) fluent.

PRACTICE 8

Choose the correct word for each blank.

1. I ________________ (use, used) to ________________ (choose, chose) a rich dessert after every dinner, but now I've ________________ (quiet, quite, quit) eating ________________ (to, too, two) much fat.
2. I ________________ (hear, here) that you ________________ (passed, past) all of ________________ (your, you're) courses.
3. Do you ________________ (know, no) ________________ (weather, whether) the family is happier now ________________ (than, then) they ________________ (were, we're, where) last year?
4. ________________ (Whose, Who's) car is parked in ________________ (are, our) driveway?
5. ________________ (There, Their, They're) performance lasted for ________________ (a, an, and) hour.
6. ________________ (Were, We're, Where) sure ________________ (to, too, two) ________________ (loose, lose) the game.
7. ________________ (It's, Its) never ________________ (to, too, two) late to ________________ (ask, axe) for forgiveness.
8. The students ________________ (were, we're, where) ________________ (been, being) tested every week.
9. The ________________ (loose, lose) atmosphere of the office is ________________ (find, fine) for ________________ (are, our) business.

10. ____________ (Your, You're) ____________ (suppose, supposed) to feed ____________ (your, you're) ____________ (knew, new) piranha ____________ (its, it's) food each day.

PRACTICE 9

Now see whether you can fill in the blanks correctly from the list below. Use each word only once.

allot	quiet	where
women	its	new
being	woman	it's
their	here	then
through	than	there
threw	who's	loose
been	except	a lot
a	lose	an

1. The child ____________ the ball ____________ the window; ____________ he ran away.
2. ____________ going to go over ____________ and tell them to be ____________ ?
3. Please put the ____________ toy you just bought back into ____________ box.
4. ____________ did they leave ____________ car?
5. Of course, we know she is ____________ honest ____________
6. They are going to ____________ funds to everyone ____________ those two ____________ ; they won't get any money.

7. I am ______________ very careful about sitting in the sun because the ultraviolet rays of the sun have ______________ blamed for causing skin cancer.

8. ______________ time for him to ______________ some weight.

9. ______________ of people like to wear ______________ baggy clothes.

10. ______________ college education is cheaper ______________ in Canada ______________ it is in the United States.

PRACTICE 10

Correct the spelling mistakes and typos in the Goldie story on page 18. There are more than thirty errors (counting the frequently misspelled *bare* for *bear* only once).

Strategy 3: Learn to Spell Contractions

In English, we sometimes squeeze two words into one. That's what contraction means: making something smaller. Notice that the previous sentence began with *that's*. *That's* is the contracted (squeezed together) way of spelling the two words, *that is*. The *i* in *is* gets left out, and it's replaced by an apostrophe ('). An apostrophe is a little comma-like mark placed *above* the line, while a comma is placed *on* the line.

It's acceptable to use contractions when you write. Some people feel that contractions are rather informal and save them for speaking or more casual writing in the same way that a person may wear jeans for some occasions and a suit for others. Both are appropriate—correct—in a particular situation. However, contractions—like khakis or jeans—are becoming more common in a wide range of settings. You should feel comfortable using contractions in your writing as long as you adhere to one important rule: **spell them correctly**.

Here are some commonly used contractions:

Be	Have	
I + am = I'm we + are = we're you + are = you're he + is = he's she + is = she's it + is = it's they + are = they're	I + have = I've we + have = we've you + have = you've he + has = he's she + has = she's it + has = it's they + have = they've	I + had = I'd she + had = she'd you + had = you'd he + had = he'd could + have = could've should+ have = should've would + have = would've
Will	**Not**	**Question Words**
I + will = I'll we + will = we'll you + will = you'll he + will = he'll she + will = she'll it + will = it'll they + will = they'll	do + not = don't does + not = doesn't is + not = isn't will + not = won't was + not = wasn't	what + is = what's why + is = why's where + is = where's who + is = who's

Could've, would've, and *should've* are especially tricky because when we say them they sound like *could of, would of,* and *should of,* and there is no such construction in English. Remember to use *'ve*—not *of*—when you write them.

Using contractions isn't difficult: Contract the two words into one and show where the letters were left out by putting in an apostrophe. (Please note, however, that the apostrophe in a contraction is used only to show where letters have been omitted. This use of the apostrophe has nothing to do with showing possession, a concept that will be discussed in Unit 3.)

The problem with spelling contractions is that they often sound exactly the same as different words with different spellings; for example, *they're/there/their, you're/your, it's/its.* Take a look at the list of deadly sound-alike words on pages 13 to 17, and you'll see just how many of these contractions there are. And, as Strategy 2 points out, a spell-check program on your computer won't catch a misused word if it's spelled correctly. You have to learn to spot them and make sure that you've got them right.

For starters, find five contractions in this section (not including the table above). Then indicate the two words that are contracted.

CONTRACTION	TWO WORDS	
________________	______	______________
________________	______	______________
________________	______	______________
________________	______	______________
________________	______	______________

PRACTICE 11

Write the contraction for the following pairs of words:

you are	______________	they will	______________
what is	______________	does not	______________
I have	______________	you will	______________
where is	______________	will not	______________
we have	______________	he had	______________

PRACTICE 12

Insert the contracted form of the words in parentheses into the blanks.

1. ____________ (I will) never speak to you again if you ____________ (do not) marry him.
2. __________ (He has) always loved you as you ____________ (should have) known.
3. ____________ (Who is) the person who ____________ (is not) coming to the party?
4. ____________ (They are) never going to learn their lesson.

5. _______________ (We have) tried to make friends with them, but _______________ (they are) always too busy to spend time with us.
6. I _______________ (could have) lost the money in the park.
7. _______________ (It is) time to leave for work, _______________ (is not) it?
8. _______________ (She had) met with him before today, but she _______________ (does not) want to discuss it now.
9. _______________ (Why is) the man going with us if we _______________ (do not) know him?
10. _______________ (It has) come to my attention that you _______________ (will not) work overtime for us next week.

PRACTICE 13

Correct the contraction mistakes in the sentences below.

1. Theyve been studying swing dancing with a teacher whos nearly seventy years old.
2. Shes said that its never too late to learn to dance.
3. Theres a man in the class who does'nt know how to dance at all.
4. Hell agree with us once weve signed the contract, wont he?
5. Im sure that the Rottweiler in the street is theirs.
6. Whys the window open if its going to rain?
7. Dont you know that you would of won the match if youd tried harder?

8. "Whos been eating my porridge?" asked the bear who's bowl wasnt quite empty.
9. Its nearly time for us to go home, isnt it?
10. Youve never been late for class before, but if youd gotten here on time you could of written the test.

READING 1

r u lol @ my convo?

We are spending a lot of time and effort learning the conventions of standard English spelling and punctuation. But if you understand the title above or can follow the "conversation" below, you are probably already familiar with the changing world of written language that instant communication on the Internet makes possible:

fluff1:	r u there?
skip707:	wuzup?
fluff1:	n2m
skip707:	ok g/g c ya

For those of you who don't use e-mail or frequent the chat rooms of cyberspace, a translation: Fluff asks Skip if she's there. Skip replies, "What's up?" Fluff responds, "Not too much." Skip signs off with "OK, got to go. See you." The title, *btw* (by the way), is "Are you laughing out loud at my conversation?"

Does this cryptic interchange signal a brave new world of instant communication where people use written language constantly, freely, and creatively? Or is it evidence of the inevitable death of written language as we know it? It is probably too soon to provide a definitive answer. What is clear, though, is that writers must know both codes; they have to be able to communicate in both "official" languages: cyber-lingo and standard written English. The Internet has opened up a wonderful way for people to connect through writing without worrying about the pitfalls of grammar, capitalization, and spelling that make writing painful for many. However, writers still must know the conventions, the "correct" versions, or they will embarrass themselves when their writing goes into the hard copy of a job application letter, business report, or sales document. Using e-mail abbreviations, symbols, lowercase letters, and acronymic spelling in those situations will have their readers *rotfl* (rolling on the floor laughing) at them. For : -) or for : - (.

Fact-Finding

What does "convo" (in the title) mean? What does "n2m" mean? What are the two "official" languages that writers need to know these days?

Main Idea

Circle the sentence that best states the main idea of the passage.

- The kind of writing people use in e-mail is destroying the written language.
- E-mail writing is easier and should replace standard written English.
- It's too soon to tell whether "cyber-lingo" is going to replace standard written English.
- Good writers need to be able to communicate in both e-mail language and standard written English.

What Do You Think?

If you use the Internet, how does your writing on-line compare to the kind of writing you do for, let's say, English class? Which kind of writing is easier to produce? Which kind of writing—on-line or traditional—can communicate more effectively?

HOW YOUR FINISHED DOCUMENT SHOULD LOOK

When you hand in a finished assignment or report, the document should be neat, attractive, and easy to read. You've worked hard on it, and you want your reader to be impressed with both the ideas you're presenting and the appearance of the paper. Taking care of these details shows confidence in your own communication skills as well as respect for your reader.

Paper: Whether you are submitting a word-processed, typed, or handwritten assignment, use standard, white, letter-sized paper. Use only *one* side of the paper.

Spacing and Margins: White space makes your paper more readable. Most academic assignments should be double-spaced (that means you have to skip a line between every line that you write on). If you are writing the assignment by hand, it is *essential* that you double-space your writing. Keep good-sized margins (about 2.5 cm) around all four sides of your paper.

Page Numbers and Title Page: Number all of the pages of your assignment, beginning with the numeral 1. The numbers usually go in the upper right-hand corner of the page (on page 1 you may choose to put it at the bottom of the page). In a paper with more than three pages, you may choose to put your last name in front of the page number (e.g., Wong 5).

Most assignments do not require a separate title page. Simply include your name, the teacher's name, the course name and code, and the date on the upper left-hand side of the first page (double-spaced). Then put the title beneath in the centre of the page. The words in the title should be capitalized except for the very short ones such as *a, an, and, of,* and *the,* unless they are the first word of the title.

Vivian Wong

Professor Rubenstein

Psychology 201

October 1, 2000

Does Parenting Matter?

Most people feel that good parenting is the most important factor in bringing up children who are psychologically healthy. The roles that mothers and fathers

1

If a title page is required, include the same information in a somewhat different order: title, your name, course, teacher, date. Centre the lines, beginning about one-third of the way down the page. Double space. Don't underline or use quotation marks in your title. Page 1 follows the title page.

Does Parenting Matter?

Vivian Wong

Psychology 201

Professor Rubenstein

October 1, 2000

READING WRITING: MORE PRACTICE

Much of the reading you come across in college textbooks and in the workplace explains details or gives you information. To get the most out of your reading, you need to ask yourself three kinds of questions when you read any passage:

1. Facts: What specific information can I find in the reading? (In this text, Fact-Finding exercises help you identify these specific facts and details.)
2. Topic/Inference: What point is this reading trying to make? What can I figure out about the subject of this reading? (Main Idea exercises point you in this direction.)
3. Opinion: Do I agree with the ideas in this reading? How do I feel about the ideas that are presented? (What Do You Think? exercises help you to sort out opinion issues.)

Turn the following paragraph into a polished-looking document. Copy the words as they are, but follow all the guidelines above in terms of spacing, appearance, margins, and title. Do it on your word processor if you use one. Also proofread for one missing end punctuation mark (and capitalization error) and six spelling mistakes. (Your spell checker won't help you find these spelling mistakes.)

READING 2

When Was Language Invented?

When did human beings invent language we really do not no how long ago our human ancestors started talking to each other. Their are no records that tell us when people began to use organized speech sounds—more then grunts and groans—to communicate with other people. Linguists (people who study language) guess that the development of spoken language occurred about 100 000 years ago. They base this estimate on to things. One, the earliest signs of civilization at this time suggest that people were talking to one another. Two, the physical remains (skeletons) reveal the brain size necessary to perform the complex tasks of language. Whenever it happened, it is undeniable that are ability to us language—to name things and to extend ourselves in time—is one of the principal things that makes us human.

Fact-Finding

Sometimes writers call attention to their ideas and hold a paragraph together by numbering points that support their ideas. Underline two facts in this paragraph that are numbered *One* and *Two*.

Main Idea

What main idea is supported by the two points you identified above?

What Do You Think?

Linguists base their theories about the development of human speech on "the earliest signs of human civilization." What might some of these early signs be? What kinds of social activity among our early ancestors would have required speech? (Hint: Think about hunting, food-gathering, and family organization.)

Proofread the next reading, and try to find nine spelling mistakes (misspellings that a spell checker won't find) and six capitalization errors.

READING 3

Our Most Remarkable Invention: Writing

If we aren't sure when human beings began to speak to each other, we have a much better idea of when they began to writ. That's because writing has permanency. It leaves it's mark while spoken language vanishes in the wind. They're are cave paintings that date back about 22 000 years, but true writing developed much latter. Humankind's most amazing invention—writing—made its appearance only about 5000 to 6000 years ago. Interestingly, it seems to have come into being at approximately the same time in far-removed parts of the world among People who had no contact with each other: in Mesopotamia (modern iraq) and in China. We have written records from both of these unrelated cultures that date back to 3500–3000 B.C.E.

The Sumerians had a highly developed civilization in Mesopotamia, and their first written symbols were used to keep agricultural records. They carved their symbols (witch we call "cuneiform" for their wedge shape) into wet clay with a sharp reed. The clay hardened to become a permanent written record of the world of these vanished people.

At around the same time, people in China developed a writing system that was very similar to the one used to write Chinese today. The earliest Chinese writing was carved into wood, shell, or bone, but later writers learned to use a "new technology," brush and ink. The result was the subtle and beautiful calligraphy of Chinese writing with its thousands of symbols.

About 5000 years ago (3000 b.c.e.), the Egyptians developed a complex writing system we have come to know as hieroglyphics. They carved these symbols into metal and stone, but they also revolutionized writing by creating strips of "paper" from the papyrus plant that grows in the Nile delta. The writing of ancient Egypt was used to keep day-to-day records, of course, but it also enabled scribes to record their complex system of history, law, religion, and literature. A parallel development was occurring in India where the earliest writing also appeared in the third millennium B.C.E.

About 3000 years ago, the Phoenicians, sailors and traders in the mediterranean, began to use an alphabet that spread with them. Cuneiform writing, Chinese characters, and hieroglyphics are ideographic writing systems. They are made up of thousands of very complicated pictographic symbols. Alphabetic writing doesn't have nearly as many symbols, and the symbols represent not ideas but the sound of the spoken language. For instance, English uses only the twenty-six characters of the Latin alphabet, but those few letters can communicate the million-or-so-word vocabulary of the language.

The Phoenician alphabet led to other Semitic alphabets, such as Hebrew and Aramaic, the languages of the bible, and arabic, the language of the Koran. It also was an forerunner of the Greek and Latin alphabets. Many linguists think that the development of the alphabet is what made reading and learning available to ordinary people who would not have had the time or capacity to learn the multitude of symbols necessary to right cuneiform or Chinese. But there is little doubt that writing, which enables us to preserve the passed and to communicate with future generations, has being the most remarkable innovation that humans have created. It has led to countless other developments that define human civilization. It's difficult to even imagine a world without writing!

Fact-Finding

Who invented writing? (Hint: Two groups of people seemed to have begun to use it at about the same time.) List, in order, the next groups mentioned in the reading who used written language. Include the dates when linguists think these civilizations started to use writing.

Main Idea

Why is writing so important? What does it enable people to do?

What Do You Think?

Writing is certainly an essential feature of human culture, although not all cultures are literate (able to read and write). What are some of the things that writing enables us to do? How do nonliterate cultures perform these tasks?

Proofread the reading below, and try to find nine spelling mistakes (misspellings that a spell checker won't find) and twenty-three capitalization errors.

READING 4

Growth of a Global Language

The english language is a baby compared to Chinese or Hebrew or Hindi or Greek. Two thousand years ago, when the Romans (led by julius caesar) arrived in Britain, the English Language did not exist. The people on the island spoke Celtic languages. Anglo-Saxon (the earliest version of English) developed about 1500 years ago, but it was spoken by a very small number of people. By 1600, William Shakespeare's time, English was spoken by around six million people, and all of them lived in britain.

However, in the next 400 years, the english language was to achieve a astonishing growth. Today it is spoken by at least 750 million people as either a first or second language. Although far more people (about 1.5 billion) speak chinese, they are mainly concentrated on one continent. English is spoken as a first or as a common second language in North America, australia, large parts of Africa, and the Indian subcontinent, as well as the British Isles.

The reasons for this growth in the use of English our complex. For one thing, People who spoke it where very good at colonizing and plundering other places. For another thing, the language itself is flexible and capable of absorbing the vocabulary, syntax, and even culture of other Languages. Hybrids (mixtures) of English and other languages have sprung up all over the world; for example, Spanglish in Los Angeles, Russlish in moscow, and Japlish in tokyo.

So for batter or worse, English has become a truly Global Language. Millions of people study it as a second language, and it's not an easy on to learn. English is buy far the international language of Business and Technology, the language of sports and hollywood, the language of air travel and Computers, of diplomacy and trade.

Of course, the predominance of english is largely a matter of history and accident. No language is "better" than any other is. But if its your language of birth, or if you've achieved the difficult task of learning it as a second language, you have a advantage in the globalized world of the Twenty-First Century. Be sure that your able to maximize this advantage by learning to use the Language confidently and correctly.

Fact-Finding

What was the earliest version of English called, and how long ago was it used? How many people use English today?

Main Idea

What are some of the reasons for the growth of English as a global language? What are some of the businesses in which English is the language of choice?

What Do You Think?

Can you speak a language other than English? If so, how important do you think your bilingualism will be in your future?

SKIMMING, ACTIVE READING, AND SCANNING

You've completed four readings, each of which deals with language in some way. You have an understanding of the ideas in each reading. Before you complete the next practice in this unit, think about the different ways in which you read.

There is a quick way of reading in which you just get a general sense of the content. This reading technique is called *skimming*. You read the passage without pausing to check difficult ideas or new vocabulary. Skimming is useful when you want to decide whether to read something in more detail. It is a good technique to use when you are doing research and are wondering whether a particular book or article will suit your purpose.

The next sort of reading you do is a slower process. It's called *active reading*. You pay close attention to the actual words, perhaps looking up the precise meaning of some words in a dictionary. You also pay attention to the arrangement of ideas. You may ask yourself questions about the content and the writer's reason for including certain details. Sometimes you have to work hard to grasp the meaning of a reading, which is why this technique is called active reading. This type of reading is useful when you have to understand a reading thoroughly.

Finally, there is a reading technique called *scanning*. When you scan a book or an article, you are looking for a specific piece of information. You know what you want to find. For example, when you use a phone book to look up a number, you scan to locate the name and number as quickly as possible. You certainly don't read every line! Scanning is useful when you need to locate a fact quickly. In fact, you used this technique when you completed the Fact-Finding exercises. There are many reading situations where scanning will serve you well. For instance, you'll get more from a textbook if you scan the table of contents and index, both of which will guide you in finding your information. A short article can be skimmed quickly to give you a sense of what to expect, and then you can scan for the precise item you need.

To complete the following practice, you will have to scan the readings. You have read the passages already, so you are familiar with them. First, ask yourself which reading is most likely to supply the information required; then scan the reading, find the information, and fill in the blank.

PRACTICE 14

Scan Readings 2, 3, and 4 to answer the questions below.

1. Human beings probably began to speak to each other about

   ____________________ years ago.

2. People who study language are known as ________________ .

3. One way to find out when speech developed is to look at ________________ to see if the brain was large enough to allow for the complex tasks of language.

4. Language gives us the ability to ________________ .

5. We know that human beings began to write about ____________ years ago because the ______________ still exists.

6. The writing of the ancient Egyptians is known as ________________, and it dates back to ________________ .

7. The earliest people to develop an ________________ for writing were probably the Phoenicians, who sailed and traded in the ________________ .

8. Using an alphabet rather than ideograms to write a language may make it possible for more people to read and write because they do not have to remember so many ________________ .

9. The ________________ has not been around nearly as long as Chinese, Hebrew, Hindi, or Greek.

10. By the time that Shakespeare was writing his plays (around 1600) about ________________ million people were speaking English.

11. English and other languages, such as ________________ and ________________ , have mixed to form unique hybrid languages in different parts of the world.

12. English has become an international language in many different fields, such as ________________ .

Writing Suggestions

1. Most of the quotations at the beginning of this unit (e.g., from the Bible and Jane Austen) are famous because they speak to deep feelings we have about life. Choose one of the quotations and write a short paragraph that provides an example of the quotation's relevance to real life.
2. Have you ever tried to learn a new language? Did you succeed? Write a short paragraph that describes some of the difficulties you encountered and what satisfaction you got out of learning to speak a second language (if you were successful).
3. What are some of the other ways to communicate nonverbally? (Nonverbally means without speaking or writing.) Body language would be one way. Write a short paragraph that describes an example of nonverbal communication such as body language.
4. If you surf the Internet, write a paragraph that explains what you use it for. Provide examples of the kind of communication you do on-line.

"And the words slide into the slots ordained by syntax."

(Anthony Burgess)

UNIT TWO

Recognizing and Writing Sentences

Unit 2 explains the key elements of the English sentence. The fundamental concepts you need to learn are listed below. (After you have finished the unit, you can refer to this box to see whether you understand the key ideas.)

1. What Is a Sentence?
2. The Subject
3. The Verb
4. Other Things You Need to Know about Sentences
   - 4.1 The Prepositional Phrase
   - 4.2 Clauses: Dependent vs. Independent
   - 4.3 Multiple Subjects and Verbs
   - 4.4 Unusual Word Order: Questions and *Here/There*
5. What We Do When We Read

WHAT IS A SENTENCE?

The basic building block of a piece of writing in English is a unit called the *sentence*. The piece of writing may be almost anything: a business letter, an essay, a short story, or a TV script, for example. Writers line up sentences into paragraphs, and then they build paragraphs into a complete piece of writing. Clearly, though, you have to know how to build a sentence to write anything well. So how do we do that? What goes into a sentence? The basic elements of a sentence are the *subject* and the *verb*. Together, the *subject* and *verb* form the engine that drives the sentence.

Read the piece of writing below. Try to indicate where one sentence ends and the next one begins, using a period (.) as a kind of stop sign between sentences and starting each new sentence with a capital letter. The first two sentences are done for you. (Warning: This exercise is a challenge! It might help to read it out loud.)

READING 1

The World's Ocean

The Earth's ocean water covers seventy-one percent of the planet. We divide the huge connecting body of ocean water into five separate oceans. The five oceans are named (from smallest to largest) the Arctic, the Antarctic, the Indian, the Atlantic, and the Pacific we also talk about "seas" as part of the world's ocean some seas, such as the Dead Sea between Israel and Jordan, do not connect to the ocean other seas such as the Mediterranean have a narrow channel to the ocean other seas share a wide opening with the neighbouring ocean as the Caribbean Sea and the Atlantic Ocean do ocean water forms the major part of our Earth it determines climate and weather patterns it also contains huge amounts of our food clearly the ocean is a major part of the reason that there is life on Earth.

Knowing where sentences begin and where they end is essential for a reader to comprehend what's written. The beginning and end of a sentence are determined not by the number of words, but by what is contained within it.

Now look at the punctuated version of the same paragraph. It's a lot easier to read and understand, isn't it? Compare the following paragraph with the paragraph where you added periods and capital letters. Does your punctuation above match the punctuation on page 43?

The Earth's ocean water covers seventy-one percent of the planet. We divide the huge connecting body of ocean water into five separate oceans. The five oceans are named (from smallest to largest) the Arctic, the Antarctic, the Indian, the Atlantic, and the Pacific. We also talk about "seas" as part of the world's ocean. Some seas, such as the Dead Sea between Israel and Jordan, do not connect to the ocean. Other seas such as the Mediterranean have a narrow channel to the ocean. Other seas share a wide channel with the neighbouring ocean as the Caribbean Sea and the Atlantic Ocean do. Ocean water forms the major part of our Earth. It determines climate and weather patterns. It also contains huge amounts of our food. Clearly, the ocean is a major part of the reason that there is life on Earth.

Let's go back to the terms *subject* and *verb* to see if we can determine how they drive and shape the sentence.

THE SUBJECT

A sentence is about something. The word or words that tell us *who* or *what* the sentence is about are called the *subject.*

Sentence	**Subject**
Fish bite.	Fish
Stars shine.	Stars
The children love the beach.	children
The waves crashed on the shore.	waves
The sea is salty.	sea

The *simple subject* is the word that tells us specifically who or what the sentence is about. Sometimes we refer to the *complete subject* as the whole set of words that describe, specify, or add some information about the subject word.

Sentence	**Complete subject**
Those ugly fish bite.	Those ugly fish
Many distant stars shine.	Many distant stars
The happy children love the beach.	The happy children
The huge waves crashed on the shore.	The huge waves
The deep blue sea is salty.	The deep blue sea

PRACTICE 1

Add a simple subject (a *who* or *what* word) to the sentences below.

1. People swim in the ocean.
2. The ______________________ did not notice the shark.
3. My ______________________ enjoyed the meal at the Key Grill.
4. A (or An) ______________________ slept all night in the backyard.
5. The blue ______________________ looked great on Rocco.

Add a complete subject (more than one word) to the sentences below.

6. ______________________ took a huge chunk out of the swimmer's leg.
7. ______________________ went on a hike in the mountains.
8. ______________________ sat in the living room watching TV.
9. ______________________ will be happy to serve you.
10. ______________________ watched the sun slowly sink into the western sky.

THE VERB

The verb is the most complex—and important—part of the sentence. The verb tells us what the subject *does* or what the subject *is*.

Sentence	**Verb**
Fish bite.	bite
Stars shine.	shine
The children love the beach.	love
The waves crashed on the shore.	crashed
The sea is salty.	is

One way to spot the verb is to look for the time word in the sentence. In other words, look for the word—or words—that changes depending on whether the verb indicates action (or being) now, in the past, or in the future. The verb is the little clock of the sentence. It is the word or set of words that changes because of time. Look at how the verb words change in the sentences below:

Present (now)	**Past (then)**	**Future (to come)**
Fish *bite.*	Fish *bit* yesterday.	Fish *will bite* tomorrow.
Stars *shine.*	Stars *shone* last night.	Stars *will shine* tonight.
The children *love* the beach today.	The children *loved* the beach last summer.	The children *will love* the beach next summer.

PRACTICE 2

Add a verb to the sentences below. Pay attention to the time of the sentence.

1. The sea <u>was</u> very quiet yesterday.
2. I __________________ this assignment by next week.
3. James __________________ the saxophone last night at a club downtown.
4. She __________________ her arm by falling off her skateboard.
5. Birds usually __________________ south to warmer weather in the fall.
6. The *Titanic* __________________ in less than three hours.
7. They always __________________ before they leap.
8. The children __________________ on the beach for hours every day last summer.
9. Daisy __________________ her birthday presents when she gets here.
10. Next week we __________________ for the missing package.

PRACTICE 3

Draw a circle around the verbs in the sentences in Practice 1.

PRACTICE 4

Draw a circle around the subjects in the sentences in Practice 2.

The verb may be a single word in the sentence, but sometimes the verb contains more than one word. Study the sentences below:

I *work* at school.	I *am working* at school.
He *works* at school.	He *was working* at school.
They *worked* at school.	They *have worked* at school.
We *worked* at school.	We *should be working* at school.
You *work* at school.	You *have been working* at school.

In the first column, the verb is a single word: *work, works, worked.* In the second column, the verb is a set of words: *am working, was working, have worked, should be working, have been working.* We will learn more about verbs in Unit 4, but for now you must remember one thing: when the verb ends with *ing,* it *cannot* stand alone as the verb of the sentence. It requires helping verbs to be complete. Used alone, without the helping verb, the *-ing* form of the verb turns a sentence into a sentence fragment. And sentence fragments are something that good writers usually avoid.

Fragment	**Sentence**
Working at school.	I am working at school.
You running on the beach.	You are running on the beach.
Tom being a good sport.	Tom was being a good sport.
Waves crashing on the shore.	Waves will be crashing on the shore.

PRACTICE 5

Add the helping verb(s) to make these sentences complete.

1. Two kids ________________ playing volleyball.
2. Fish ______________________ swimming in the shallow water last night.
3. ________________ you shopping at the mall yesterday?

4. The old man ________________ doing all the work.

5. Her friends ________________ being very nice about the mistake.

6. You ________________ not leaving without me.

7. The moon ________________ shining very brightly tomorrow night.

8. I ________________ leaving for Vancouver next week.

9. The children ________________ watching less television.

10. You ________________ working harder in this course.

PRACTICE 6

Identify the simple subject with an "S" and put a circle around the complete verb in the sentences in Practice 5.

PRACTICE 7

Now go back to the paragraph that you punctuated on page 42. Underline the simple subject and circle the verb in each sentence.

OTHER THINGS YOU NEED TO KNOW ABOUT SENTENCES

So far, the sentences we've been looking at have been pretty straightforward. They proceed from subject to verb (Fish bite = S–V), or perhaps from subject to verb to something that completes the meaning of the sentence.

The children love the beach. = S–V–completer
The sea is salty. = S–V–completer

However, there are a lot of ways to write sentences. Good writers use many different sentence patterns to communicate their meaning. Read the unpunctuated paragraphs in Reading 2 on the next page. Add capital letters and periods (or question marks) where sentences begin and end. The first three sentences are done for you.

READING 2

Sea Questions

People often refer to the ocean as "the deep blue sea." When we hear these words, questions pop into our minds. How deep is the ocean? The average depth of the ocean is about three kilometres where is it deepest in 1962 oceanographers explored and measured the deepest part of the ocean in the Mariana Trench near the Philippines it has a depth of eleven kilometres you and I may need a comparison that we can use for reference to this great depth if the highest mountain in the world (Mt. Everest at over 8800 m) were placed in the Mariana Trench almost three kilometres of water would still cover it

Why is the ocean blue the colours of the sea show us whether much life exists there the deep blue water of the ocean far from land reveals empty seas where little plant or animal life exists this ocean water looks blue because the sun shines on tiny particles in the water when more plant life mixes with the water near the coast the water looks greener there is more abundant animal life near abundant plant life the colour of the water is a clue about the amount of life in it.

The sentences above are more complex grammatically than the sentences in Reading 1 on page 42. To understand them—and the grammar of sentences generally—you need to learn about a few more key sentence elements:

- prepositional phrases;
- dependent and independent clauses;
- multiple subjects and verbs; and
- unusual word order: questions and *here/there*.

The Prepositional Phrase

One part of the sentences in Reading 2 that may have confused you is known as the *prepositional phrase*. The first thing to learn is that a *phrase* is defined as a group of related words that does *not* contain a subject and a verb. See the examples below:

a thin grey line
howling prairie winds
to the lighthouse
running, laughing children
below the surface of the water

Each of these examples contains words that are related; they communicate some meaning. But they cannot be considered sentences because they do not have the essential engine that drives a sentence: a subject and verb. Therefore, we call them *phrases*. (When we talk about hearing the phrases of a song, we mean just a few notes—not the whole song. When we write a phrase, we are writing part—not all—of the sentence.)

The second thing to learn is that a *prepositional phrase* is a special kind of phrase, but one that is difficult to define. Basically, a prepositional phrase is a group of related words that contains a preposition and a *noun* (the name of a person, place, or thing) or *pronoun* (a word that stands in for a noun, such as *it, her, he, me, us*). But what is a *preposition*? Prepositions often express position (*on, at*), direction (*over, under*), or movement (*to, from*). Perhaps the best way to explain prepositions is by showing you some typical prepositions in sample phrases.

Typical prepositions	**Typical prepositional phrases**
across	across the street
after	after the war
at	at the college
below	below the surface
between	between you and me
by	by the edge
during	during the week
for	for us
from	from prison
in	in a hammock
near	near the pool
of	of the water
on	on the shore
over	over the mountains
through	through the crisis
to	to the lighthouse
with	with her

Get to know what prepositional phrases look like. Then remember the most important rule about them: **the subject and verb are never in a prepositional phrase.** A prepositional phrase can be part of a sentence, but it is not, by itself, a complete sentence.

Prepositional phrases can get really tricky when they go between the subject and verb as the sentences below show:

The kids with the dog laughed at us.
Gusts of wind blew the sand in our faces.

You might think that the nouns *dog* and *wind* are the subjects of the sentences, but if you look closely, you'll see that they are part of the prepositional phrases *with the dog*, *of wind*. And the subject, we repeat, is *never* in a prepositional phrase. The subject of the first sentence is *kids* (the verb is *laughed*). The subject of the second sentence is *gusts* (the verb is *blew*). There are other prepositional phrases in the sentences. Can you spot them?

PRACTICE 8

Put a preposition in the blanks below. Circle the prepositional phrase.

1. We went for a walk on the beach.
2. The woman smiled ________ me.
3. The words ________ the love song made her cry.
4. ________ the river and ________ the woods.
5. I sent an e-mail message ________ my friend ________ Vancouver.
6. ________ time ________ the meeting.
7. ________ next week, you will finish the lesson.
8. Sam danced ________ the woman ________ the red dress.
9. The name ________ the child ________ the doll is Robin.
10. ________ the night we saw her face ________ the window.

PRACTICE 9

Now go back to Practice 8 and identify the simple subject in the sentence with the letter "S" and the verb with the letter "V." Two of the word groups are not sentences. Circle their numbers.

PRACTICE 10

Find five prepositional phrases in Reading 2, "Sea Questions."

Clauses: Dependent vs. Independent

Another kind of word group can sometimes confuse you when you are trying to understand sentences. A *clause* is a group of related words that contains a subject and verb. Isn't that the same thing as a sentence? Well, yes and no. An *independent clause* has a subject and verb; it can stand alone as a complete sentence. A *dependent clause* has a subject and verb, but it has another piece that means it can't stand alone as a sentence. Unit 5 will tell you a lot more about combining dependent and independent clauses. But for now, here's the equation:

IC (independent clause) = complete sentence
DC (dependent clause) = not a complete sentence

(By the way, did you notice a group of words in the paragraph above that is not a sentence?)

What is it that makes a group of words with a subject and verb into a dependent clause? Let's go back to the first sentences (independent clauses) we looked at in this unit. Notice that when we *add* certain words to the sentence (interestingly, making the group of words longer) we change the meaning in a way that makes the clause dependent on another clause to complete its meaning.

Independent clause—IC	**Dependent clause—DC**
Fish bite.	If fish bite
Stars shine.	When stars shine
The children love the beach.	Because the children love the beach
The waves crashed on the shore.	Before the waves crashed on the shore
The sea is salty.	Since the sea is salty

When stars shine, what? *Since the sea is salty*, what? These groups of words need another clause—an independent one—to be complete sentences. The independent clause can go before or after the dependent clause. Sometimes the dependent clause even fits inside the independent clause (look below at Practice 11, sentences 6 and 14, for dependent clauses that begin with *that* and *who*). The order of clauses can vary. What can't vary is the requirement to join dependent clauses to independent ones. **A dependent clause all by itself is not a complete sentence.** It is another kind of sentence fragment error.

If fish bite, we leave the water. (DC/IC)

David gets out his telescope when stars shine. (IC/DC)

Because the children love the beach, they can play there for hours. (DC/IC)

We built a sandcastle before the waves crashed on the shore. (IC/DC)

Since the sea is salty, we don't drink it. (DC/IC)

There are a number of words that we use to begin dependent clauses. In the sentences above, you see *if, when, because, before,* and *since* introducing dependent clauses. The list below includes more of these words and shows them used in dependent clauses.

Dependent clause word	**Dependent clause**
after	after we finish our dinner
although	although he never has much money
as	as the man talked
as long as	as long as the rain continues
even if	even if the sun shines
that	that we tried
until	until the show is over
unless	unless you have the ticket
what, whatever	whatever you want
when, whenever	whenever the baby smiles
where, wherever	wherever you go
whether	whether he knew it or not
while	while the teacher is out of the room
who	who spoke to us

PRACTICE 11

Add an independent clause to each of the dependent clauses from the list above. The pattern may be IC/DC, DC/IC, or the DC may come within the IC (in sentences 6 and 14).

1. After we finish our dinner, the entertainment will begin.
2. ______________________________ although he never has much money.
3. As the man talked, ______________________________.
4. As long as the rain continues, ______________________________.
5. ______________________________ even if the sun shines.

6. The ________________ that we tried ________________________ .
7. _____________________________________ until the show is over.
8. Unless you have the ticket, ________________________________ .
9. _____________________________________ whatever you want.
10. Whenever the baby smiles, ________________________________ .
11. ____ wherever you go.
12. Whether he knew it or not, _______________________________ .
13. ___________________________________ while the teacher is
    out of the room.
14. __________________ who spoke to us ______________________ .

PRACTICE 12

Add a dependent clause to the independent clauses below.

1. We will go out for dinner as soon as <u>everyone is here</u>.
2. Anne has a difficult time making decisions because
   ____ .
3. After _______________________________ , I will buy you a ticket.
4. While ________________________________ , the police drove by.
5. The party will be a success if ______________________________ .
6. The professor who ____________________ is an excellent lecturer.
7. Although __________________________ , no one knew the man.
8. Sharks are often found wherever ____________________________ .
9. Unless __________________________________ , it will be difficult
   to find a good job.
10. Last night we stayed out until ______________________________ .

PRACTICE 13

Identify the simple subject ("S") and the verb ("V") of the dependent clauses in Practice 11 and the independent clauses in Practice 12.

Did you notice anything about the punctuation of the sentences in Practices 11 and 12? Some of them have commas; others don't. Where do you use a comma with dependent and independent clauses? When the independent clause comes first, do not put a comma between the clauses. When the dependent clause comes first, put a comma between the clauses. (We will learn more about punctuation in Unit 5, but remember this rule for now.)

IC DC **DC , IC**

PRACTICE 14

Now go back to Reading 2, "Sea Questions." Identify a sentence that has a dependent clause followed by an independent clause. Then find a sentence consisting of an independent clause followed by a dependent clause. Underline the sentences and identify the subjects and verbs in each of the clauses.

Multiple Subjects and Verbs

Sometimes a sentence contains two subjects (officially called a *compound subject*). In the first sentence below, *Wanda* and *Charley* are both subjects of the verb *gave*. In the second sentence *mother* and *father* serve as the multiple subject of the verb *are taking*. Notice that each word (Wanda/Charley/mother/father) could be a subject on its own.

Wanda and Charley gave me a snorkeling lesson.
My mother and father are taking a vacation.

The sentences below have similar meanings, but they do not have a multiple subject. *Along with Charley* is a prepositional phrase, so the subject can't be found in it. What is *as well as their best friends* in the second sentence?

Wanda, along with Charley, gave me a snorkeling lesson.
My parents, as well as their best friends, are taking a vacation.

Verbs can also be found in multiples. Note that a multiple verb (or *compound verb*) is *not* a main verb with its helpers (*are taking*). In a multiple, two or more verbs are joined together and usually linked with *and* or *or*. Any verb in a multiple can stand on its own in the sentence. The sentences below have a single subject (*Wanda, parents*) but multiple verbs (*swims and snorkels, hiked and sailed*):

> Wanda swims and snorkels every day.
> My parents hiked and sailed on their vacation.

Double multiples are also possible. In the following sentences, *Wanda and Charley, parents and best friends* serve as multiple subjects; *prepare and eat, hiked and sailed* are multiple verbs.

> Wanda and Charley prepare and eat only healthy food.
> My parents and their best friends hiked and sailed on their vacation.

Unusual Word Order: Questions and *Here/There*

As we've pointed out before, there is no single method that a writer must use to compose good clear sentences. Usually, the word order of the sentence moves from *subject* to *verb* to something else that completes the meaning of the verb. However, writers can change the usual word order to suit their meaning, as long as they make sure they have a complete subject and verb in the independent clause. One place where the word order is always changed is in a sentence that asks a question.

> Do you like sunshine?
> Where did Walter go?

In the first sentence, the subject, *you*, goes between parts of the verb, *do like*. The non-question word order would be *You do like sunshine*. In the second sentence, *Walter* is the subject of the verb *did go*.

Occasionally writers change the word order of sentences that are not questions. For instance, sentences that begin with *here* or *there* use an inverted word order. The important thing to remember is that *here* and *there* are **never** the subject or verb of the sentence.

> Here is your lunch.
> There will be time for questions later.

In the first sentence, the subject is *lunch* and the verb is *is*. In the second sentence, *time* is the subject and *will be* is the verb. (What is *for questions*?)

PRACTICE 15

Add the subject or verb that will complete these sentences. You can add more than one word if you choose.

1. <u>Did</u> Peter <u>finish</u> his homework?
2. There is ______________________ on television tonight.
3. ____________________ and ____________________ fought like cats and dogs.
4. Are ____________________ taking mathematics next semester?
5. Here ____________________ the recipe for chocolate cake.
6. The good guy and ______________________ never shook hands after the argument.
7. We __________________ and __________________ two videos last night.
8. There __________________ two people in the boat.
9. Why ____________________ you always __________________ in school?
10. There are ________________ and __________________ in the swimming pool.

PRACTICE 16

Identify the simple subject ("S") and verb ("V") in the sentences in Practice 15. Remember three important things about sentences:

- subjects and verbs can be multiples (multiple verbs are different from single verbs with helpers);
- the word order of questions is different; and
- *here* and *there* are never the subject or verb of a sentence.

PRACTICE 17

Now go back to Reading 2, "Sea Questions," which you punctuated on page 48. Look at it again and reconsider the subject and verb of each sentence, including sentences with dependent and independent clauses. Would you change any of the punctuation that you added the first time? Now compare your revised version with the punctuated paragraph below. Analyze the differences between it and your own.

READING 2

Sea Questions

People often refer to the ocean as "the deep blue sea." When we hear these words, questions pop into our minds. How deep is the ocean? The average depth of the ocean is about three kilometres. Where is it deepest? In 1962 oceanographers explored and measured the deepest part of the ocean in the Mariana Trench near the Philippines. It has a depth of eleven kilometres. You and I may need a comparison that we can use for reference to this great depth. If the highest mountain in the world (Mt. Everest at over 8800 m) were placed in the Mariana Trench, almost three kilometres of water would still cover it!

Why is the ocean blue? The colours of the sea show us whether much life exists there. The deep blue water of the ocean far from land reveals empty seas where little plant or animal life exists. This ocean water looks blue because the sun shines on tiny particles in the water. When more plant life mixes with the water near the coast, the water looks greener. There is more abundant animal life near abundant plant life. The colour of the water is a clue about the amount of life in it.

Fact-Finding

Where is the deepest part of the ocean? How deep is it? What colour is ocean water when there is a lot of plant life in it?

Main Idea

A paragraph develops one main idea. Which paragraph focuses on the depth of the ocean? Which focuses on the colour? In which sentence are both of these concepts introduced?

What Do You Think?

What is the value of exploration or scientific study of remote regions of the Earth? Is it worth the money, effort, and risk required to explore the bottom of the ocean or the top of Mt. Everest, for example? Why or why not?

READING WRITING: MORE PRACTICE

Up to this point in Unit 2, we have been looking at the fundamental grammar of the sentence and at individual sentences in isolation. However, when we read and when we write, we block sentences together into paragraphs to determine both specific details and overall meaning. The readings and exercises that follow will help you achieve several goals:

- reinforcement of your understanding of sentence structure;
- improvement of your reading comprehension; and
- introduction to the shape and scope of paragraph structure.

Here's how the next three readings work. Read the selections that follow. At the end of each reading, you will find a series of words, phrases, or clauses. Each of them fits into one of the blank spaces in the reading. Your task is to read the paragraphs for understanding and then find the word or set of words that fits into the blank space. Be careful about the punctuation. The first reading is done for you. Read it over carefully to see how the process works.

READING 3

Sea Turtles

Sea turtles live (D) in all but the very coldest parts of the ocean. They have low streamlined shells and very large powerful flippers (rather than legs) that enable them to swim huge distances. Sea turtles (A) hatch from eggs on the shore. If they are male, they never return to land unless they are sick or injured. If they are female, they come back to shore only to lay eggs (or if they are sick or injured). Even though sea turtles swim across thousands of kilometres of ocean, females manage to return to the warm tropical beach where they were hatched (B) to lay their own eggs. The female sea turtle climbs up on shore, digs a hole, and deposits (F) about a hundred eggs. Then she returns to the ocean. Two months later, 4-cm-long baby turtles hatch. They erupt from their nest together and scurry down the beach (C) to the sea. The hatchlings must avoid (E) both land and sea predators. Sea turtles that reach maturity can be huge; for example, (G) an adult leatherback turtle may weigh as much as 600 kg.

A. . Sea turtles
B. where they were hatched
C. scurry down the beach
D. live
E. . The hatchlings must avoid
F. climbs up on shore, digs a hole, and deposits
G. ; for example,

Fact-Finding

When do sea turtles come onto the land? How large are baby sea turtles? Does the mother sea turtle look after them?

Main Idea

Circle the phrase that best expresses the main idea of "Sea Turtles." What is most of the paragraph about?

- sea turtles as an endangered species
- sea turtles as long-distance swimmers
- how sea turtles reproduce
- the size of baby sea turtles

What Do You Think?

Do you know the difference between an endangered species and a threatened species? Can you provide examples of creatures that are at risk? Is it worth the time and money necessary to protect animals and plants that are threatened with extinction? Why or why not?

Now read the paragraphs on the sinking of the *Titanic* and fit the correct word or words (from the list below the paragraph) into the right blank. Again, be careful to include the punctuation.

READING 4

The *Titanic*

The RMS *Titanic* set sail from Southampton, England, on April 10, 1912. It was the ship's first voyage, and the *Titanic* was the largest and most luxurious ship ever built. She ______________________________ 2228 passengers and crew. Although many passengers were poor emigrants who traveled in steerage, a large number ______________________________ enjoyed the lavish upper decks of the ship. Most people thought that the *Titanic* was unsinkable.

Three days later the ship struck an iceberg about 550 km off the shore of Newfoundland. The *Titanic* was traveling at near top speed ______________________________ In less than three hours, the ship broke in half and sank to the bottom of the Atlantic. The *Titanic* was carrying fewer than half the lifeboats that it needed. Only 705 people survived the sinking. All the rest (over 1500 people) ______________________________ to death in the icy water.

The remains of the *Titanic* were not found until 1985 when Dr. Robert Ballard ______________________________ located it 3810 m below the surface. His pictures of the broken ship and its debris scattered across the ocean floor captivated people's imaginations. The most luxurious and technologically advanced ship of its day was destroyed by a sinister natural phenomenon ______________________________ of the great unsinkable ship remains a powerful symbol for all of us nearly 100 years after the *Titanic* slid beneath the cold Atlantic waves.

A. . The sinking
B. carried
C. , an oceanographer,
D. drowned or froze
E. of extremely wealthy and powerful people
F. even though the crew had been warned about dangerous icebergs in the area.

Fact-Finding

Writers often use numbers and statistics to clarify the ideas they are trying to communicate. In "The *Titanic*," find all of the sentences that have dates or numbers in them, and underline the numbers. Why do you think that the writer has included these numbers?

Main Idea

A paragraph develops one main idea. Then a writer orders the paragraphs in a way that makes sense. Decide which main idea is developed in each of the three paragraphs of "The *Titanic*," and number them 1, 2, or 3.

_____ finding the remains of the *Titanic*
_____ when the *Titanic* sailed and who was on it
_____ how the ship sank

What Do You Think?

There have been many ship, plane, and natural disasters that have killed large numbers of people. Millions have been wiped out in twentieth-century wars. So why do you think that one ship's sinking—the *Titanic* disaster—has had such a powerful hold upon people's imaginations for nearly a hundred years?

The paragraphs below detail the source and power of gigantic tidal waves. Put the correct word or words from the list below into the correct blank. Include the punctuation.

READING 5

Tsunami Waves

We call giant waves "tidal waves," but they are not really produced by the regular tides of the ocean. The correct name is *tsunami* ______________________________ *Tsunamis* are caused by earthquakes or volcanic eruptions in the depths of the ocean floor. In the deep waters of the open ocean, a *tsunami* is usually no more than a metre high. People on a ship cannot feel a *tsunami* in deep water, nor can the waves be seen ______________________________ However, in deep water the *tsunami* waves travel at an astonishing 950 km an hour!

When a *tsunami* reaches the shallow water near a coastline, it can become a monstrously high wall of water. Its speed decreases, but ______________________________ The crest ______________________________ may reach a height of thirty metres and strike the land with devastating force. A *tsunami* crashed into Papua New Guinea in 1998, killing thousands of people. As this tragedy and many other examples show, *tsunamis* are a very dangerous threat to people and property on islands and coastlines.

In 1883, the volcanic eruption of Krakatoa (between the islands of Java and Sumatra) generated gigantic waves of thirty-five metres. Over a thousand villages ____ were swept away, and at least 36 000 people perished because of the *tsunamis* caused by Krakatoa's eruption. In 1896, a *tsunami* ______________________________ ______________ more than 27 000 people dead. In 1946, a submerged earthquake in the Aleutian Islands near Alaska caused a *tsunami* that shook the entire Pacific. The waves, traveling at speeds over 750 km/h, ____ Hawaii in less than five hours. Waves over fifteen metres high crashed into the Hawaiian Islands, killing hundreds of people. Less destructive waves ______________ __________________________ reached the shores of North and South America as well as Australia, almost 11 000 km away. After this disastrous quake-induced set of waves, a *tsunami* warning system was set up in the Pacific ____ they can wreak enormous devastation on people and coastal environments.

A. , a Japanese word meaning "harbour wave."
B. reached
C. on nearby islands
D. from the air.
E. from this Alaskan *tsunami*
F. its height and destructive potential increase tremendously.
G. of a *tsunami*
H. crashed into Japan and left
I. . Although such waves are relatively rare,

Fact-Finding

How many different *tsunamis* at specific times and in specific places does "*Tsunami* Waves" tell you about? Underline each of them.

Main Idea

The main ideas of the first two paragraphs of "*Tsunami* Waves" are included below. Determine the main idea of the third paragraph.

Paragraph 1: *tsunamis*—their cause and the way they travel in the ocean
Paragraph 2: the size and danger of *tsunamis*
Paragraph 3: ______________________________

What Do You Think?

In Canada we don't experience *tsunami* waves, but nature does present challenges. What kinds of climatic or seismic events can have devastating effects in the Canadian environment?

WHAT WE DO WHEN WE READ

What is reading? You might answer that question by saying that reading is recognizing words on the page and being able to say them, but reading is actually a lot more than that. Reading is a process of getting meaning from written words. When you read, you don't simply say the sounds the words represent, nor do you stop to define each word as you come across it. Reading is an integrated process, a result of thinking. You actively create meaning from the writer's words as you read and understand them.

For example, look at the title of Reading 5, "*Tsunami* Waves." Did you know what the word *tsunami* meant when you first read it? Even the word *waves*, which was probably more familiar to you, has two distinct meanings: one is related to the movement of water, the other to a hand gesture.

Now, look at the opening sentences of "*Tsunami* Waves":

> We call giant waves "tidal waves," but they are not really produced by the regular tides of the ocean. The correct name is *tsunami*, a Japanese word meaning "harbour wave."

What meaning do you get from these sentences? For one thing, you're now sure that the "wave" refers to the ocean—not to a waving hand. The first independent clause in the first sentence tells us that the waves we are talking about are very large: "giant," in fact. The second independent clause begins with *but* and tells us that the giant waves are not caused by the normal ocean tides. They must be something out of the ordinary. The second sentence tells us what these huge waves are called (*tsunami*) and the language from which the word is taken (Japanese).

It didn't take you nearly as long to figure out the meaning of the two sentences as it did to read this explanation of how you'd done it. Active reading usually occurs beneath the processes of conscious thought. We read words, relate them to what we know, see how the writer has shaped the thoughts, and integrate all of these processes to determine meaning. Keep these ideas at the back of your mind as you read the following short essay.

The paragraphs below are going to take you on a vacation to Atlantic Canada. Put the correct words from the list below into the correct blank. Include the punctuation.

READING 6

An Ocean Vacation

Thinking about the ocean and ocean creatures has probably put you in the mood for a seaside vacation. So let's go "down east" to the Bay of Fundy, the 150-km inlet of the Atlantic Ocean between New Brunswick and Nova Scotia that is famous for its fast-running tides. In parts of the Bay of Fundy, the difference between high and low tides is as great as twenty-one metres, the highest in the world. It is also an important part of the migratory patterns of several varieties of whales. Whales, of course, ______________________, and their immensity and mysterious beauty make people long to see them. Whale-watching adventures—like the one we're on—are a summertime staple in the Bay of Fundy.

We've checked in to a pretty guesthouse in the town of Digby, Nova Scotia, on the shores of the Bay of Fundy. We've spent two days exploring the historic sites of Annapolis Royal and savouring the famous Digby scallops. Now it's time to see the whales! We board a ten-metre boat along with seven other eager whale watchers. We've brought along binoculars, sunglasses, sun-screen, camera, raingear in case the clouds gather, and a tasty picnic lunch. Our guide, Captain Brian, provides ongoing commentary telling us about the whales ______________________ He also assures us that his crew abides by the guidelines established to prevent harassment of the whales. Our boat won't be chasing, herding, or helping to encircle the whales. It will travel parallel to the whales and maintain a respectful distance from the animals. ______________________ from whale hunting (now mostly outlawed) or pollution. Whale watchers must take special precautions not to disturb or pester the creatures.

We are marvelling at the beauty of the Bay of Fundy as we sail along its sandstone and lava cliffs when suddenly the captain points us in the direction of what looks like sea spray. It's not sea spray, however, but the balloon-shaped spray of a humpback whale exhaling breath through its blowhole. Before long, we're watching a pod (that means group) of twelve- to eighteen-metre-long humpbacks as they cavort in the waves. Humpbacks like to clown around; they "spyhop" (lift their heads and eyes above the surface to look at us), wave their flippers, and slap their tails. We're also treated to the sight of a finback whale, nearly twenty-four metres long. The finback is the fastest whale in the ocean, ______________________. We are delighted by the whales we've seen, and after two hours of watching them, our boat heads back toward Digby. That's when we spot a pair of right whales, mother and nursing calf, lying on the ocean's surface. The right whale was given its name because nineteenth-century whalers dubbed it the "right" whale to kill and hunted it nearly to extinction. There are only about 350 right whales left today, and they are at great risk because of their slowness and their tendency to swim near the surface in shipping lanes as they migrate from their North Atlantic feeding grounds to their winter calving grounds off the coast of Georgia and Florida. We feel awe as we look at this seventeen-metre leviathan and her baby, so huge and yet so fragile.

Whale watching is becoming a very ______________________________ ______________, providing economic growth for seaside towns and environmental education for the people who enjoy it. As we head home after our whale-watching adventure, we agree that it has been as exciting an ocean vacation as we can imagine.

A. swimming up to forty-eight kilometres per hour
B. and other wildlife we're likely to see.
C. popular eco-tourism activity
D. are the largest creatures on our planet
E. Many species of whale are threatened or endangered

Fact-Finding

What is the Bay of Fundy noted for, apart from its high tides? Do people still hunt whales? What does a whale do when it "spyhops"? How many right whales are left today?

Main Idea

In your own words, write the main idea of paragraphs 2 and 3. Paragraphs 1 and 4 are done for you.

Paragraph 1: why the Bay of Fundy is an interesting vacation spot
Paragraph 2: ______________________________
Paragraph 3: ______________________________
Paragraph 4: watching whales has been a fascinating eco-tourism adventure

What Do You Think?

Can you think of other kinds of eco-tourism activities? Where do people like to go to see unusual or remote parts of the world? What is the appeal of such a trip? Does this kind of adventure interest you? Why or why not?

PRACTICE 18

Write your own sentences using the facts and ideas you encountered in Readings 1–4. Try not to just copy the sentences in the readings; use your own words where it's possible. Make sure that your sentences have a complete subject and verb.

1. The largest ocean ______________________________________

   ____ .

2. We usually speak of five different __________________________

   even though one continuous body of ocean water actually covers

   ____ .

3. The world's ocean affects ______________________________

   ____ .

4. The average depth _____________________________________

   about three kilometres.

5. In ______________________________________ found out that

   the Mariana Trench ___________________________________

   ____ .

6. ____ is the mountain

   ____ is the highest

   ____ .

7. Although male sea turtles _______________________________

   ____ , female sea

   turtles ____ .

8. The *Titanic* left ______________________________________

   with ______________________________________ on board.

9. About 550 ______________________________________ , the

   ship ______________________________________ in less than

three hours, taking ______________________________

to the bottom of ______________________________ .

10. The wreckage of the *Titanic* ______________________________

______________________________ .

PRACTICE 19

Complete the paragraphs below by filling in the blanks with details that you read in Readings 5 and 6. Use your own words where possible.

Waves

Earthquakes and volcanic eruptions on the ocean bottom cause ______________ known as ______________. If you were on a boat in the open ocean when ______________________ , you ______________ feel it. However, it could still be traveling at ______________ speed. *Tsunamis* become very dangerous when ______________________________ where they increase tremendously in height. *Tsunami* waves as high as ______________ can ______________ the shore. ______________________ can be incredibly destructive. The *tsunami* waves created by ______________ killed more than 36 000 people in 1883. In 1946 an undersea earthquake ______________________ Islands near Alaska caused *tsunami* waves that crashed into Hawaii in less than ______________ , wiping out ______________________. People who live ______________ must be aware of the danger of ______________________.

Watching Whales in Maritime Canada

The Bay of Fundy is part of the ______________ Ocean, and it flows between ______________ and ______________. It has the ______________ tidal range in the world, as great as ______ metres. Whale watching is a ______________ eco-tourism activity in the Bay of Fundy. Good whale-watching guides make sure that the boats do not ______________ the whales. They keep a respectful

________________ from the animals. A group of whales is known as a ________________. Humpback whales like to ________________________. The fastest-swimming whale is the ____________. The right whale is slow and swims near the surface in shipping lanes; therefore it is ____________________________.

Writing Suggestions

1. Did you see the movie *Titanic*? Write a paragraph describing what you remember best about the film and how it affected you.
2. Have you ever been in a large storm or other natural disaster? Write a paragraph describing what happened and how it affected you.
3. Have you ever seen a whale or other large ocean creature? Write a paragraph describing your experience.
4. What is your idea of a perfect ocean vacation? Write a short paragraph describing it.

"The beginning of all learning is the study of names."

(Aristhenes)

UNIT THREE

Working with Nouns and Pronouns

Unit 3 examines nouns and pronouns and provides more work on the subject of a sentence. The concepts you need to know are listed below. (After you finish this unit, you can refer to this box to see whether you understand the key ideas.)

1. Nouns
   - 1.1 Plurals—More than One
   - 1.2 Subject–Verb Agreement
   - 1.3 Nouns That End with *ing*
   - 1.4 Using Commas to Separate Words in a Series
   - 1.5 Showing Possession
2. Pronouns
   - 2.1 Reflexive Pronouns
   - 2.2 Using Subject/Nonsubject Pronouns
   - 2.3 Subject–Verb Agreement
   - 2.4 Pronoun–Antecedent Agreement
   - 2.5 Pronoun Consistency
   - 2.6 Possessive Pronouns
   - 2.7 Indefinite Pronouns
3. Rewording

READING 1

The Importance of Names

In every cultural tradition, there are stories about the creation of the world and the naming of the things in it. Among the Blackfoot people of Alberta, Napi ("Old Man") is the creator. At first there was only water until Napi formed the Earth from a clump of mud that he took from the bottom of the great lake. Then he created the animals, and next men and women. He taught men and women the names of all things on the Earth and how to live among them. In the Judeo-Christian tradition, Adam, the first man, is given responsibility for naming all the things on the Earth, under the waters, and in the heavens. In the Hindu tradition, Prithu, the first ruler, was the one who named the Earth and all that is in it. Our earliest heroes are those who named.

NOUNS

You know what a noun is: it's a *word that names a person, place, or thing*. There are two sorts of nouns.

1. A *proper noun* names a particular person, place, language, day, month, or religion. (Nell, Dasgupta, Saskatoon, Nova Scotia, Algonquin College, French, Wednesday, October, Islam). Proper nouns are always capitalized.
2. A *common noun* names things. Common nouns are not capitalized unless they begin a sentence. There are two sorts of common noun.
   a. *Concrete nouns* name objects that you can experience through your senses (table, roti, mother, fish, supermarket).
   b. *Abstract nouns* name emotions or ideas (love, boredom, war, infancy, information). The things these nouns name are *not* perceived through your senses; in other words, you could never see or touch these things although you understand what they are.

PRACTICE 1

Underline all the nouns in the following sentences. Use two lines for proper nouns and one line for common nouns.

1. Jack and Jill went up the hill.
2. This little piggy went to market.

3. Mary had a little lamb.

4. Twinkle, twinkle little star.

5. The north wind does blow and we shall have snow.

6. Jack Sprat could eat no fat.

7. Boys and girls come out to play, for the moon does shine as bright as day.

8. Lucy Locket lost her pocket; Kitty Fisher found it.

9. Little Bo Peep has lost her sheep and doesn't know where to find them.

10. Old King Cole was a merry old soul.

Plurals—More than One

As you know, nouns can be singular or plural. In most cases making a noun plural is very simple: you just add *s* to the end of the word. Look at sentence 7 in Practice 1 above: *boys* and *girls* are both plural words.

An easy way to recognize nouns is to look for one of the words that usually comes before them. The marker words are *a, an, the, this,* and *that* for singular nouns, and *the, these,* and *those* for plural nouns.

A baby cries a lot.	Babies cry a lot.
An apple is red.	Apples are red.
The book is on the desk.	The books are on the desk.
This sneaker is mine.	These sneakers are mine.
That car is speeding.	Those cars are speeding.

PRACTICE 2

Add your own appropriate nouns to each of the following sentences. Watch out for singular and plural markers.

1. The ________ of the _______ woke me up from my ______ on the ________.

2. I like ___________ , ____________ , and ____________ on my pizza.

3. _________ likes to ride a __________ at the __________.

4. Whenever ____________ sees the ____________, she is happy.

5. If I win the ______________, I'll get a ______________ and a ____________ right away.

6. We have to leave the ____________ now if we want to catch the ____________.

7. ____________ wants those ____________ over there.

8. I want a _____________ for Christmas.

9. The little _________ runs in the __________ all the time.

10. A ____________ is my favourite kind of ____________.

Irregular Plurals

A few words are exceptions to the plural spelling rule. Look at the plural of *baby* (*babies*) in the examples on page 71. As Unit 1 pointed out, most of the time a spell-check program will catch spelling errors. However, it's useful to be able to prevent the mistake from happening in the first place, and the following rules and Practice 3 will make it easy for you to change singular nouns into plural ones.

Rule 1: A singular word that ends in y—drop the *y* and add *ies*.

fantasy fantasies

Rule 2: A singular word that ends in *s, ch, sh, x,* or *z*—add *es* to the end of the word.

box boxes

Rule 3: A singular word that ends in *f* or *fe*—drop the *f* or *fe* and add *ves*.

wife wives

PRACTICE 3

Make the following words plural; then write a sentence for each plural word.

1. party ______________________________

____

2. buzz ______________________________

____

3. responsibility ______________________________

____

4. thief ______________________________

____

5. kiss ______________________________

____

6. library ______________________________

____

7. country ______________________________

____

8. dish ______________________________

____

9. knife ______________________________

____

10. loaf ______________________________

____

11. army ______________________________

____

12. watch ______________________________

____

13. scarf ______________________________

____

14. strawberry ______________________________

____

15. wish ______________________________

____

Exceptions to the Exceptions

The following two words simply add *s* to make them plural:

roof	roofs
chief	chiefs

There is a set of words that make their plurals in very different ways. Here are some of the more common examples:

Singular	**Plural**
man	men
woman	women
child	children
foot	feet
tooth	teeth
sheep	sheep
goose	geese
mouse	mice
ox	oxen
oasis	oases

PRACTICE 4

Add an appropriate singular word from the list above to each of the following sentences. Then rewrite each sentence using the plural form of the noun.

1. The ______________ runs in the Toronto Rat Race every year.

____

2. My front __________ looks crooked.

____

3. That little _________ scares most adults.

____

4. This __________ likes to read.

____

5. Your ________ fits the slipper, Cinderella.

____

6. An ______ works as a beast of burden in many parts of the world.

____

7. An _________ seems a welcome sight in the desert.

____

8. That __________ wants to be a member of the legislature.

____

9. This Canada __________ migrates south every year.

____

10. The _________ grazes on grass.

____

In all of the sentences in Practice 4, the nouns you had to add were the subjects of sentences, but you know that nouns can be nonsubjects and so be part of the sentence completer, too.

Write your own definition of the subject of a sentence. Compare your version with those of your classmates. Now check Unit 2 (page 43) for the definition given there.

PRACTICE 5

Read the following passage and underline all the nouns in it. Then identify each noun you underlined as proper/common, plural/singular.

First Woman in Space

Does the name Valentina Tereshkova mean anything to you? She was the first woman in space. Before she was recruited into the Soviet space program in 1961, Valentina Tereshkova was an amateur parachute jumper. After an intensive training period lasting two years, Tereshkova was ready for blast-off. As a Soviet cosmonaut, she orbited Earth for three days in June 1963. Later that year, Valentina Tereshkova married another cosmonaut, Andrian Nikolayev. Their baby, born in 1964, aroused great interest as the first, and so far only, child ever to be born to parents who have both been in space. After retiring from the Soviet space program, Tereshkova became a goodwill ambassador for the United Nations and later entered politics.

Subject–Verb Agreement

When two people agree about an issue, their opinions match; they share the same idea. The subject and the verb of a sentence have to agree as well, but what do they have to agree about? They have to agree in terms of number. If the subject is singular, the verb must be singular. If the subject is plural, the verb must be plural. Actually, the difference between singular and plural matters in one verb tense only. Look at the table below. It uses pronouns as subjects—which will be explained later in the unit—but it shows how the verb changes to agree with its subject. Look especially at *he, she,* and *it.*

Person	**Singular**	**Plural**
First	I work	we work
Second	you work	you work
Third	he works she works it works	they work

When you have a singular noun (third person) as the subject of a present tense verb, the verb ends in *s*. See the examples on the next page.

Singular	Plural
That boy play**s** basketball.	Those boys play basketball.
My mother visit**s** her doctor once a year.	My mother and father visit their doctor once a year.
A good joke make**s** me laugh.	Good jokes make me laugh.
Cindy Crawford look**s** good in that red dress.	Cindy Crawford and Tyra Banks look good in those red dresses.
A happy child smile**s** frequently.	Happy children smile frequently.
Canada welcome**s** many American tourists each year.	Canadians welcome many American tourists each year.
A snowflake feel**s** cold.	Snowflakes feel cold.

That seems easy enough doesn't it? Unfortunately, subject–verb agreement is a minefield of potential mistakes for many people. Of course, when the subject and verb are separated from each other, you are more likely to make mistakes with subject–verb agreement. Even if there are words between the subject and the verb, the agreement rule remains in effect.

Complete/Simple Subject Review

In Unit 2 you studied the complete and simple subject. Let's review them in the following practice.

PRACTICE 6

Underline the complete subject and circle the simple subject in each sentence.

1. Suddenly, at 2:11 a.m., James woke up.
2. The humidity of the night had made him hot and sticky.
3. The uncomfortable and stifling heat hadn't woken him.
4. James could feel something tickling his chest.

5. A great, black, hairy, eight-legged tarantula spider crawled across James' chest.
6. The spider and James looked at each other for a moment.
7. James, with infinite care and great precision, brushed the spider onto the floor with his hand.
8. In a shoe next to the bed, the poisonous tarantula landed.
9. One long, hairy leg carefully probed the floor around the shoe.
10. The trembling, relieved man watched as the spider scurried away.

PRACTICE 7

In the following set of sentences, underline the simple subject and the correct verb in parentheses.

1. The cost of new homes in this area (goes, go) up steadily.
2. The choice of which videos to get (is, are) up to you.
3. My sister in the hospital (enjoys, enjoy) visitors.
4. The mess on your bedroom floor and in the closet (needs, need) to be cleaned up.
5. The old man with three dogs (likes, like) to walk for at least an hour twice a day.
6. My neighbours who have six children (wants, want) a bigger house.
7. New steps that encourage more investment (has, have) to be found.
8. *Titanic*, one of the most expensive movies ever made, still (attracts, attract) an audience.
9. A snack before dinner (ruins, ruin) your appetite.

10. These offices down the hall (belongs, belong) to the detective agency.

PRACTICE 8

Complete the following sentences with an appropriate verb in the present tense. Do not use the verb *be* (*is*/*are*).

1. My brothers ________ home every Christmas.
2. These groups ________ rap.
3. The bridesmaids ________ beautiful in those pink dresses.
4. Those Canadians ________ summer more than winter.
5. Happy children ________ frequently.
6. Snowflakes ________ cold.
7. Shapes ________ a number of sides.
8. Sixteen moons ________ around the planet Jupiter.
9. Rick and Jane ________ to my cottage every summer.
10. Those cars ________ gas.

PRACTICE 9

Change the sentences you completed in Practice 8 to singular sentences. You have to be careful with subjects and verbs.

1. ____
2. ____
3. ____
4. ____
5. ____
6. ____

7. ____

8. ____

9. ____

10. ____

PRACTICE 10

Identify and correct any verb that doesn't agree with its subject in the following paragraph.

Tony like ice cream a lot. His favourite flavours include mint chocolate chip and chocolate mousse. These two varieties both involves chocolate. Tony think that mint chocolate chip is a refreshing experience, and chocolate mousse taste rich and creamy to him. His girlfriend, Penny, dislike all ice cream, so Penny eats fresh fruit instead. Tony and Penny never agrees about desserts. However, Penny still believe Tony is a really sweet guy. Maybe all those ice creams makes him so sweet.

PRACTICE 11

Make the following sentences singular. This means you will have to change the subjects and the verbs. In some sentences you also have to change the marker word that comes before the subject. Here is an example.

My best friends visit me every day.
<u>My best friend visits me every day</u>.

1. My brothers think about work all the time.

____

2. Snakes scare little boys more than girls.

____

3. Those girls dislike spiders.

____

4. Rolling stones gather no moss.

____

5. Holidays provide many opportunities to relax.

____

6. Massages relieve tension and stress.

____

7. These women often attend rock concerts in the summer.

____

8. The students think that grammar is easy.

____

9. Grammar rules seem hard to grasp at first.

____

10. Canadians believe in law, order, and good government.

____

PRACTICE 12

Complete the following sentences based on the subjects you are given. The first one is done for you. Be careful with subject–verb agreement.

1. Michael and Peter have been best friends since first grade.
2. Bacon, eggs, and toast ______________________________
3. Basketball ______________________________
4. Spiders, snakes, enclosed spaces, great heights, and the number thirteen ______________________________
5. Vampires and werewolves ______________________________
6. Peanut butter and jelly ______________________________

7. True love ________________________________

8. Red, orange, yellow, green, blue, indigo, and violet ____________

____

9. *Star Wars* ________________________________

10. The subject of a sentence ____________________

Nouns That End with *ing*

Sometimes nouns look like verbs: *playing, swimming, sailing, dancing, writing, reading* are all common activities. However, an *-ing* word is not a verb unless it follows a form of the verb *be.* (See Units 2 and 4.) So what are the words listed in the first sentence? You have to look at their function in a sentence, at what the words actually do and mean.

Peter is reading.
Peter loves reading.
Reading is Peter's hobby.

In the first sentence, the word *reading* is part of a verb. It follows a form of *be.* It tells what Peter is doing now. In the second and third sentences, the word *reading* is a noun. It tells what activity or thing Peter loves or enjoys doing. (An *-ing* noun is officially called a *gerund.*)

PRACTICE 13

Indicate whether the word *in italics* in each of the following sentences is a noun or part of a verb.

1. Children love *playing* in the snow.

2. I am *writing* an essay for Mr. Buchanan.

3. *Shopping* is my sister's favourite hobby.

4. Cindy is *swimming* Lake Ontario next week.

5. The *writing* on the wall has been cleaned off.

6. *Swimming* is my favourite summer sport.

7. The *readings* for next class are listed on the handout.

8. Ali is *playing* the drums in my brother's band.

9. We have been *reading* for about twenty minutes.

10. They are *going* to Florida during March break.

Remember that when you encounter an *-ing* word in a sentence, you have to think about its function—the work it is doing—to determine how to classify it.

Try your own hand at classifying *-ing* words in the following practice.

PRACTICE 14

In each of the following sentences, classify the *-ing* word as a noun or part of a verb.

1. The child tripped when he was running to his mother.
2. I was following your directions, but I still managed to get lost.
3. The information should help your understanding of the issue.
4. Going to the dentist is hardly my idea of fun.
5. Frowning uses more muscles than smiling.
6. I am finding this exercise easier than I thought it would be.
7. The teacher is droning on and on.
8. The buzzing of the flies kept me awake.
9. Visiting your grandmother often requires tact and patience.
10. Is Nick coming to your party next week?

PRACTICE 15

Write a sentence of your own for each of the following words. Use each word as a noun, not as part of a verb.

1. singing

   ____

2. selling

___

3. sleeping

___

4. going

___

5. painting

___

6. dancing

___

7. running

___

8. playing

___

9. waiting

___

10. sailing

___

Using Commas to Separate Words in a List or Series

When you include a list of more than two items in a sentence, put a comma between the items.

> Sun, surf and sand are all part of a great day at the beach.
>
> A herpetologist studies snakes, lizards, alligators or other reptiles.
>
> Violins and cellos are both stringed instruments. (No comma is needed here because there are only two items in the series.)

Actually, there are two correct ways to punctuate the first two sentences above. First, you can place commas between the items, but omit the comma before the *and* or the *or*. This is the pattern in the first two examples above. Second, you can add the comma before the *and* and *or*.

Sun, surf, and sand are all part of a great day at the beach.

A herpetologist studies snakes, lizards, alligators, or other reptiles.

Punctuation standards in Britain prescribe that the comma be omitted before *and/or*. Punctuation usage in the United States prescribes the second: insertion of a comma before the final item in a series joined with *and/or*. In Canada, we get a choice: use the comma before *and/or*, or leave it out. You decide. But once you have decided which pattern of punctuation you prefer, use it consistently. Don't switch back and forth.

The comma rule about items in a series applies to a list of nouns or to other kinds of words. As long as there are more than two items in a series, use commas to separate them.

Jackie wants to go shopping with you, him(,) and me. (pronouns)

Rodolfo is singing, dancing(,) and acting his way to stardom. (verbs)

Robin is going to spend this year learning math, studying computers(,) and looking for a job. (phrases)

PRACTICE 16

Insert commas where necessary in the following sentences. Be consistent in your use (or non-use) of the comma before the final item joined with *and/or*.

1. My favourite sports are swimming jogging biking and basketball.
2. The sign told us not to feed the birds squirrels raccoons or bears.
3. Math data processing accounting and business are the other courses I am taking this semester.
4. Billy loves to celebrate April Fool's Day and Halloween.
5. The salad we ordered was made of Boston lettuce black olives diced potatoes crunchy green beans fresh tuna and hard-boiled eggs.
6. Most of us hope to be able to earn a good salary live in a comfortable home and raise a happy family.

7. We found lots of interesting things in the back seat of Ferdinand's car: a Superman cape a martini shaker two dumbbells a Ouija board a miniature Swiss chalet and a lobster trap.
8. Convenience stores are not supposed to sell cigarettes or other forms of tobacco to children.
9. Your house will sell faster if you weed the flower beds fix the front door paint the living room and tidy up the basement.
10. The project will be completed quickly whether you choose Lisa Eric Bart Roseanna or me as your partner.

Showing Possession

There is another occasion when we add *s* to the end of a word. This has nothing to do with plural nouns or verb endings.

An apostrophe *s* (*'s*) is added to the end of a noun to show possession.

When something is owned or possessed by a noun we can use an *of phrase*, or write *belonging to*. However, most of the time we use an apostrophe and *s* to show ownership. The owner word ends in *'s*.

Jane*'s* book is on the table.

This means: The book *belonging to* Jane is on the table.

Louise*'s* cats are friendly.

This means: The cats *owned by* Louise are friendly.

David*'s* brothers are twins.

This means: The brothers *of* David are twins.

The baby*'s* teeth are beginning to grow.

This means: The teeth *of* the baby are beginning to grow.

The gerbil*'s* nose twitched a lot.

This means: The nose *belonging to* the gerbil twitched a lot.

The crowd*'s* roar was loud.

This means: The roar *of* the crowd was loud.

My neighbour*'s* house has been renovated.

This means: The house *belonging to* my neighbour has been renovated.

What do you do if the word already ends in *s*? You just add the apostrophe after the *s* on the end of the owner word.

We wish we could solve the problem *of* the boys.
We wish we could solve the boys*'* problem.

The exam *of* the students was scheduled at 3:30.
The students*'* exam was scheduled at 3:30.

PRACTICE 17

Eliminate each possessive phrase by using an apostrophe *s* (*'s*).

1. the time of a week ____________________
2. the tail of my cat ____________________
3. the date of the contract ____________________
4. the noise of the air conditioner ____________________
5. the sound of the rain ____________________

PRACTICE 18

Eliminate each possessive phrase by using an apostrophe; the owner words already end in *s*.

1. ideas of the boys ____________________
2. the dog of the Jones ____________________
3. the voices of their guests ____________________
4. the cries of the twins ____________________
5. the wife of Charles ____________________

PRACTICE 19

Rewrite the sentences using *'s* to show ownership in place of the possessive phrase. Here is an example.

I haven't seen the new baby of my sister yet.
<u>I haven't seen my sister's new baby yet</u>.

1. I don't like the cooking of my grandmother.

____

2. Can I borrow the book belonging to David?

____

3. That house is owned by Frank.

____

4. I'll see you in the time of two weeks.

____

5. The car belonging to Linda was broken into last night.

____

6. The scent of the flowers was sweet.

____

7. The colour of your jacket clashes with your pants.

____

8. The noise of the children was too loud to ignore.

____

9. The bark of his dog is worse than its bite.

____

10. The toppings of one pizza were pepperoni, mushroom, onion, and hot peppers.

____

PRACTICE 20

Add possessive apostrophes where appropriate in the following sentences. Be careful not to confuse plurals and possessive words.

1. History provides a catalogue of famous names, but we don't always know each names story; do you know about Helen of Troy?
2. She has become known as the worlds most beautiful woman.
3. Helens story took place around 3000 years ago in ancient Greece.
4. A young Trojan prince named Paris fell in love with her.
5. Secretly, Helen and Paris ran away to his fathers kingdom of Troy.
6. Helens husband, King Menelaus of Sparta, threatened Troy with war if Helen did not return to him.
7. However, Helen loved Paris, and so she refused her husbands demand.
8. When the war began, it was said that Helens beautiful face had launched a thousand ships.
9. Soon Troys army was mobilized by King Priam to defend the city against the Greeks invasion.
10. The Greeks and the Trojans fought bitterly for ten years.
11. The Greeks defeated the Trojans by tricking them with a wooden horse.
12. After so much bloodshed, each sides soldiers were probably grateful when the war ended.

PRONOUNS

What is a pronoun? A pronoun is a word that stands for or takes the place of a noun. (A *pro*noun stands in *for* the noun.) A noun names a person, place, or thing, but a pronoun refers to a noun or another pronoun. Just like nouns, pronouns can be singular/plural and subject/nonsubject.

	Subject	**Nonsubject**
First person singular	I	me
Second person singular	you	you
Third person singular*	he she it	him her it
First person plural	we	us
Second person plural	you	you
Third person plural	they	them

*Pronouns can also express gender:

masculine – he, him; feminine – she, her; neuter – it.

PRACTICE 21

Read the following passage and underline the pronouns you find in it.

The Modern King of Troy

For centuries it was believed the stories of the Greek and Trojan heroes written about by Homer in *The Iliad* and *The Odyssey* were make-believe. However, a German archaeologist, named Heinrich Schliemann, proved the ancient city of Troy had actually existed. As a child, he had loved the ancient Greek myths and heroic legends, and he desperately wanted to believe they were based in fact, not fantasy. Using clues he found in Homer's writing and in the Greek myths, he spent his adult life searching for the location, and then unearthing the ruins, of the city of Troy. Finding it became a mission he never gave up on, and in 1870 he found the site of the ancient city of Troy. It was near the Dardanelles, part of modern day Turkey. Excavations of the site uncovered a walled city, a great fortress, and a royal palace. Many artifacts were also uncovered, including a magnificent jewelled headdress; Schliemann believed Helen herself might actually have worn it.

Reflexive Pronouns

Did you recognize the pronoun *herself*? When we add *-self* or *-selves* to the end of a pronoun, we can use it to refer to the subject again in the same sentence. *-self* pronouns are called *reflexive pronouns*, and they are used to add emphasis to the subject of the sentence.

I can do it by *myself.*
They helped *themselves* to the chocolate cake.
He will meet you at the station *himself.*
We can see *ourselves* out.
Help *yourself* to the salad.

PRACTICE 22

In the space provided in each sentence, write a pronoun to take the place of the noun in parentheses. Here is an example.

(friends) ______________ are always there for you.
They are always there for you.
You can rely on ______________ .
You can rely on them.

1. (mother) a. Dave asked ______________ to lend him $50.

   b. ______________ gave Dave $100.

2. (city) a. ______________ has a population of three million.

   b. More people live in ________ than five years ago.

3. (woman) a. ______________ is in my accounting class.

   b. I see ______________ in my math class too.

4. (players) a. ______________ practised for the big game.

   b. The next game was crucial for ______________ .

5. (son) a. His father gave ______________ an allowance.

b. ______________ works for the weekly allowance.

6. (turtle) a. He keeps ______________ in an aquarium.

b. ______________ is his favourite pet.

7. (love) a. We all need ______________ in our lives.

b. ______________ makes the world go round.

8. (success) a. ___________ doesn't happen without hard work.

b. Most people desire ______________ .

9. (Ms. Grant) a. ______________ doesn't tolerate slackers.

b. You have to pay attention to ______________ .

10. (boys) a. The coach rewarded ______________ with a meal at McDonald's.

b. ______________ won their soccer match.

PRACTICE 23

Read the following passage and insert appropriate pronouns into the blank spaces.

A Canadian First

Roberta Bondar has made __________ a place in the history books. __________ is the first Canadian woman to go into space. Bondar was born in Sault Ste. Marie in 1945, and even as a small girl __________ dreamed of becoming a pilot. __________ had a distinguished academic career before becoming a member of the Canadian Space Agency. Roberta Bondar earned a B.Sc. in zoology and agriculture, following __________ with a Masters degree in experimental psychology. Next __________ gained a Ph.D. and M.D. in neurobiology. During this time, Roberta Bondar also learned to scuba dive and to fly. The pilot's licence, formidable academic credentials, and superb physical conditioning made __________ a natural candidate for the Canadian Space Agency, which works in partnership with NASA. __________ was in the first group of Canadian astronauts to be selected, and NASA trained __________ as an astronaut. __________ was on January 22, 1992, that Roberta Bondar blasted off into space as a Payload Specialist aboard the shuttle *Discovery*. During the eight days __________ was in space, Bondar was responsible for the health and well-being of the shuttle crew, as well as for conducting research into the effects of weightlessness on the human nervous system. Now a professor of space medicine at Ryerson Polytechnic University and associate professor of medicine at McMaster University, Dr. Bondar has earned __________ place among a very select and small group of women who have been in space.

Using Subject/Nonsubject Pronouns

Recognizing these pronouns isn't difficult; it's using them correctly that causes the problems. Look at this sentence:

> My brother and I are allergic to shellfish.

When you speak, you might say, "My brother and me are allergic to shellfish." However, this is not standard English; you can't use *me* as the subject of the verb when you are writing. Because this error only seems to occur when there is a multiple subject, a good way to check whether your pronoun use is correct is to take away the first subject along with the word *and*; that is, remove *my brother and*. You wouldn't say, "Me are allergic to shellfish," would you?

The flip side to this error occurs with multiple nonsubjects. Look at this sentence:

> My parents gave Anne and me a loan.

Sometimes you might be tempted to say, "My parents gave Anne and I a loan." Check to see whether it's correct. You wouldn't say, "My parents gave I a loan," would you? Now you can see that it's not standard English to say, "My parents gave Anne and I a loan." The correct choice is *me*.

PRACTICE 24

Choose the correct pronoun in parentheses for each of the following sentences.

1. Mom taught Matthew and (he, him) how to fish.

2. You and (I, me) like the same things.

3. (She and I, Her and me) were totally bored.
4. The manager gave Stacey and (I, me) a bonus.
5. Mr. Roach spoke to Tom and (I, me) after class.
6. Fires have always fascinated Kate and (he, him).
7. The skaters and (we, us) spectators were frozen.
8. Winston and (they, them) are going on vacation next week.
9. She couldn't see Danny and (I, me) hiding behind the sofa.
10. Eva and (I, me) have been friends for a long time.

PRACTICE 25

Complete each of the following sentences by adding an appropriate pronoun.

1. Mike and ________ always complete our assignments on time.
2. Paula asked my sister and ________ to be her bridesmaids.
3. Did ________ really enjoy the ski trip by yourself?
4. ________ and your family are all invited.
5. We gave ________ and your partner a head start.
6. I've always liked ________ .
7. It's time for ________ and our pets to leave.
8. Frank and ________ want you to come to dinner.
9. That professor gives ________ too much homework.
10. You and ________ have to get together soon.

PRACTICE 26

Complete the following sentences by adding an appropriate pronoun.

1. The idea was for Hans and ________ to take the subway.
2. The information was given to Laura and ________ .

3. She and ________ will be your representatives.

4. You and ________ are really late for our class.

5. The new job has been a success for both George and ________ .

6. I showed the photo to Annette and ________ yesterday.

7. You'll have to do better if ________ want to convince ________ .

8. I was afraid he and ________ would get into trouble.

9. You and ________ understand each other.

10. Those jeans fit ________ but they are too tight for ________ .

Subject–Verb Agreement

Just like nouns, subject pronouns have to agree with their verbs in terms of number: singular or plural. **When you have a third person singular pronoun as the subject of a present tense verb, the verb ends in *s*.**

Person	Singular	Plural
First	I go	We go
Second	You go	You go
Third	She goes He goes It goes	They go

Try this practice with subject–verb agreement.

PRACTICE 27

Choose the correct form of the verb in parentheses for each sentence.

1. She (makes, make) us feel so proud of her achievement.

2. It (is, are) a long time since we have seen our grandmother.

3. You (says, say) you can do it yourself.
4. It (is, are) time for us to leave if we (wants, want) to catch the last bus.
5. He (spends/spend) his money as soon as he (gets, get) it.
6. We (learns, learn) our attitude to life from our parents.
7. (Is, are) you sure it (is, are) your coat? It (looks, look) a lot like mine.
8. They (picks, pick) up their papers from her office.
9. The dog (wags, wag) its tail furiously whenever it (sees, see) me.
10. We (enjoys, enjoy) skiing; it (makes, make) winter our favourite season.

PRACTICE 28

Write complete sentences of your own based on the following subjects.

1. we

 ____

2. you and I

 ____

3. he and his dog

 ____

4. she

 ____

5. they

 ____

6. it

 ____

7. I

____

8. Jack and you

____

9. he

____

10. that girl and her sisters

____

PRACTICE 29

Read the following passage and then rewrite it, changing all plurals to singular forms. You can make your commuter male or female, but make sure your use of gender is consistent. The first sentence is written for you after the passage.

The Heroic Commuter

Commuters are modern day heroes whose quests are to get to work on time. Like knights of old, they battle the elements and overcome obstacles just to get to work. They are the victims of rush hour. They crawl out of bed around 6 a.m. and grab quick cups of coffee. Then they rush off to the station. If they are lucky, they find parking spots right away and make it to the platforms before the trains pull out. Of course, if the commuters are on time, the trains are late! Next, the commuters struggle to find places on the trains. Often no seats are available, so the commuters find standing-room-only spots. Of course, the poor commuters are never able to reach the poles or overhead handles, but since they are unable to move there are no chances for them to fall over. They endure these awful conditions for nearly an hour. When the commuters finally arrive at work, it's no wonder they feel exhausted.

The commuter is a modern day hero whose quest is to get to work on time.

How did you do? It's a tricky exercise, isn't it? You had to pay attention not only to subjects and verbs, but also to all the other words that complete the sentence. Did you make mistakes with *him/them* or *a/the*?

Pronoun–Antecedent Agreement

As you know, a pronoun takes the place of or refers to a noun (name of a person, place, or thing). The word the pronoun stands for or refers to is called a *pronoun antecedent*. (*Antecedent* simply means coming before.) Here is the pronoun rule:

A pronoun must agree with its antecedent in terms of person, number, and gender.

Lorne lost his watch.

In this sentence *Lorne* is the antecedent of the pronoun *his*.

The students missed their teacher.

In this sentence *students* is the antecedent of *their*.

A pronoun must agree with its antecedent in terms of person, number, and gender. *Lorne* is singular and masculine; so is *his*. *Students* is plural and masculine/feminine; so is *their*.

Most of the time you follow this rule without even thinking about it. Look at the previous sentence, for example. You would never say, "Most of the time, you follow this rule without even thinking about him." Let's unpack this sentence and see why you wouldn't use *him*, *her*, *you*, or *them* instead of *it*. What is the pronoun *it* referring to? In this sentence *it* refers to *this rule*. Now, *this rule* is third person, singular, and neuter, so you choose the only pronoun that fits those categories: *it*.

PRACTICE 30

In each of the following sentences, circle the correct pronoun in parentheses and the antecedent of that pronoun.

1. We should all do (your, our) own work on this assignment.
2. Have you all finished (your, their) lunch?
3. When John finishes cooking, (he, it) always cleans up right away.
4. Finish reading the book before (you, I) start your report.
5. If Jane does well this semester, (she, they) is going to take time off next year.
6. When Louise stroked the cat, (she, it) began to purr.

7. The ball hit a spectator and hurt (it, him).

8. The girl carried (her, his) own books.

9. Children should respect (her, their) parents.

10. Do you believe in following (his, your) intuition?

There is another part to this pronoun agreement rule: *vague pronoun reference.* If you describe something as vague, you mean that you don't really understand it because you are not given enough clear information. Vague pronoun reference means the pronoun doesn't refer clearly to any word in the sentence. A vague pronoun will confuse your reader.

> Mike told Eric he was going bald.
>
> She loves working with children in the childcare centre, and one day she would like to have one.
>
> When Don looked at the frog, he croaked.

These sentences all contain a vague pronoun reference, leaving the reader wondering:

> To whom does the word *he* refer? Is Mike or Eric going bald?
>
> What does *one* refer to? What would she like to have? A child or a childcare centre?
>
> To whom or what does *he* refer? Did Don or the frog croak?

To correct the problem and make a vague pronoun clear, you may have to rewrite part of the sentence:

> Mike said Eric was going bald.
>
> She loves working with the children at the childcare centre, and one day she would like to have a child of her own.
>
> When Don looked at the frog, it croaked.

PRACTICE 31

Rewrite any sentence where the pronoun use is vague and the meaning is unclear. Here is an example:

> In England, they call the trunk of a car the boot.
>
> <u>English people call the trunk of a car the boot</u>.

1. Gordon told Sam he would probably fail.

____

2. Jill told Marie she should get her hair cut.

____

3. When Jeff saw the dog, he wagged his tail.

____

4. Kyle loves watching hockey games on TV and he wants to do it professionally.

____

5. Bruce thought of Hamid because he owed him a favour.

____

6. Marcia finished stirring her coffee, rinsed the spoon and drank it.

____

7. At Laurier Academy they have to wear uniforms.

____

8. Jackie loves numbers and she hopes to make a career of it.

____

9. Dean took the pepperoni off the pizza and ate it.

____

10. When my car hit the van, it didn't stop.

____

Pronoun Consistency

A pronoun indicates the point of view of the writing. *I* is first person, *you* is second person, and *he*, *she*, and *it* are third person. You shouldn't change from one person to another unless your meaning demands the change. If you switch person in the middle of a sentence or paragraph for no apparent reason, your reader may get lost because you have changed the point of view. Using pronouns consistently is important if you want to keep your reader with you.

If a student wants to succeed in this course, you should study hard.

This sentence begins in third person (*a student* – she/he), but switches to second person (*you*). How will your studying help him or her succeed? The sentence doesn't make sense. It is confusing for the reader or listener because the pronoun *you* doesn't refer accurately to a student.

Don't mix persons unless your meaning requires it.

Go back to the reading at the beginning of this unit, "The Importance of Names." The last sentence changes the point of view. Why do you think this change is acceptable?

PRACTICE 32

Choose the correct pronoun in parentheses to complete each sentence.

1. Any woman could be a blonde if (you, she, we) would just lighten up.
2. If you want to organize a paragraph (I, you, one) need a topic sentence.
3. We should read the instructions carefully before (you, he, we) assemble the bookcase.
4. A review of the problem indicates that (he, it, they) could have been prevented.
5. Just because you got an A on an assignment, that doesn't mean (one, you, we) should stop trying.
6. He can't make an omelette if (you, one, he) doesn't break a few eggs.
7. How can one appreciate the finer things of life if (you, one, we) doesn't know what they are?
8. A college graduate who can't write a grammatical sentence should be ashamed of (myself, yourself, herself).

9. I enjoy parachute jumping because it's the quickest way (I, you, we) can land.

10. When we got out of the house, the fresh air invigorated (one, you, us).

Possessive Pronouns

You already met a lot of these pronouns in Unit 1 when you studied the Deadly Sound-Alikes. Pronouns do not use an apostrophe to show possession the way that nouns do (*Mike's* beer); pronouns have special forms that are possessive in themselves (*his* beer). There are two sorts of possessive pronouns: those that are followed by a noun (This is *our* house.) and those that are not followed by a noun (This house is *ours*.). Possessive pronouns follow the pronoun antecedent rule too.

Possessive pronouns do not use an apostrophe to show possession.

Possessive Pronouns	**Followed by noun**	**Not followed by noun**
First person singular	my	mine
Second person singular	your	yours
Third person singular	his her its	his hers its
First person plural	our	ours
Second person plural	your	yours
Third person plural	their	theirs

PRACTICE 33

Use a possessive pronoun in place of the noun in italics in each sentence. Here is an example:

> *Denvil's* mother works in a library.
> His mother works in a library.

1. This is *Brandon's* new car.

   ____

2. That isn't *Mark's* essay; it's *Julia's*.

   ____

3. I enjoyed *Tom and Jerry's* ice cream.

   ____

4. The cottage on Fox Island is my *grandparents'*.

   ____

5. The *cat's* whiskers twitched at the sight of the bird.

   ____

6. We listened to *Professor Mary Grabowski's* lecture.

   ____

7. The *bird's* squawk was barely audible.

   ____

8. We ate our own cakes, not your *friends'*.

   ____

9. *Mom's* sweater is in the family room.

   ____

10. The *car's* motor stalled as the lights turned green.

    ____

PRACTICE 34

Add the correct possessive pronoun to each of the following sentences.

1. Jake's mother told him to do __________ homework.
2. She licked __________ ice cream cone carefully.
3. We like ketchup on __________ french fries.
4. You should check __________ work before handing it in.
5. I found __________ gloves in the driveway.
6. My cat chases __________ own tail.
7. They returned __________ library books yesterday.
8. How can he hear anything over the noise of __________ stereo?
9. She drove __________ car into a ditch.
10. The team scored __________ first goal of the season.

PRACTICE 35

Correct any errors in pronoun use you find in the following sentences.

1. Him and me are going to the concert tomorrow.

   ____

2. Its not your's; its mine.

   ____

3. My supervisor and me will attend the meeting.

   ____

4. We should know which car is our's.

   ____

5. The cat licked it's dish clean.

   ____

6. It looks like it's going to rain.

____

7. Is this book her's?

____

8. Frank will give Jane and I a ride home.

____

9. Although its only been a week since its tuneup, I think this car needs maintenance.

____

10. You and him are welcome any time.

____

PRACTICE 36

Read the following passage and then add appropriate pronouns to it. Be consistent in your use of pronouns.

A Great Mother

Simone has a wonderful mother. When I tell __________ this story __________ will understand why __________ admire Mrs. Raduca. When Simone was five years old, __________ felt that one of the measures of maturity was to walk home from school by __________ . For __________ , the most embarrassing moment each day was when ______ mother arrived to take __________ home. __________ was certain all the bigger children thought __________ was a baby.

__________ family lived quite close to __________ school. __________ begged and pleaded with __________ mother, promising to look carefully before crossing the one road on the way home from school. Finally __________ mother agreed, and __________ wrote a letter to Simone's teacher that explained Simone was allowed to come home by __________ . After Simone's teacher read the letter, she smiled broadly and told the little girl that __________ could walk home alone.

At that time Simone couldn't read, and __________ never knew that __________ mother was following __________ home each day at a safe distance. Years later, when Simone did discover the truth, __________ felt grateful that __________ mother had been sensitive enough to respect __________ independence.

Who and *Whose*

Who refers to people, and *whose* is a possessive pronoun. Don't use a possessive apostrophe *s* with *who*. Check Unit 1 for apostrophes used as contractions.

PRACTICE 37

Circle the correct word in parentheses to complete each sentence.

1. (Who's, Whose) coming to dinner tonight?
2. (Who's, Whose) turn is it to pitch?
3. (It's Its) time to take a break.
4. Do you know (who's, whose) dog that is?
5. I think (it's, its) a shame Leo couldn't come with us.
6. I wonder (who's, whose) knocking at the door.
7. (Who's, Whose) going to get the beer?
8. (Who's, Whose) beer is this?
9. The horse won (it's, its) race.
10. (Who's, Whose) your favourite movie star?

Indefinite Pronouns

Look at the chart on the facing page, which contains a list of indefinite pronouns. The pronouns listed in the chart are indefinite because they refer to people or things that are not specified. They are used for making generalized statements:

Everybody knows that.

Now, here is the part that people have difficulty with: *indefinite pronouns are always third person singular subjects*. You know what that means, don't you? Present tense verbs agree with their subjects by ending in *s*.

-*one* words	**-*body* words**	**-*thing* words**	
no one	nobody	nothing	each*
anyone	anybody	anything	either*
everyone	everybody	everything	neither*
someone	somebody	something	none*

**Each, either, neither,* and *none* are often followed by a phrase that begins with *of*.

> *Each of* us deserves a chance.
> *Either one of* the purses matches those shoes.
> *Neither of* the brothers is eligible for the award.

The only exception is *some of*. This phrase takes a plural verb because *some of* means more than one.

PRACTICE 38

Write a sentence in the present tense for each of the following subjects.

1. anybody

   ____

2. everyone

   ____

3. neither of the twins

   ____

4. nothing

   ____

5. each

____

6. no one

____

7. something

____

8. some of

____

9. each one of

____

10. none of

____

11. someone

____

12. anything

____

The use of indefinite pronouns can lead not only to subject–verb agreement errors, but also to pronoun agreement errors.

When we speak, we can say things like the following:

Everyone has their own way of getting the job done.
Anyone who has a question should raise their hand.

In both cases the word *their* is plural, and so it doesn't agree with its singular antecedent. We can't write this way.

It's worth mentioning that if you use a plural pronoun, you can avoid the dilemma of *his/her*. When you don't know the gender of the person the pronoun refers to, an alternative solution is to change the subject pronoun.

We all have our own way of getting the job done.
Most people have their own way of getting the job done.
People with questions should raise their hands.
If you have a question, raise your hand.

PRACTICE 39

Complete each of the following sentences by inserting a correct pronoun.

1. Every snowflake has __________ own shape.
2. All snowflakes have __________ own shapes.
3. Someone has borrowed my book, and I want __________ to return it.
4. Everybody in the theatre leaped to __________ feet and cheered.
5. Nobody is expected to complete __________ assignments before the weekend.
6. If anybody calls, tell __________ I'm busy.
7. Any man who wants to create an impression should wear __________ tuxedo.
8. Each girl brought __________ own soccer ball.
9. No one wants to lose __________ job.
10. Every boy tried __________ hardest to make the team.

PRACTICE 40

Complete each of the following sentences by adding appropriate pronouns.

1. Little Red Riding Hood lost __________ way through the woods.
2. Batman whacked the Joker on __________ funny bone and broke __________ .
3. __________ hand did Luke Skywalker grab?
4. Count Dracula is originally from Transylvania, but now __________ lives in Hollywood.
5. Children have adopted "D'oh!" as part of __________ own speech although __________ was originally Homer Simpson's cry.

6. Aladdin, who had been rubbing __________ lamp for some time, was relieved when __________ genie finally appeared.
7. The third little pig was the one that built __________ house of bricks.
8. Don't __________ wonder what happens to the clothes Superman takes off when __________ transforms from Clark Kent?
9. Will Smith stars in blockbuster movies; __________ have made lots of money for __________ .
10. Scully shot at the shadow, which turned out to be __________ partner, Mulder.

READING WRITING: MORE PRACTICE

So far in Unit 3, we have worked on recognizing nouns and pronouns and using them correctly. In the following readings, you will find four very different heroes. Read each of the selections for understanding. As you read, put each phrase or clause from the list that follows the reading into the correct blank.

READING 2

A Nobel Peace Prize Winner

What do you think of when you come across the word *hero*? Is it someone who was brave beyond expectations, a character in a story or cartoon, an average person who achieves something in spite of the odds, someone who contributes something to our way of life? All of these are possible heroes. One Canadian who achieved ______________________________ ______________________________ Before being elected prime minister of Canada in 1963, Lester Pearson was awarded the Nobel Peace Prize. ______________________ for his work in the United Nations. He began working there in 1943, and he created refugee relief programs and ______________________ Pearson believed the gap between the rich and the poor nations must be closed. As a diplomat, he helped to restore peace in many areas around the world, ______________________ Pearson was responsible for the creation of the United Nations Peacekeeping force; under his leadership, ______________________ This is a tradition most Canadians still feel proud of today. A lot of people don't remember his achievements and their effect on our country's international status; they just know there's an airport named Pearson in Toronto. Now you know why.

A. he received this award in 1957
B. Canada became the first nation to designate certain battalions of its armed forces to be used as international peacekeepers
C. including Israel, Korea, and the Suez Canal
D. heroic stature in the international arena was Lester B. Pearson
E. helped establish the Food and Agriculture Organization, which works to eliminate world hunger

---

Fact-Finding

Answer each of the following questions in a sentence of your own.

1. What award did Lester Pearson win?
2. Where did Pearson work before he became prime minister of Canada?
3. What force did Pearson create at the United Nations?

Main Idea

What is this reading about? In one to three sentences of your own, write the main idea of this passage.

What Do You Think?

1. Do you think Canadians are proud of their role as an international peacekeeper?
2. Did you know about Lester Pearson before you read this passage?

Reading 3

The Great One

Wayne Gretzky only had one dream in his life: to be a professional hockey player. In 1967, when he was only six years old, he scored ______________________ The rest of his teammates were ten years old, so he was the youngest and smallest on the team. Gretzky played for a team in the Brantford Atom League called the Steelers. During the next couple of years, Gretzky established himself as the star player in his league even though the other players were older and bigger than he was. ______________________ in a story about him in a local newspaper; this name was soon transformed into its current form: "The Great One." When Gretzky was fourteen, his parents allowed him to move to Toronto to play junior hockey. This was the only opportunity for him to continue playing hockey at his level of ability. Although ______________________ Gretzky quickly became the star of this league too. During this time, Gretzky grew very close to his "foster family," the Cormishes, and he remains so to this day. Of course, he missed his own parents and younger brother, Brent. He saw them only on weekends when they could come down to Toronto, or if they attended one of his games.

It was when he made the move to the Soo Greyhounds that Gretzky acquired his other trademark: the number 99. Originally he had wanted the number 9 because of ______________________ Gordie Howe, Maurice Richard, and Bobby Hull, but that number was already taken. The coach persuaded Gretzky to try 99, and ______________________ At the end of 1977, Gretzky signed his first professional contract: $1 million to play in the WHA for the Indianapolis Racers. Unfortunately, Gretzky had a poor start with this team and after only eight games, ______________________—the Edmonton Oilers. This was the start of a great career in the NHL, and Gretzky's status as a hockey hero. Now, even though Wayne Gretzky has retired, all across North America young hockey players covet the number 99.

A. it has been his number ever since
B. in 1970, he was officially given his first nickname, "The Great Gretzky,"
C. he was traded to the team where he achieved his first professional success
D. his first goal in team play
E. its association with his own hockey heroes
F. his teammates and opponents were in their late teens and early twenties

REWORDING

This useful technique is also called *paraphrasing,* and it means "putting it in your own words." Helping you understand what you have read or heard is the main reason for rewording. After all, if you can express an idea for yourself, in your own words rather than repeating it exactly, you understand it.

Rewording or paraphrasing is an activity you engage in all the time. When you tell someone about your day, or when you share a conversation you've had with a friend, you reword what has been said to you. You put the information into your own words.

There are a number of benefits to rewording. First, in order to put something into your own words, you have to think it through and to comprehend it. Rewording helps you understand difficult ideas. Second, the process of rewording improves your control of sentence structure and adds to your vocabulary. Third, rewording is a way of taking down information and of getting the facts straight.

To reword a sentence, you have to understand the message the sentence is giving you. You may have to find new words to replace nouns or verbs in the sentence, so you may have to consult your dictionary. You may have to change the sentence structure of the original idea in order to put it into your own words.

Let's try rewording a sentence from the reading about Wayne Gretzky.

> The rest of his teammates were ten years old, so he was the youngest and smallest on his team.

What is the information here?

> Other players were ten years old
> Wayne was smaller and younger

Work those facts into a different sentence structure. For example:

> At age ten, the other players on his team were all older and bigger than Wayne.

Fact-Finding

Find three facts about Wayne Gretzky in the article above and write them in three sentences of your own.

Main Idea

What is this reading about? In one to three sentences of your own, write the main idea of this passage.

What Do You Think?

Do you admire Wayne Gretzky? Is there a celebrity whom you regard as a hero? Why?

Wayne Gretzky is a hero to many people because of his extraordinary success and achievements. In the next reading you deal with a different kind of hero, the leading character in a story. The leading character in a fictional work doesn't have to be noble and successful, or even admirable, for us to use the term *hero*.

There is one word in this story that you may not know. It is *calabash*. A calabash is a large gourd whose shell is used as a container.

Reading 4

Anansi and Common Sense

Long ago, Anansi the spiderman came up with a plan to increase his power and wealth. Anansi decided to collect all the common sense in the world. Then, whenever there was a problem, ______________________________ ______________ Not only would this mean that he would be recognized as the wisest of creatures, ______________________________ Anansi desired respect and wealth. Well, for a long time Anansi collected all the common sense he could find ______________________________ ____________ So that no one would find his precious store, Anansi decided to hide the calabash at the top of the tallest tree. He strapped the calabash to his belly and began the arduous climb up the tree. Now that calabash was bulky, ______________________________ He couldn't climb the tree, no matter how hard he tried. As he groped and struggled at the bottom of that tree, he heard someone laughing; turning back, Anansi saw a small boy.

"How ridiculous you are," said the boy. "If you have to climb that tree, you should put the calabash on your back."

Anansi was so filled with rage when he realized __________________ __________________ that he threw the calabash to the ground. It smashed into millions of bits, and so now nearly all of us in the world have our share of common sense—thanks to Anansi.

A. so he couldn't get a firm hold on the tree and he couldn't move his knees above his waist
B. people would turn to him for help
C. and then he put it into the biggest calabash he could find

D. but he could charge a lot for his sensible advice and so he would become rich
E. there was a piece of common sense he did not own

Fact-Finding

What sort of character is Anansi? Choose three words to describe him, and use information from the reading in your own words to prove that your choice of descriptive words is appropriate.

Main Idea

What do you think this story is about? In one to three sentences of your own, write the main idea of this story.

What Do You Think?

1. Anansi is a well-known hero in Caribbean folktales. Do you know any folktales?
2. Why do you think folktales are told, and why have they endured for so many years?

READING 5

Terry Fox

We probably all recognize the name Terry Fox, and some of us may even take part in one of the many annual Terry Fox runs. These runs, ______________________________ raise millions for cancer research, but do you know why these annual events are named after him? In 1976, when he was just eighteen years old, Terry Fox discovered he had cancer in his knee. The cancer destroyed the bone and his right leg was amputated above his knee. Following the amputation, while ______________________________ Fox came up with his idea of fundraising for cancer research. Once he was fitted with an artificial leg he began the slow and arduous process of learning to walk all over again.

It took him two years to learn to walk, and by 1978, he was training seriously for his goal; ______________________________ His run was called "The Marathon of Hope," and he found corporate sponsors that supplied him with a vehicle, gas, shoes, and money. In 1980, Fox was running quickly enough to believe he was capable of fulfilling his dream, so in April he set out from St. John's, Newfoundland; ______________________________ He expected to arrive in Vancouver by November. He ran from Newfoundland through Nova Scotia, Prince Edward Island, and New Brunswick. Then in Quebec, ______________________________ then it was on to Ottawa, Toronto, and Thunder Bay. All along the way, people would line the streets as he ran through their towns. Every night when he stopped running, Fox would address the crowd, speaking about the need for cancer research. The money poured in from across Canada.

However, the run was not easy for Fox. ______________________________ Even his good leg suffered from the gruelling run he was undertaking. He had an enlarged heart that caused him shortness of breath and dizziness. On the approach to Thunder Bay, Fox began to develop more alarming symptoms. He had a racking cough and debilitating pains in his chest. After ______________________________ His cancer had returned in both lungs. Fox went home to Port Coquitlam, B.C., not by running, as he had hoped, but by air. Even in hospital, while undergoing chemotherapy treatments, Fox continued to focus public attention on the need for cancer research.

He died on June 28, 1981, one day before his twenty-third birthday. His Marathon of Hope had been an enormous success. He had raised more than $24.7 million for cancer research in just 143 days. Terry Fox had run into the hearts of Canadians and they made him their hero.

A. he developed blisters and sores on his stump that bled onto his prosthesis
B. he was in hospital undergoing a long process of radiation and chemotherapy treatment
C. which are named after him
D. he was prepared to run fifty kilometres a day to raise money for his cause
E. his route followed the course of the St. Lawrence into Montreal
F. it was to raise $1 million by running across Canada
G. his arrival in Thunder Bay, Fox was taken to hospital for a check-up

Fact-Finding

Find three facts about Terry Fox in the article above and write them in three sentences of your own.

Main Idea

What is this reading about? In one to three sentences of your own, write the main idea of this passage.

What Do You Think?

What sort of hero is Terry Fox? How does he compare to Wayne Gretzky, Anansi, Lester B. Pearson, or any of the other heroes in this unit?

Writing Suggestions

1. In eight to twelve sentences, discuss your name. Define its meaning, say who chose your name and why. Think about whether you like your name, whether it suits you. Explain why or why not.
2. Find and photocopy an article that gives you more information about one of the people in this chapter. Read it carefully and rewrite some of the information you found interesting. Write eight to twelve sentences, and submit the photocopy along with your writing.
3. Is there someone you regard as a hero? In eight to twelve sentences, write about that person, explaining why you believe he or she is a hero.
4. Who is your favourite fictional hero? It could be someone from TV, movies, books, or cartoons. Explain why you enjoy this character in eight to twelve sentences.

"A verb has a hard enough time of it in the world."

(Mark Twain)

UNIT FOUR

Using Verbs

Unit 4 explains how to use verbs correctly. The fundamental concepts you need to learn are listed below. (After you have finished this unit, you can refer to this box to see whether you understand the key ideas.)

1. Recognizing Verb Tense
2. The Infinitive
3. *Be, Have, Do*
4. Making Verbs Negative
   - 4.1 Using Negative Words
5. Simple Verb Tenses
   - 5.1 The Present Tense
   - 5.2 The Past Tense
   - 5.3 The Future Tense
6. Participle Tenses
   - 6.1 *Be* + *-ing* Verb
   - 6.2 *Have* + Past Participle
7. Consistency of Verb Tenses
8. The Passive Voice
   - 8.1 Forming the Passive Voice
9. Answering Questions

READING 1

Sharing a Language

I remember my very first day as a teacher. It was in the Midlands area of England. I knew that the people who live there have their own distinctive accent, but I was unprepared for the dialect of English they spoke. A *dialect* is a version of a language with its own vocabulary and rules of grammar. As I walked nervously into a class of thirty-eight eager seven-year-olds, I was asked the following question. "Are you our new teacher?" The difficulty was the question didn't sound like that to me at the time. This is what I actually heard: "Am yow us niow taychur?" You can see the grammar rules here are not those of standard English. We don't use *am* with *you*; we don't say *us* instead of *our*. My problem wasn't simply the pronunciation: *yow* instead of *you*; *taychur* instead of *teacher*. I was presented with a different version of the language from the one I grew up with in Yorkshire (where, incidentally, people have their own pronunciation and dialect). In effect, these children were bilingual; they understood my standard English perfectly, but spoke to one another in their dialect. I spent a lot of time during my first week of school smiling and nodding at the children, all the time hoping that what they were telling me wasn't a tale of family tragedy.

Have you ever had trouble understanding someone because of their use of spoken English? When you are talking to other people, their facial expressions help you figure out their meaning. Of course, you can also ask them to repeat something you don't understand. When information or ideas are in writing, you can't stop and ask what the meaning is. As a reader, you are on your own. If a writer uses incorrect grammar or nonstandard English, the reader may not understand the communication. An understanding of the forms and functions of the verbs in standard English is vital if you want to communicate successfully.

The passage, "Sharing a Language," shows you that English has many variations. However, when we want to communicate clearly we have to use standard English.

There are many dialect forms of verbs that can't be used in standard English. There are also slang expressions, involving the use of verbs, that are acceptable in speech but shouldn't be used in standard, written English.

We may say each of the following in informal situations:

I'm gonna see you later.
I ain't bothered.
It don't affect me.
I be here all day.

He knowed what to do.
She done her best.
We been waiting a long time.
I seen you do it.

What you can't do is write or speak like this if you want your communication to be professional.

It should be clear to you just how important it is to have a firm control of the forms of the verb if you want to be understood easily. This is true whether you are writing a single sentence, an essay, a report, a letter, a memo or making a presentation.

RECOGNIZING VERB TENSE

In Unit 2 you examined the role of the verb in a sentence. You also learned that the verb is the time marker (clock) of the sentence. How does the verb mark time in a sentence? The form of the verb changes. We change the *base form* of the verb, or we place a *helping verb* before the base form to create a different tense. *Tense* is the form of the verb as it expresses different times. The *base form* is the verb itself (e.g., *exercise*).

Examine the sentences below to see how the base form (*exercise*) changes to express different tenses. Sometimes a helping verb is also needed. Can you tell which of these sentences are past, present, or future?

I exercise every day.

You exercised last week.

He exercises on weekends.

We will exercise tomorrow.

They are exercising now.

She has exercised for a month.

I am exercising at the moment.

You had exercised since 5 p.m.

He has been exercising for a long time.

We have exercised all the muscle groups.

They will be exercising next week.

She was exercising yesterday.

You probably relied on the additional time words, such as *now*, *yesterday*, *tomorrow*, *next*, and *after,* to pinpoint the time frame. In each case, the form of the verb also had to change to express the time period.

Let's consider the time changes in the following sentences:

I *enjoyed* the meal last night. (past tense)
I *enjoy* a meal with my friends. (present tense)
I *will enjoy* the meal next Sunday. (future tense)

We can combine a variety of tenses to provide information, as you can see in the examples below. Can you identify the tense of each of the highlighted verbs?

> Last year I *worked* as a cashier in a grocery store. Now I *work* in a clothing store. I *will work* here until I graduate from college.
>
> Students who *enjoyed* high school usually *enjoy* college, but they all think they *will enjoy* their chosen profession more.

The form of each verb expresses its tense. What does each tense look like?

- The present tense is the *base* form of the verb (*exercise, enjoy*).
- The past tense adds *-ed* to the base form if the verb is regular (*exercise + ed, enjoy + ed*).
- The future needs *will* or *be going to* in front of the base form (*will exercise, are going to enjoy*).

PRACTICE 1

Underline the verbs and identify their tenses in the following sentences. For example:

> Ottawa <u>is</u> the capital of Canada. *(present)*

1. Amazingly, we like grammar.
2. Many people experienced problems with verb tense.
3. I will understand tense after this unit.
4. The verbs seem easy to identify.
5. Except for my spelling, I make no mistakes.
6. I need your help with this problem.
7. Jeff will finish the assignment.
8. You proofread your work carefully.
9. We worked on this exercise for a few minutes.
10. Did you enjoy this practice?

THE INFINITIVE

The infinitive is the *base form* of a verb with *to* in front of it. For example:

to be
to look
to have
to listen

As we begin to work with verb tenses, let's be clear about the one form of the verb that has no tense. It is called the *infinitive*. *Infinite* means having no time, being eternal, lasting forever. The infinitive form of the verb doesn't express time, and we add it to other verbs to make a complete verb phrase.

This is how you use it in a sentence:

He wants to be an astronaut.
I like to look at other people.
She wants to have more money.

PRACTICE 2

Complete the following sentences by inserting an appropriate infinitive.

1. The children love _____________ in the park.
2. My dog seems _____________ at strangers.
3. The teacher wants us _____________ .
4. Deciding whom _____________ to a party is not easy.
5. The manager asked me _____________ on Saturday.
6. I enjoy the weekends when I get the chance _____________ .
7. _____________ or not _____________ , that is the question.
8. She plans _____________ next year.
9. You always try _____________ to your parents.
10. We want you _____________ happy.

BE, HAVE, DO

There are three verbs you have to know thoroughly if you want to have total control of verb tenses and verb use. The three verbs are *be*, *have*, and *do*. They are the most frequently used verbs in English. They are verbs in their own right, but they are also the helping verbs for other tenses.

They are all *irregular*. Regular verbs add *-ed* to form their past tenses. Irregular verbs form their past tenses in other ways. Study the table below:

Tense	Subject	Be	Have	Do
Present	I	am	have	do
	You	are	have	do
	He/she/it	is	has	does
	(and all singular nouns)			
	We	are	have	do
	You	are	have	do
	They	are	have	do
	(and all plural nouns)			
Past	I	was	had	did
	You	were	had	did
	He/she/it	was	had	did
	(and all singular nouns)			
	We	were	had	did
	You	were	had	did
	They	were	had	did
	(and all plural nouns)			
Future	I	will be	will have	will do
	You	will be	will have	will do
	He/she/it	will be	will have	will do
	(and all singular nouns)			
	We	will be	will have	will do
	You	will be	will have	will do
	They	will be	will have	will do
	(and all plural nouns)			

Look at *do*. Notice the spelling for third person singular: *does*. With *do* and *go* you have to add *-es* to the verb, not just *-s*.

> She *does* too much for them.
> He *goes* to work on weekends.

Be careful also not to write *dose*! This is a common spelling mistake.

PRACTICE 3

Refer to the table opposite if you need to as you do the following practice. Choose the correct form of *be*, *have*, or *do* in each sentence.

1. It __________ (be) time to start work now.
2. My dog __________ (have) a passion for chocolate cookies which I share.
3. We __________ (do) this exercise for homework last night.
4. I __________ (be) happy to meet you yesterday.
5. She __________ (be) working in the library right now.
6. They __________ (have) a new baby a week ago.
7. You __________ (do) a lot of writing tomorrow.
8. It __________ (be) your turn to babysit next time.
9. Marlene __________ (have) never gotten married because she wants a man who __________ (do) his share of the housework.
10. He __________ (have) a new job that he enjoys.

Look at the chart on page 124 again. You can see that *be* is the most irregular verb. The third person singular and the first person singular have their own forms of the verb *be* in both the present and the past. Always pay close attention to the verb *be*.

PRACTICE 4

Choose the correct form of the verb in parentheses for each sentence.

1. Dorinda (is/are) my best friend.
2. We (was/were) the first to find out about it.
3. Michael and Peter (was/were) on vacation.
4. The trees in my garden (is/are) tall.
5. The silver birch tree (was/were) swaying in the wind.
6. The dog next door (was/were) barking all night.
7. It (is/are) my favourite movie.
8. When I (was/were) a child, yellow (was/were) my favourite colour.
9. You (is/are) the one I trust.
10. This restaurant (is/are) very popular.

PRACTICE 5

Complete the following sentences with the appropriate present tense form of the verb *be*.

1. She __________ a manager of a dress shop.
2. My husband __________ an engineer.
3. He __________ very tired today.
4. It __________ nearly time to go.
5. My kids __________ at their grandmother's house today.
6. I __________ on my way home right now.
7. It __________ sunny at the moment.
8. You __________ my inspiration.
9. That gas station __________ open at 6:30 every morning.
10. The same students __________ in the back row again.

PRACTICE 6

As you read the passage, write the correct form of *be*, *have*, or *do* in each blank space.

My Favourite Teacher

My favourite teacher __________ Mr. Desmond. Even now after all these years, I __________ very strong memories of him. He __________ my teacher in grade five. Every morning, before the announcements and "O Canada," he __________ stretches with the class. He used to say that the physical exercises __________ our wake-up call, and that we __________ to get the blood moving to our brains. He also __________ a great sense of humour and __________ strange things in class. I __________ never forgotten about projectiles and velocity because he threw chalk or balls of paper at us when we __________ noisy. Then he __________ an impromptu lesson on the science of throwing. He __________ six feet four inches tall, so he __________ a powerful presence in a class of ten-year-olds. He never __________ to shout or even raise his voice to get our attention; every kid in his class wanted to pay attention to him. He was a great teacher.

PRACTICE 7

As you read the passage, write the correct form of *be*, *have*, or *do* in each blank space.

Coaching a Team

Coaching a little league soccer team __________ a big responsibility. Yvonne and Terry __________ the coaches of a team of five- to six-year-olds, and they __________ eighteen children on their team. Because a soccer team __________ only eleven players on the field at a time, the coaches __________ to make a lot of substitutions to ensure that every child __________ an opportunity to play. This __________ not as easy as it sounds because the team also wants to win its games. Yvonne __________ the one with experience as she __________ a coach last year, and she __________ such a great job the league asked her to come back again. Terry still __________ a lot of doubts about her ability as a coach, but with Yvonne's encouragement and help she __________ a lot of fun on game night. The team __________ a game once a week. Because the children on the team __________ so young, each game __________ only one hour long. The game __________ two twenty-minute halves and a break of about ten minutes for the children to __________ drinks and snacks. Before each game, Yvonne and Terry __________ warm-up exercises with the children for half an hour. First Terry __________ stretches with the team, and when she __________ the children's attention, she and Yvonne __________ a lap around the field with them. Then Yvonne __________ in charge of ball-control activities. The three activities __________ dribbling, passing, and shooting. The team and the coaches __________ a lot of fun each week. They hope the team __________ champions next month.

MAKING VERBS NEGATIVE

Do is a very useful little verb that is often employed when you want to make a negative statement. You attach *do/does/did* to the word *not* and place them before the *base form* of your main verb. You do all this without thinking about it most of the time. A problem you may encounter with negation is making sure you use the correct form of *do*. *Do/does* are present tense; *did* is past tense. Look at the chart on page 124 again.

I like chocolate.
I *don't* like chocolate.

Tony's girlfriend loves him.
Tony's girlfriend *doesn't* love him.

The cat sat on the mat.
The cat *didn't* sit on the mat.

You know that *not* is usually a contraction (*n't*):

do not	=	don't
does not	=	doesn't
did not	=	didn't

Make sure you place the apostrophe in the correct position. Remember: an apostrophe replaces the missing part of a word.

Have is another helping verb that can become negative when it is used with *not* (*n't*).

I've got time right now.	I haven't got time right now.

The very irregular verb *be* can also be attached to *not* (*n't*) to make it negative.

I am happy.	I'm not happy.
You are happy.	You're not happy.
He is happy.	He isn't happy.
She was happy.	She wasn't happy.
We were happy.	We weren't happy.
She will be happy.	She won't be happy.*

* The contraction *won't* doesn't make much sense does it? Nonetheless, it is correct.

PRACTICE 8

Make the following sentences negative.

1. It is time to go now.

   ____

2. He was late for his appointment yesterday.

   ____

3. You can give me a hand with the laundry.

   ____

4. They were watching TV last night.

   ____

5. The Leafs played well in their last game.

   ____

6. She likes reading mystery novels.

   ____

7. We went for a meal at that new Indian restaurant.

____

8. The VCR is working now.

____

9. You will be late for your practice.

____

10. Denton enjoys journal writing.

____

Using Negative Words

The other way to make a negative statement doesn't affect the verb. Instead you use a negative word, such as *no one, nobody, none, no, never*. For example:

> No amount of money can repay you. (An amount of money can't repay you.)
>
> I never want to see you again. (I don't want to see you ever again.)
>
> None of us care any more. (We don't care any more.)
>
> Nobody knows about it. (There isn't anybody who knows about it.)
>
> No one likes Peter. (There isn't any one who likes Peter.)

The Double Negative

This error happens when you combine the negative verb with one of the negative words. Apart from driving English teachers nuts, this error makes your expression redundant and contradictory. You are not saying what you mean.

> **wrong:** I don't never want to see you again.

This actually says, "I do want to see you again." As in math, two negatives equal a positive. The two negatives cancel each other out. **Do not use double negatives.**

PRACTICE 9

Write ten negative sentences based on the following subjects and verbs. For example:

children like
Most children don't like Brussels sprouts.

1. he lost

   ____

2. it feels

   ____

3. she wrote

   ____

4. we found

   ____

5. they have forgotten

   ____

6. the mayor makes

   ____

7. they thought

   ____

8. the children sang

   ____

9. it went

   ____

10. everyone has

    ____

Negative Prefixes

Other negative words are formed by the addition of *negative prefixes* to verbs, nouns, and adjectives. What are negative prefixes? *Dis-*, *il-*, *im-*, *in-*, and *ir-* are a few examples.

Let's look at the example in Practice 9. The sentence could be made negative by changing the verb from *like* to ***dislike***.

> Most children don't like Brussels sprouts.
> Most children dislike Brussels sprouts.

Likewise, *fashionable* can be made negative by adding *un-*. *Un* placed in front of a word means *not.* It makes the word *fashionable* express its opposite meaning.

PRACTICE 10

Make each of the following words negative by adding the appropriate prefix (consult your dictionary if you are not sure which prefix belongs with which word), and then write a sentence for each negative word.

1. possible ______________

   ____

2. regular ______________

   ____

3. logical ______________

   ____

4. respect ______________

   ____

5. reliable ______________

   ____

6. legal ______________

   ____

7. able ______________

____

8. lock ______________

____

9. perfect ______________

____

10. legible ______________

____

11. appear ______________

____

12. capable ______________

____

SIMPLE VERB TENSES

For some of you, there is a lot of work to be done in this part of Unit 4. Others of you will find that you don't typically make mistakes with verb tenses; if this is the case, you may not need to do all of the practices.

The Present Tense

If you want to discuss a daily activity or situation now, you need the *simple present tense*; you also use this tense if you are providing facts or making a generalization.

You know how to make this tense: it's the base form (the verb itself). There is one important rule to remember with the simple present tense:

The third person singular present tense verb ends in *s*.

PRACTICE 11

Choose the correct present tense form of the verb for each sentence.

1. A friend in need (seems/seem) a friend indeed.
2. A couple (consists/consist) of two people.
3. Some people (believes/believe) that love (makes/make) the world (goes/go) round.
4. We (chooses/choose) our friends, but we (inherits/inherit) our relatives.
5. I (possesses/possess) a variety of friends.
6. I really (enjoys/enjoy) going out with some of my friends.
7. I (calls/call) this sort of friend a "goodtime friend."
8. We all (relies/rely) on these friends for our entertainment.
9. We (gets/get) in touch with some friends only a few times each year.
10. I (calls/call) these friends "distance friends."
11. You probably (knows/know) people you just (chats/chat) with regularly.
12. I (considers/consider) them "casual friends."
13. Finally we (comes/come) to the category of best friends.
14. Although I (likes/like) all my friends, I (considers/consider) only two as best friends.
15. A best friend (shares/share) everything with because you (trusts/trust) her with your most intimate secrets.

Look at sentence 5 in Practice 11. The verb, *possess*, ends in an *s* already. For this reason you have to add *-es* to make the third person present tense form. This spelling rule applies to the other verbs that end in *s*, *sh*, and *ch*.

She kisses her boyfriend every morning.
The little boy wishes he could fly.
He watches the late night news.

Practise this spelling rule in the following sentences. Be careful: not all the verbs need *-es*.

PRACTICE 12

Write the appropriate present tense form of the verb in parentheses.

1. My daughter ____________ (rush) to greet me after school.
2. Fred ____________ (lunch) in the cafeteria most days.
3. She ____________ (use) too much perfume.
4. Charlene ____________ (fuss) too much.
5. He ____________ (crush) beer cans in one hand.
6. She usually ____________ (miss) her 8:30 class.
7. My brother always ____________ (lose) his car keys.
8. Your dog ____________ (chase) cars.
9. My mother ____________ (patch) my favourite jeans.
10. Dave ____________ (pass) the ball to the end zone.
11. Dan rarely ____________ (express) his feelings.
12. That student ____________ (ask) intelligent questions.
13. Our teacher never ____________ (punch) three holes in the handouts.
14. The plough ____________ (push) the snow to the sides of the highway.
15. That child ____________ (catch) colds easily.

PRACTICE 13

Write a simple present sentence for each of the following verbs. Use the subject in parentheses. The first one is done for you.

1. worry (he)

   He worries about his family.

2. find (I)

   ____

3. surprise (you)

   ____

4. walk (she)

   ____

5. try (Leonardo)

   ____

6. smile (they)

   ____

7. think (my mother)

   ____

8. reply (Marie)

   ____

9. seem (it)

   ____

10. make (we)

    ____

Did you spell the verbs correctly in sentences 5 and 8?

When *y* at the end of a word is pronounced, adding *-s* to that word changes the spelling from *-y* to *-ies*. For example:

hurry	=	hurries
dry	=	dries

Practise this spelling rule in the following sentences. Be careful: not all the verbs need *-ies*.

PRACTICE 14

Write the correct form of the verb in parentheses.

1. Peter ____________ (fry) the onions before serving them.
2. He never ____________ (play) his stereo quietly.
3. Maria always ____________ (say) the right thing.
4. My sister often ____________ (cry) at weddings.
5. A new baby certainly ____________ (try) your patience.
6. On Fridays, Neil ____________ (stay) home.
7. My brother ____________ (try) out for every team at school.
8. That man ____________ (lie) through his teeth.
9. A heavy snowfall ____________ (delay) all flights out of the airport.
10. The rule ____________ (apply) to all verbs.

The Past Tense

The *simple past tense* expresses activities or situations that began and ended before now. You know how to make the simple past tense. If the verb is regular, add *ed* to the end of the base form of the verb.

The past tense is where you are most likely to encounter problems with *irregular verbs*. The present and future tenses seem relatively straightforward, but the past form is not always predictable. Irregular verbs make their past tenses in different ways that you have to remember. These verbs often have a past participle that is different from their past tense form. (Participles will be discussed later in this unit.) For example, for the verb *go* the past tense is *went*, and the past participle is *gone*. If you confuse the two forms, you will write in a way that is incorrect and confusing.

You'll find a list of the common irregular verbs and their forms in Appendix B. It's been included because many people are not familiar with the forms of irregular verbs and their spelling.

PRACTICE 15

Write the past tense of the following verbs. Be careful with spelling. You should consult Appendix B any time you encounter a verb whose form or spelling you are unsure of.

1. think ____________________
2. begin ____________________
3. choose ____________________
4. sleep ____________________
5. speed ____________________
6. throw ____________________
7. teach ____________________
8. eat ____________________
9. feel ____________________
10. wear ____________________

PRACTICE 16

Write a sentence for each of your past tense verbs in Practice 15.

1. ____________________
2. ____________________
3. ____________________
4. ____________________
5. ____________________
6. ____________________

7. ______________________________

8. ______________________________

9. ______________________________

10. ______________________________

Watch out for verbs whose base form ends in *y*. The same spelling rule for adding *-ed* is the same as the one for adding *-s*.

PRACTICE 17

Make the following sentences past tense.

1. They walk to the pool every day.

   ____

2. He usually plays second base.

   ____

3. We hurry to school on Mondays.

   ____

4. You worry too much about the future.

   ____

5. Carlene sings with the choir.

   ____

6. The dogs run in the park.

   ____

7. I drink diet cola.

   ____

8. The sun rises in the east.

   ____

9. I write a letter to my girlfriend every day.

____

10. The premier throws the first pitch at the game.

____

PRACTICE 18

Write the correct past tense of the verb given in parentheses before each sentence.

1. (hear) I ____________ Louise asked Dan to marry her.
2. (say) He ____________ "yes."
3. (take) She ____________ him home to meet her mother.
4. (think) Dan ____________ Louise's mother was wonderful.
5. (feel) He ____________ Louise would be a great wife.
6. (draw) They ____________ up plans for the wedding.
7. (choose) Louise ____________ her mother's birthday for their wedding day.
8. (have) They ____________ a big, formal wedding.
9. (wear) Louise ____________ a traditional white dress and long veil.
10. (buy) Dan and his best man ____________ tuxedos for the ceremony.
11. (be) Three of Louise's friends ____________ bridesmaids.
12. (cost) The celebration ____________ a lot of money.
13. (drink) The wedding guests ____________ a champagne toast to the bride and groom.
14. (make) Dan's mother ____________ the wedding cake.

15. (eat) Everyone ____________ at least one slice.

16. (bite) Dan ____________ a huge chunk of the wedding cake.

17. (get) The couple ____________ a lot of beautiful wedding presents.

18. (go) They ____________ to Hawaii for their honeymoon.

19. (come) Dan and Louise ____________ home last week.

20. (bring) Dan ____________ his mother and mother-in-law some pearl earrings.

PRACTICE 19

Write a sentence for each of the following verbs. Use the past tense.

1. study

   ____

2. be

   ____

3. eat

   ____

4. catch

   ____

5. do

   ____

6. win

   ____

7. forget

   ____

8. see

____

9. write

____

10. bury

____

The Future Tense

This tense expresses events or situations that are in the future.

To make the *simple future* tense, we add a helping verb, *will*, in front of the base form of the main verb. The main verb doesn't change.

> We *will* see you later.
> Mark *will* find his way here.
> My mother *will* buy me a new coat.

There is another way to express the future: *be* + *going to* + main verb.

> He *is going to* meet his boss at 3 p.m.
> I *am going to* visit Jamaica this summer.
> We *are going to* participate in the marathon next week.

PRACTICE 20

Write a future tense sentence for each of the following verbs. Use *going to*.

1. go

____

2. fly

____

3. read

____

4. manage

____

5. keep

____

6. feel

____

7. look

____

8. fill

____

9. help

____

10. fall

____

PRACTICE 21

Complete each of the following sentences using either form of the future tense (*will* or *be going to*).

1. After I go shopping, ______________________________

____

2. Before you can run in the marathon, ______________________________

____

3. She feels that ______________________________

____

4. The letter ______________________________

____

5. If you are quiet, ______________________________

____

6. The decision ______________________________

____

7. They can choose what ______________________________

____

8. Whatever Mark has ______________________________

____

9. This fall ______________________________

____

10. Later in the week ______________________________

____

PARTICIPLE TENSES

So far in this unit, we have reviewed the simple verb tenses: present, past, and future.

I work   I worked   I will work

But there are other ways to form verb tenses in English that express subtly different senses of time.

I am working   I have worked   I will be working

We call these constructions the participle tenses, and we form them with the helping verbs *be* and *have.* (That's one of the reasons we have been working so hard on these words in this unit—they are part of a lot of verb tenses.)

Be + *-ing* Verb

In Unit 2, you learned that you cannot use the *-ing* form of the verb alone as the verb in the sentence. In Unit 3, you learned that an *-ing* word can also be a noun. The *-ing* verb must always be used with the correct from of *be*. Here are some examples.

I am working   I was working   I will be working

The *-ing* verb (along with a form of the verb *be*) is used to indicate an action in progress or to emphasize how long an action lasts.

I was waiting for twenty minutes.
He is taking a long time to find the book.
Kesha Forbes will be managing the office for the next two weeks.
Donna was laughing while she watched Joe.*

* A specific time wasn't given here; instead we can figure out that Donna laughed *for as long as* she watched Joe.

Look at those examples again and you can see that when you want to change from past to present or future, you change the form of the helping verb *be*, not the main verb. You choose *am*, *are*, *is*, *were*, *was*, or *will be* when you want to express past, present, or future. The present participle, *-ing*, is used to emphasize an action in progress, happening over time.

PRACTICE 22

Write a sentence for each of the following verbs. Use an *-ing* verb with a form of the verb *be*. For example:

(study) I am going to study in the library tomorrow.
or He was studying so hard, he didn't hear the phone ring.

1. play

____

2. meet

____

3. prepare

____

4. carry

____

5. swim

____

6. feel

____

7. come

____

8. listen

____

9. work

____

10. run

____

PRACTICE 23

Add an independent clause to each of the following to make a complete sentence. Use any appropriate verb tense.

1. When I see you, _______________

____

2. Until you changed her diaper, _______________

____

3. Although Laura is saving money, _______________

____

4. We always hold hands when _______________

____

5. After she finishes the book, ____________________

____

6. My neighbours were playing their stereo so loudly that ________

____

7. While we were at the movie, ____________________

____

8. Jack is being silly, so ____________________

____

9. Although it is sunny at the moment, ____________________

____

10. You make me laugh when ____________________

____

The verb *be* presents many students with difficulties. In particular, the present and past participles *being* and *been* are confused. You probably remember these from Unit 1 (page 19). *Being* (the present participle) has to be added to *am/are/is/was/were* to make a complete verb; *been* (the past participle) has to be added to *have/has/had* to make a complete verb.

The following practices should help clear up this confusion.

PRACTICE 24

Underline the correct participle in each of the following sentences.

1. It has (being/been) a long time since I last saw you.
2. My little brother was (being/been) a nuisance.
3. I have (being/been) looking for you.
4. We were (being/been) ignored by the waiter.
5. They had (being/been) for a strenuous hike.
6. That apartment has (being/been) vacant for two months.

7. Your clothes have (being/been) on the floor since Monday.
8. I hope you have (being/been) happy here.
9. The cake is (being/been) made by my aunt.
10. I am (being/been) assigned to your group next week.
11. You have (being/been) right all along.
12. It has (being/been) snowing for hours.
13. It is (being/been) printed right now.
14. It has (being/been) printed already.
15. She has (being/been) my friend since we were in kindergarten.

PRACTICE 25

Complete each of the following sentences. In each case use an appropriate form or tense of the verb *be*.

1. Today, my friend Rodney ___________ very happy.
2. Last week my mother ___________ fifty-three.
3. This ___________ a wonderful year for my family so far.
4. My grandparents had never ___________ to Banff before.
5. My little brother Jack ___________ very moody at the moment.
6. I ___________ twenty-three next month.
7. I wonder what the new millennium ___________ like.
8. We ___________ sorry Aunt Mary ___________ sick yesterday.
9. He ___________ five years older than I ___________ .
10. I hope you have ___________ well since our last meeting.

PRACTICE 26

Write ten sentences of your own. Use either *being* or *been* as part of the verb.

1. ______________________________
2. ______________________________
3. ______________________________
4. ______________________________
5. ______________________________
6. ______________________________
7. ______________________________
8. ______________________________
9. ______________________________
10. ______________________________

Have + Past Participle

The *past participle* is the form of the verb that is used with *have/has/had*. The good news is that, most of the time, the past participle is the same as the simple past tense: just add *-ed*. Verbs that do this are regular verbs.

I work	I have worked	I had worked

The bad news is that some verbs use a past participle that is different than their simple past. These are called *irregular verbs*. There aren't many of them, but they are some of the most common verbs in our language. Check Appendix B for a list of these irregular verbs.

I eat	I ate	I have eaten
I see	I saw	I have seen
I go	I went	I have gone

Be, *have*, and *do*—those useful helping verbs—can confuse you because they are irregular verbs themselves.

I am	I was	I have been
I have	I had	I have had
I do	I did	I have done

When do you use this past participle verb tense? There are two occasions. First, you use it when you want to discuss something that began in the present and still continues.

I have worked hard all semester.

Second, you use it when you want to discuss something that happened recently.

Michael has changed since he began his new job.

PRACTICE 27

Write the correct past participle of the verb given in parentheses before each sentence.

1. (become) Donna has __________ a mother for the first time.
2. (choose) She had __________ the name Michael for her baby.
3. (tell) Donna had __________ all her friends.
4. (say) She had __________ this name often to her bulge.
5. (hear) Even the nurses had __________ about Donna's choice of name.
6. (give) Donna has __________ birth to a girl.
7. (think) She has __________ about the problem of the name all night.
8. (take) It has __________ her a while to find a solution.
9. (speak) Donna realized she had only __________ the name.
10. (write) She had never __________ it down.
11. (give) Donna has __________ her baby the name Mykela.

12. (say) Once you have _______________ the name aloud, you'll know why.

Be very careful not to leave out *have, has,* or *had* with the past participle form of the verb. It is nonstandard to speak—and incorrect to write—sentences like this:

I done it. He seen it. They gone.

Check Appendix B or your dictionary if you are not sure about the form of the past participle of a particular verb.

PRACTICE 28

Correct the verbs in the following sentences if necessary.

1. I seen Diane last night.
2. No one done a better job than Jason on the assignment.
3. I broke my arm when I fell from the ladder.
4. Paul come to the party alone last night.
5. He grown a lot since I last seen him.
6. Mary and Joanna gone to the library to study.
7. She caught the ball with her left hand.
8. Mike begun college before Labour Day.
9. They eaten all the chocolate cake I was saving for dessert tonight.
10. He wrote to his uncle asking for more money.

As Unit 1 (page 27) points out, contracting *have* + past participle can result in a spelling mistake. Because *'ve* sounds like the word *of,* you may make the mistake of writing *of* as part of the verb.

wrong: I could of helped you with that project.

wrong: Penny should of known better than to trust Lloyd with her new Ferrari.

In both of these examples, *of* is used as if it were a verb, which it isn't. It's a preposition. The sentences should read:

I could've helped you with that project.

Penny should've known better than to trust Lloyd with her new Ferrari.

PRACTICE 29

Correct the following sentences if necessary.

1. When I've spoken to him, I'll let you know.
2. You broken your arm.
3. She should of given him a piece of her mind.
4. Peter gone to Las Vegas on the four o'clock flight.
5. Madison chosen her clothes carefully.
6. They could of taken the last bus home.
7. A thief has stolen all my money.
8. The sun must of risen, but there are too many clouds to be sure.
9. I done my best work for you.
10. He would of written the answers carefully if he had enough time.

PRACTICE 30

As you read this passage, underline the verbs.

Images from the Past

Angela was helping her mother to tidy the closet in the spare room. She came across a box of old photographs that she hadn't seen before. Most of the photographs weren't in colour. They were in black and white. Angela thought these photos hadn't been taken recently. However, when she looked at the photos more closely, she felt a certain young woman in many of them looked just like her. Angela didn't have the same hairstyle or wear such unfashionable clothes. Apart from these facts, the young woman could have been Angela, but that was impossible. Angela had no idea who the woman was, so she asked her mother. Angela's mother went through a couple of the photos and laughed. She told Angela that they weren't pictures of Angela, but of her grandmother.

PRACTICE 31

Rewrite "Images from the Past" in the present tense. This could be your first sentence:

Angela is helping her mother to tidy the closet in the spare room.

PRACTICE 32

The following passage provides a check of your skill with tenses and subject–verb agreement. Choose the correct tense and form of each verb in parentheses.

Reading Trouble

Ever since he ___________ (be) a little boy, Frank ___________ (love) to read. Back then books ___________ (open) new worlds for him. He ___________ (identify) with the heroes in novels, so he ___________ (solve) mysteries or he ___________ (have) adventures in his imagination. Nowadays, he always ___________ (read) on the subway, but last night when he ___________ (read) a book, he ___________ (become) very engrossed in it. He ___________ (concentrate) so hard that he ___________ (miss) his stop. By the time he ___________ (realize) this, he ___________ (go) five stops beyond his destination. Of course he ___________ (hurry) to get off the train at the next station. He ___________ (be) angry and embarrassed. He ___________ (feel) that everyone ___________ (notice) his mistake. That ___________ (be not) true. No one ___________ (pay) any attention to him. When he ___________ (get) off the train, he ___________ (be) lucky. A train that ___________ (go) in the other direction ___________ (arrive) at the platform only a minute later. Frank ___________ (be) able to board it and to return to his station. He ___________ (read not) on his return journey.

PRACTICE 33

As you read the passage, underline the verbs. There are ten subject–verb agreement errors in this passage. Go back over the passage to find and correct them.

Date—Anyone?

My great-grandmother, who is still as lively as a cricket, love to tell stories of when she was young. She was born in 1918, so society have undergone a lot of changes in her lifetime. For example, when she was a young woman, dating were a completely different experience. After all, who was a suitable date? Of course, my mother and I still disagrees about this issue, but for my great-grandmother the rules was rigorous. My great-grandmother was not permitted to date anyone whom her parents considered unsuitable. Suitable young men came from the same social class; that is, they was working in a job similar to her father's. If a young man wanted to date my great-grandmother, he have to be introduced to and approved by her parents. Finally, if any man was capable of meeting her parents' requirements of family background, education, and employment, he was permitted to "walk out with" her. Even this have a catch to it. A chaperone always accompanied the couple on the date. My great-grandmother tell wonderful stories about how she and her dates was able to avoid the chaperone and actually get to know each other. After all, my great-grandmother didn't want to marry a stranger.

Multiple Meanings All the words below are taken from the passage "Date—Anyone?"

date Of course you know what this word means. However, *date* is a word with multiple meanings, so you have to check the context (the surroundings) to be sure you have the correct meaning. For example:

> What is the *date* today?
> This *date* is a delicious, sweet fruit.
> I have a hot *date* tonight.

The word *date* has three completely different meanings as a noun and it can also be used as a verb. When you look up a new word in the dictionary and see that it has multiple meanings, you must make sure you select the meaning that fits your context.

cricket This word has multiple meanings too. What are they? Write a sentence of your own to show each meaning.

suitable This adjective has only one meaning. What is it? The word *suit* has multiple meanings. Write a sentence of your own to show each meaning.

same/similar These two words are often mistaken for each other. In fact, they have distinct meanings. Explain the difference between them.

catch How many meanings does this word have?

chaperone What does this word mean? What language did it come from?

PRACTICE 34

Read the following list of activities. You will notice that the verbs are all in the present tense. Write a complete sentence for each activity in the past tense as if the events happened to you yesterday. You will end up with a story that uses a consistent verb tense. (*Consistent* is an adjective that means staying the same. There is more work on verb consistency on page 158.)

This could be your first sentence:

Yesterday morning, my clock radio came on at 6:30.

6:30 clock radio on

____

6:33 open eyes

____

6:34 realize it's the wrong station ... opera!

____

6:36 re-tune radio

____

6:40 weather forecasts heavy rain

____

6:45 crawl out of bed

____

7:00 finish in the shower

____

7:10 still trying to find clean shirt

____

7:15 discover there is no coffee, juice, or milk

____

7:20 drink water

____

7:30 car doesn't start

____

7:45 soaking wet, waiting for the bus

____

8:10 go to donut store for caffeine and calories

____

PRACTICE 35

Rewrite your sentences in the present tense as if the events are happening now, but this time write your sentences about Susan. Again, your use of verb tense will be consistent. Remember you need to add *-s* to the verb if Susan (third person/she) is the subject.

This could be your first sentence:

Every morning at 6:30, Susan's clock radio comes on.

6:30 clock radio on

____

6:33 open eyes

___

6:34 realize it's the wrong station ... opera!

___

6:36 re-tune radio

___

6:40 weather forecasts heavy rain

___

6:45 crawl out of bed

___

7:00 finish in the shower

___

7:10 still trying to find clean shirt

___

7:15 discover there is no coffee, juice, or milk

___

7:20 drink water

___

7:30 car doesn't start

___

7:45 soaking wet, waiting for the bus

___

8:10 go to donut store for caffeine and calories

___

CONSISTENCY OF VERB TENSES

Being consistent does not mean being rigidly uniform. Generally, if you begin in the present tense, you should continue to use it throughout your writing. Sometimes, however, the meaning of the sentence or paragraph requires a writer to move to a different time and tense. Watching a movie that flashes back and forth between timeframes without a clear reason is a jolting experience for the audience. As a careful writer, you should consider your reader and use verb tense consistently; that is, change tense only when your meaning requires it.

Check your control of verb consistency in the next practice.

PRACTICE 36

Complete the following sentences. Choose appropriate verbs in the correct tense for each one. The sentences are not related.

1. Yesterday he ______________, but tomorrow he ____________.
2. They ____________ you later today if they ______________ their work.
3. She ____________ chocolate now, but when she ____________ a child she __________.
4. The moon ____________ around the earth. It ____________ the moon twenty-eight days to complete its cycle.
5. Before we ______________ her, we ___________ blondes _________ more fun.
6. When he _________ seven, he _________ karate. Now he _________ a black belt.
7. Next year I _________ Mexico. I _________ hot weather and the beach.
8. The dog _________ when it _________ me. It always _________ that.

9. You _________ the first person to visit our new home since we _________ last week.

10. Jennifer _________ to see *Hunks from Outer Space*, but I _________ that movie _________ boring.

PRACTICE 37

Choose the correct verb for each sentence. The sentences relate to each other, so the first verb choice will control the rest. The first sentence is done for you.

1. Good neighbours <u>are</u> (are/were) hard to find.
2. I know most of us _________ (get/got) along with our neighbours.
3. Usually we _________ (do/did) this because we _________ (have/had) to.
4. However I _________ (am/was) truly fortunate in my next door neighbours.
5. Five years ago, when I _________ (move/moved) into my house, the whole family _________ (come/came) round to help me.
6. The eldest son in the family still _________ (cuts/cut) my grass in the summer.
7. In the winter, he _________ (shovels/shovel) the snow for me.
8. You probably _________ (wonder/wondered) what I _________ (do/did) to help my kind neighbours.
9. I _________ (share/shared) vegetables and flowers from my garden with them, and they _________ (keep/kept) their bikes and sleds in my garage because their garage _________ (is/was) always full.

10. As long as we remain good neighbours, I am sure we ________ (be) friends.

How did you do? You should have found that sentence 5 was different from the other sentences. Why is that? Well, the phrase at the beginning of that sentence is a time marker that requires a specific tense. The phrase changes the timeframe. In each of the other sentences you are providing information that is still current. Sentence 10 also provided a change of tense because you had to move to the future.

PRACTICE 38

Read the following passage and add the appropriate tense of each verb in parentheses. Be careful and check for time markers.

First Day

Even today, Luke vividly ______________ (remember) his very first day in school when he ______________ (be) five years old. His memory of that day ______________ (be) so clear even now because he ______________ (have) such an embarrassing experience back then. On his first day, he ______________ (arrive) at school at 9 a.m., and by 9:30 he ______________ (be) desperate to go to the washroom. He ______________ (know) that he ______________ (have) to ask permission. Of course, the teacher ______________ (say) yes and Luke ______________ (go) to the washroom. That ______________ (be) the start of his embarrassment. At the age of five, Luke ______________ (know) how to go to the bathroom by himself, but he ______________ (go) to the girls' washroom. Luke ______________ (do not know) boys and girls ______________ (have) their own washrooms in school. When he ______________ (come) back into the classroom, some of the children ______________ (begin) to tease him. This ______________ (make) Luke unhappy and he ______________ (cry) so much that the teacher ______________ (send) him home at recess.

PRACTICE 39

Read the following passage and correct any errors in verb form you discover.

Cooking with Grandma

My favourite childhood memories relate to my grandma and the way she teach me to cook. With my grandma, I study baking since I was a little boy. When I was too small to see over the top of the counter, I love to stand by my grandma when she will be cooking. If she was baking a sponge cake, I hear the eggs as she crack their shells and whisked them up. Then she bend down with the bowl and showed me the golden egg froth. She put aside the frothy eggs and beats butter and sugar together. When she added the flour, I see she work hard to blend the mixture. As soon as she had mixed the eggs and some vanilla into her mixture, it was my turn. Grandma carefully place the bowl on my lap and I holds it tight. My grandma convinces me that without my effort the cake doesn't rise. While my grandma greased the cake pans and checks the oven temperature, I stir that batter with all my strength. Once the cake is in the oven, my favourite part came: cleaning the bowl.

THE PASSIVE VOICE

An active person is someone who gets involved in life, someone who participates in whatever is going on. On the other hand, a passive person tends to let life go by. A passive person usually stands back from the action and lets others do things. The two verb voices are like active and passive people.

Look carefully at these two sentences.

1. My mother gave the ring to me.
2. The ring was given to me by my mother.

The two sentences contain the same information, but there are differences between them: the word order and the verb form are different. The result of these differences is that the emphasis in each sentence is altered. Can you see how the first sentence stresses the mother while the second focuses more on the ring?

Sentence 1 is an *active voice* sentence. It is the sort of sentence you generally use. Most writing involves the use of the active voice. In an active voice sentence the subject (*mother*) performs the action of the verb (*gave*), and the verb agrees with its subject.

> Ben always runs the last leg in the relay.
> He won two gold medals yesterday.

In each of these example sentences, the subjects (*Ben, he*) perform the actions (*runs, won*). The subjects and verbs agree.

Sentence 2 is a *passive voice* sentence. In a passive voice sentence the subject (*ring*) is the result of, or receives the action of, the verb (*was given*). The verb agrees with its subject. The doer of the action may be identified in a *by* phrase (*by my mother*) or may not be mentioned at all.

> The last leg of the relay is always run by Ben.
> Two gold medals were won by him yesterday.
> Grapes are grown in the Niagara region.

In each of these example sentences, the subjects (*leg, medals, grapes*) receive the action (*is run, were won, are grown*). The subjects and verbs agree, but notice the second verb (*were*) has to become plural to agree with *medals*. The doers of the actions are identified in a *by* phrase (*by Ben, by him*) in the first two examples. In the third example, no specific grower is mentioned; it's a general statement.

Forming the Passive Voice

The passive voice is made by adding a form of *be* to the past participle of the main verb.

> A famous Toronto landmark *is located* on the corner of Front and Yonge.
>
> The Hockey Hall of Fame *is being expanded.*
>
> An international exhibit *has been planned.*
>
> Last year, the Hockey Hall of Fame *was visited* by over one million people.

The passive voice isn't used as frequently as the active voice, but there are occasions when you will choose to use it instead of the active voice. There are three specific instances when you choose to use the passive voice.

The first instance when you choose the passive voice is when you want to emphasize the result or receiver, not the doer, of the action. For this reason, it is often used in lab reports or accounts of experiments.

My tree was blown down by the strong winds last night.

The new funding formula was passed by a narrow majority.

Penicillin, that wonderful drug, was discovered by Sir Alexander Fleming.

In the first example, the tree is more important than the wind. In the second example, the new funding formula is emphasized, not the narrow majority. In the third example, the focus is on penicillin, not Fleming.

PRACTICE 40

Rewrite each of the following sentences to make them passive voice. Compare your version with the original. Which do you prefer in each case? Can you say why?

1. Roger ate all of the chocolate chip ice cream.

   ____

2. That boy caught the ball.

   ____

3. The dog buried that huge bone last week.

   ____

4. The storm destroyed my beautiful red rose bush.

   ____

5. The snake mesmerized the terrified rabbit.

   ____

PRACTICE 41

Rewrite each of the following sentences to make them active voice. Compare your version with the original. Which do you prefer in each case? Can you say why?

1. Consensus on the new subway line was reached late last night by city council.

   ____

2. The dilapidated, old house on the corner is being renovated by my uncle.

   ____

3. Mark was bitten by his own dog yesterday.

   ____

4. That poor little bird has been mauled by my cat.

   ____

5. The award for Student Achievement in Engineering has been donated by Drillco this year.

   ____

The second occasion when you choose the passive voice is when you don't know who the doer of the action is.

My house was built in 1890.
A fire was started in the West End early this morning.
The letter will be mailed as soon as possible.
It is forbidden to walk on the grass.
The *Titanic* has been discovered deep in the Atlantic.
At this moment, Bob is being given a tetanus shot.

PRACTICE 42

Rewrite each of the example sentences above as active voice sentences. Compare your version with the original. Can you say which one you prefer and why?

1. ______________________________
2. ______________________________
3. ______________________________
4. ______________________________
5. ______________________________
6. ______________________________

The third reason for choosing the passive voice is when you want to avoid identifying the doer. It is also used when no one wants to take responsibility for an action. As you can imagine, this is a popular choice when you are accused of something! In these cases, a *by* phrase is deliberately not included.

The milk was spilled.
My car was involved in an accident.
It has been decided to discontinue your line of credit.

PRACTICE 43

Make each of the following sentences passive voice and avoid identifying the doer in each case.

1. Fidelma hit the stop sign with her car last night.

   ____

2. Lynn has lost the directions to the camp.

   ____

3. I ate the last piece of chocolate cake.

   ____

4. The bank manager is closing your account.

   ____

5. The teacher bored the restless students.

   ____

READING WRITING: MORE PRACTICE

The next three readings provide you with an opportunity to recognize verbs at work in longer passages. The first passage employs the passive voice extensively while the second uses a variety of present tense verbs, and the third is predominantly written in the past tense.

Reading 2

Food for Thought

The information was adapted from *Social Studies* by Michael Kesterton.
Reprinted with permission from *The Globe and Mail.*

Many social changes are based on scientific research and are a result of teamwork. Take, for example, the well-known baby food, Pablum. In the early part of the twentieth century, nutritional food was too expensive for many people. As a result of poor nutrition, many children were being maimed by, or even dying from, diseases that are rarely even heard of today. One of these diseases is rickets. It is caused by poor nutrition, particularly in childhood. Rickets was so prevalent that close to a thousand cases a year were seen at the Toronto Hospital for Sick Children. In 1920, Dr. Alan Brown, a pediatrician, was hired by the hospital. The decision to hire him was based on his claim that he would reduce the annual rate of child deaths by fifty percent. Because he understood the role of good, inexpensive nutrition in healthy child development, Dr. Brown ensured that two of his colleagues with a special interest in nutrition were also hired by the hospital. So Drs. Theodore Drake and Fred Tisdall joined his team. As a result of Dr. Brown's influence, breast-feeding was encouraged and the pasteurization of milk was promoted by the hospital. Breast milk is, of course, free. The pasteurization of milk meant that people would have milk that was free from harmful bacteria, and which didn't sour so quickly.

Throughout the 1920s the three doctors researched the effects of vitamins and minerals not only in promoting healthy growth, but also in preventing disease. In 1930, a nutritional, new baby food was created by this team of doctors. It was called Pablum. This name was taken from the Latin word for food, *pabulum*. Pablum was a mixture of wheatmeal, cornmeal, and oatmeal. The bland flavour of the meal was used to mask the taste of its other active ingredients: wheat germ, brewer's yeast, alfalfa, bone meal, iron, and copper. The original version of Pablum was produced as a biscuit, and in trial taste tests, Pablum was certainly enjoyed by its consumers. Parents and doctors could now be sure that children were getting the right sort of nutrition.

On the advice of friends, the doctors sold the food commercially. It was mass-produced as a cereal that took only seconds to prepare. The fact that Pablum was now a mushy cereal meant it could be eaten by just about anyone but newborn babies. The child death rate due to poor nutrition began to drop. Not only children ate Pablum. In fact, Dr. Drake's widow ate Pablum for breakfast every morning until 1974, when she discovered sugar was being added as a sweetener. Sugar had not been included in the original recipe because the doctors feared it would encourage tooth decay.

The doctors made sure that all the royalties from the commercial sale of Pablum were assigned to the Hospital for Sick Children in Toronto. This was where their team had found a place to work on its research. In recent years, the word *pablum* has been included in the dictionary. If you look it up, you will find its meaning is listed as *bland*. Pablum might taste bland, but the effects of this Canadian creation were anything but! In most countries around the world, Pablum is enjoyed as a nutritional meal. Pablum revolutionized child nutrition.

PRACTICE 44

1. Find five passive voice sentences in the passage "Food for Thought." Copy them out and then rewrite each one as an active voice sentence.

2. Using your five examples, think about the three reasons for choosing the passive voice. Decide whether the use of the passive voice is appropriate in each case.

You probably had to check the meaning of a number of words. Or you skipped over them, guessing at their meaning because of their context.

Maimed, *rickets*, and *prevalent* are dealt with in the section on answering questions, but they represent the sort of word whose meaning you assume you know while you are reading. This is called *reading from context*. It's a useful tool, but you should always check to see whether your assumed meaning is accurate.

promote Be careful with this word. In this context, it doesn't mean to raise in status and increase responsibility, which is what we normally mean by it. What does it mean?

pasteurize What does this word mean? Where does it come from?

Answering Questions

Often when you have read an informative piece of writing, you are asked to provide facts from the article or think about and discuss certain details.

If you are asked a direct question, there is an easy and effective way to answer it. Turn the question around and use it to start your answer. Then you add the required fact that you locate in the article and you have completed the task.

What were the results of poor nutrition at the beginning of the twentieth century?

Okay? Now turn the question around:

The results of poor nutrition at the beginning of the twentieth century were

Next you locate the facts. Looking at the opening sentences of "Food for Thought," you have a few facts to choose from:

being maimed by diseases
dying from diseases
rickets

Before you add these facts to your beginning, make sure you understand them. Finally, don't simply copy your information word for word; rewrite it in your own words. You practised this skill in Units 2 and 3.

Do you understand the word *maimed*? If not, look up its meaning. Its meaning is given in the dictionary as *mutilate, cripple*. Choose the meaning you think is most appropriate. What about *rickets*? Its meaning is *a softening of the bones, especially the spine, associated with a deficiency of vitamin D.*

Now complete your sentence:

The results of poor nutrition at the beginning of the twentieth century were diseases such as rickets that could cripple or kill children.

Now that is a great sentence! Let's try one more.

How prevalent was rickets in 1920?

Before you turn this question around, what must you do?

Well, what does *prevalent* mean? If you had to look it up, you would find *prevalent* means *commonly or generally existing or occurring.*

Okay, now turn the question around:

In 1920, rickets commonly occurred

Now we have to show how common it was. Find the information in the article:

close to a thousand cases a year were seen at the Toronto Hospital for Sick Children

Don' t copy it word for word.

In 1920, rickets was so common that nearly one thousand children were treated at the Toronto Hospital for Sick Children alone.

Sometimes the question and answer are so short, you can't avoid using the same words:

> Who were Dr. Brown's colleagues?

The only problem you might have with this question is spelling the names correctly, so be careful.

> Dr. Brown's colleagues were Dr. Theodore Drake and Dr. Fred Tisdall.

Now try on your own.

Fact-Finding

Answer each of the following questions in a complete sentence.

1. Why was Dr. Alan Brown hired?
2. Why was pasteurization of milk promoted by Dr. Brown?
3. Why did the doctors think vitamins and minerals were important nutritionally?
4. How long did it take the doctors to create Pablum?
5. Why did the doctors call their new food Pablum?
6. What was in Pablum?
7. What was the commercial form of Pablum?
8. Why did Dr. Drake's widow stop eating Pablum after forty-four years?
9. What still happens to the royalties from the sale of Pablum?
10. Explain what this sentence means: "Pablum might taste bland, but the effects of this Canadian creation were anything but!"

Main Idea

What is this passage about? In five to eight sentences of your own, write the main ideas of this passage.

What Do You Think?

1. The passage describes the process by which Pablum changed child nutrition and shows how teamwork was an important factor in that process. What do you think the benefits of teamwork are?
2. Did you know about this important Canadian contribution to child nutrition before reading this passage?

Reading 3

Moving Meaning

Body language means the innumerable movements we make that convey information. Sometimes we choose to express our meaning by our gestures. In Canada, for example, we express "no" by moving our heads from side to side. However, in India a similar gesture means something like, "please continue talking; I'm interested." These movements are often made unconsciously, but there are many gestures we make quite consciously to express our meaning without words. If you make a fist with the thumb pointing up, in most parts of the world you are indicating things are fine or "good luck." Just don't try it in Malta or Turkey, or you could find yourself in an unwanted amorous situation! Perhaps the most famous gesture in the world at the moment is the "Titanic salute." In this case, the makers of the movie were being anachronistic. The raised middle finger was not used as a gesture in the early twentieth century.

In all parts of the world an initial greeting displays the hands, but in many cultures people do not shake hands with each other. For example, in Arabic countries people raise their right hands to their own foreheads to make a greeting. In Japan people clasp their own hands before they bow, while in the Indian subcontinent, the hands are pressed together and raised to the face in greeting. Each of these forms of greeting makes the hands visible to others. Perhaps originally these greetings showed that people were unarmed and came in peace. Think of another famous gesture made popular by Hollywood: the raised open palm commonly displayed in Westerns.

In North American culture, many consider direct eye contact to be respectful, but in most cultures dropping the gaze shows respect. For example, in many parts of the world you would not look directly at an elder relative or a figure of authority such as a teacher. This use of eye contact can be misinterpreted or lead to misunderstanding. In addition, there is the duration of the look to consider. If you sustain direct eye contact for too long, it becomes a stare, and that is usually interpreted as rude or even as hostile. Finally, there is the dropped eye gaze. Try it. You'll soon realize this is the basis of the flirtatious look.

As you can see, there are many gestures that convey meaning. There are even more unconscious movements that can tell another person what you are really thinking or feeling at any given time. Slumping in your seat conveys exhaustion or boredom; folding your arms across your chest suggests resistance to another person; leaning towards the person you are speaking to sends a message of agreement while leaning away implies the opposite. Just think for a moment about your personal space. How close can another person stand to you before you feel uncomfortable? It varies with the circumstances, doesn't it? If you know and like the other person, you accept a closer stance than if a stranger in an elevator, for example, gets too near to you. Your body has a language all of its own.

Fact-Finding

Answer each question in complete sentences and support your answers with references to the reading.

1. What is body language?
2. In India, how would you be misunderstood if you shook your head in response to a question?
3. Explain "unwanted amorous situation" in your own words.
4. What does *anachronistic* mean? In your own words, rewrite the sentence in which it appears, substituting another expression for *anachronistic*.
5. How many examples of greetings can you find in the second paragraph?
6. What reason is given for most greetings displaying the hands?
7. What sorts of eye contact are discussed?
8. How can you begin flirting with someone, according to this reading?
9. Which part of the world believes direct eye contact is not disrespectful?
10. What would your boss think if you slouched with your arms folded while the two of you were talking?
11. If you see a couple sitting side by side on a sofa, but leaning away from each other, what would you assume about their relationship?

Main Idea

What is this passage about? In five to eight sentences of your own, write the main idea of this passage.

What Do You Think?

1. What other common gestures can you think of?
2. How do you use eye contact?
3. Do you greet different people in different ways?
4. How close to you can others stand before you feel crowded?

READING 4

How the Buffalo Was Saved

Aboriginal people have always had a close relationship with the earth and its creatures. Traditionally, they have a spiritual responsibility to care for the earth as a living creature itself. This is very different from the tradition the European settlers brought with them as they established themselves in Canada. The native peoples of Canada hunted and trapped, but did not disturb the ecological balance in doing so. The settlers, following the voyageurs westward, brought a belief that nature was theirs to use. They also had guns and railways, which enabled them to use up the creatures of the plains quickly. In less than fifty years of European colonization, the great herds of buffalo that had roamed the plains for thousands of years were almost extinct.

When the United States and Canada established their international border in 1873, Michel Pablo, a Blackfoot, found himself living officially in the United States. He lived on the Flathead reserve in Montana where his ancestors had hunted the buffalo for more than ten thousand years. In 1880, he realized that the buffalo would no longer exist unless some action was taken. He rounded up a few buffalo calves and kept them, like cattle, on the reserve. By the early 1900s, he was responsible for the largest herd of buffalo anywhere in the world. In 1906, the buffalo were threatened yet again because Michel Pablo's people lost their reserve to settlers. Without the land to roam, the buffalo faced extinction.

In 1905, Alberta had joined Canada as a province and the Canadian government was establishing a series of national parks in western Canada. The Canadian government offered to buy the herd if Michel Pablo could deliver it to Wainwright, Alberta. Pablo and a crew of native cowboys set out on the long roundup that summer. They drove the 400 buffalo across the foothills and the plains from Montana to Alberta for $250 a head.

Today the descendents of that herd live in Wood Buffalo National Park in northern Alberta, where they roam freely. These buffalo represent over half of the buffalo alive today in the world. Michel Pablo was a man with a vision who saved an entire species from extinction.

Fact-Finding

1. Reword the relationship of the aboriginal people with nature.
2. How would you describe the attitude toward nature of the European settlers?

3. How much money did Michel Pablo and his cowboys make in the summer of 1906?
4. In your own words, record an event for each date that is mentioned in the reading.

Main Idea

In your own words, tell what Michel Pablo did.

What Do You Think?

1. How do you feel about the environment? Do you believe we have a responsibility to preserve ecosystems and animals? Why or why not?
2. Which national or provincial parks have you visited in Canada? What was your experience there?

Writing Suggestions

1. Write eight to twelve sentences of your own about your best friend. Use the present tense.
2. Write eight to twelve sentences of your own about a childhood memory. Use the past tense.
3. Write eight to twelve sentences about your ambitions or plans for the future. Use the future tense.
4. Write eight to twelve sentences about a teacher you remember well. Explain why that teacher made such a strong impression on you.
5. In eight to twelve sentences, discuss your favourite team game.
6. In eight to twelve sentences, discuss your attitude to the environment.

"The making of clear and beautiful sentences in harmony with the movement of thought is high art."

(Stephen Leacock)

UNIT FIVE

Combining Sentences

Unit 5 explains how sentences can be combined in order to make them clearer and better able to express your intended meaning. The concepts you need to learn are listed below. (After you finish the unit, you can look at the box to see whether you understand the key ideas.)

1. Coordinating Conjunctions
2. Punctuating to Coordinate: The Semicolon
3. Coordinating with a Semicolon and Transition Words
4. Subordinating Conjunctions
5. Punctuating to Subordinate: The Comma

COMBINING SENTENCES

READING 1

Swimming the Lake

In September 1954, sixteen-year-old Marilyn Bell captured most Canadians' imaginations. She became the first person to swim Lake Ontario. This swim was a grueling 51.5 kilometres. She had to swim from Youngstown, New York, on the south shore of the lake to Toronto on the north shore. Marilyn Bell was a young high-school girl in Toronto. She was a determined marathon swimmer. She had won a forty-kilometre ocean race in Atlantic City, New Jersey, in July 1954. The Canadian National Exhibition offered $10 000 to American marathon swimmer Florence Chadwick to swim Lake Ontario. Bell and her coach, Gus Ryder, thought that a Canadian should be given the chance to become the first person to accomplish this swim. The CNE didn't agree. On September 9, Marilyn Bell plunged into the twenty-degree water along with Chadwick, the authorized swimmer. Both swimmers had their crews. Bell's effort wasn't sanctioned by the officials at the CNE.

It was a chilly and rainy night. The women faced long hours of swimming in the darkness in high waves. By 4:45 in the morning, Florence Chadwick, violently seasick, had to be taken from the water. She was rushed to Toronto for medical care. Bravely, Marilyn Bell continued to fight off lamprey eels. They attached themselves to her in the cold, dark lake. She too was sick from the huge rollers and the fumes from oil spills and boats. By midmorning heavy winds had driven her off course. She recovered herself. She kept stroking. Cold and exhausted, Bell scarcely knew what she was doing by evening. She swam on supported by the efforts of her coach and team. By this time, thousands of Canadians were cheering for her. They listened to her progress on the radio. Crowds of people lined the shore. Flotillas of boats came out into the lake as she neared her goal. After twenty-one hours in the dark waters of Lake Ontario, Marilyn Bell touched the north shore. She completed her crossing.

The next year Marilyn Bell became the youngest person to swim the English Channel. At eighteen she became the youngest person to cross the treacherous Juan de Fuca Strait. It is between Vancouver Island and the Olympic Peninsula in Washington. The Canadian public was captivated by the strong and courageous young woman. She remained a modest, intelligent, and personable hero of Canadian sport.

The paragraphs in Reading 1 have very short, choppy sentences. They are basically correct as sentences go; there is nothing really *wrong* with them. They just sound kind of childish, and they aren't very interesting to read. The paragraph fails to show the connections between the ideas that are being explored.

Combining sentences is an important way to improve our writing and to show the connections between our ideas. One way to combine sentences is to coordinate them. We should review an important concept that was covered in Unit 2, where you learned the difference between independent and dependent clauses. As a brief reminder, clauses are groups of words that have a subject and verb. An independent clause can stand alone as a sentence. A dependent clause can't stand alone as a sentence (even though it has a subject and verb) because it has a word that makes its meaning dependent on another clause.

Most Canadians love hockey.	(Independent clause: subject–*Canadians*, verb–*love*)
Most Americans love baseball.	(IC: s–*Americans*, v–*love*)
Although most Canadians love hockey.	(Dependent clause because of *although*)
While most Americans love baseball.	(DC because of *while*)

COORDINATING CONJUNCTIONS

To coordinate something is to share it among equals. For example, if you're in charge of the night shift at the restaurant where you work, you're the boss. If you share that responsibility with another person, you're coordinating bosses. You're both in charge.

To coordinate sentences means to combine independent clauses, which are equal in terms of their ability to stand alone as sentences.

Most Canadians love hockey, and most Americans love baseball.

This sentence combines the two choppy little sentences you saw above into one longer sentence that shows the connection between the two ideas. The link used here is a comma (,) and the word *and*. *And* is what is called a *coordinating conjunction*. *Conjunction* means to join something, to link it together. And *coordinating* means that the things linked together are equal (independent clauses in this case).

There are only seven coordinating conjunctions in English: *and*, *but*, *or*, *nor*, *for*, *yet*, and *so*. These are the only words strong enough, so to speak, to combine independent clauses (with a comma). Because there are so few, they're easy to remember. Try this memory trick: the first letters of all seven spell out the "word" FANBOYS.

F or

A nd

N or

B ut

O r

Y et

S o

Would other coordinating conjunctions work in the combined sentences below? How about *so, or, for*? Why or why not? What are the differences in meaning?

Most Canadians love hockey, but most Americans love baseball.
Most Americans love baseball, yet most Canadians love hockey.

And

And is a kind of plus sign, *also, in addition*

Most Canadians love hockey, and more Americans are learning to enjoy it.

But

But puts the sentence in reverse, *except, in contrast*

Most Canadians love hockey, but many Americans just can't see the puck.

Or/Nor

Or provides an alternative, *either*. So does *nor* but it's a negative alternative, *neither*.

We will watch hockey on TV tonight, or we will go to a baseball game.

We won't watch hockey on TV tonight, nor will we go to a baseball game.

(Notice that *nor* is used with *not* verbs and that the word order of the second independent clause changes when it's used: *nor will we go*.)

For

For suggests a reason for something, *because*

> Some people find baseball boring, for it is a slow and subtle game.

Yet

Yet is similar to *but, nevertheless*

> Yuri was a big strong skater, yet he couldn't make the team.

So

So means as a result, *therefore*

> Baseball is a slow and subtle game, so some people find it boring.

And, but, or, nor, for, yet, and *so* are the seven coordinating conjunctions that have the power to combine independent clauses. However, they require one more piece of artillery: the comma. Don't forget the comma when you are combining sentences with a coordinating conjunction. Here's the formula:

	, and	
	, but	
	, or	
Independent clause	, nor	independent clause
	, for	
	, yet	
	, so	

PRACTICE 1

Combine these independent clauses by putting a comma and the appropriate coordinating conjunction in the blank. Don't forget the comma. The first one is done for you.

1. Their father was born in Canada, but their mother was born in the United States.
2. Hockey is the Canadian national sport ______________ baseball is the national game in the U.S.

3. She joined the Canadian Forces to see the world _____________ the only place she saw was Petawawa, Ontario.
4. The computer lab at school was closed on Saturday _____________ I couldn't finish my assignment.
5. Both Cindy and Elsa are short _____________ their sister Wendy is very tall.
6. I will ask my teacher for help _____________ she is usually kind and helpful.
7. He didn't learn to play hockey here _____________ did he learn it in Russia.
8. Michael has always wanted to be a sports reporter _____________ he enrolled in Ryerson's journalism program.
9. Would you like to join me for a game of pool _____________ would you prefer to play street hockey?
10. We were frightened by the noise in the basement _____________ we didn't find anything unusual down there.

PRACTICE 2

Combine your own independent clause with each of the independent clauses below, using a comma plus the coordinating conjunction specified in parentheses. Make sure that the two clauses are logically related. The first one is done for you.

1. (and) He was accepted at the University of British Columbia, and he will be moving to Vancouver in September.
2. (but) I studied math for hours every night _________________

____

3. (so) All of the roads were covered with ice ____________________

____

4. (for) Frank had always wanted to be a model __________________

____

5. (or) We could stay home tonight ____________________________

____

6. (and) Lucy's grandparents came here from China _____________

____

7. (yet) I love to eat pizza __________________________________

____

8. (nor) Maria doesn't play golf _______________________________

____

9. (but) ____

________________________ we haven't seen a movie in a long time.

10. (and) ____

________________________________they became very good friends.

PRACTICE 3

Combine each of the sentence pairs into one sentence with two independent clauses, using a comma and an appropriate coordinating conjunction. (Be careful about the wording if you use *nor*.) The first one is done for you.

1. Roger decided to get into shape.

   He joined a fitness club.

   Roger decided to get into shape, so he joined a fitness club.

2. We vacationed in Jamaica last winter.

   We visited Prince Edward Island in the summer.

   ____

3. Minh's mother speaks English.

   His father speaks Vietnamese.

   ____

4. In 1954, sixteen-year-old Marilyn Bell became the first person to swim Lake Ontario.

   She later swam the English Channel and Juan de Fuca Strait.

   ____

5. Pat started college to study nursing.

   She finished with a degree in engineering.

   ____

6. The family worked day and night in their store.

   They wanted to achieve a higher standard of living.

   ____

7. I don't have any interest in hockey.

   I don't have any interest in baseball.

   ____

8. Carolyn wanted to meet a new man.

   She put a personal ad in the newspaper.

   ____

9. Carolyn got a lot of phone calls.

   The men all sounded a little weird.

   ____

10. Sarah earned the highest marks in her program.

    She got free tuition for next year.

    ____

PRACTICE 4

Each of these clauses is complete by itself, but you can combine them to make more interesting sentences. Match the independent clauses and combine pairs—using *and, but, or, nor, for, yet, so,* and a comma—and write ten new sentences on the lines below. Be sure to capitalize correctly. The first one is done for you.

Jean works during the day	he never drives it
Gary applied for a job at Burger King	he was too scared to look into the gorge
I don't like spicy foods	Ron visited Niagara Falls for the first time
David may go to Red Deer College	he may attend the University of Manitoba
the snow fell all night	she grew up in Whistler, B.C.
her husband works at night	most Canadians are proud of them
the plot twists always keep me interested	he got it
the roads were impassable in the morning	I love to read mystery novels
Linda knows how to ski	Jack bought a fancy sports car
I don't like sweet foods	our peacekeeping forces are respected in the world

1. Jean works during the day, but her husband works at night.
2. ______________________________
3. ______________________________
4. ______________________________
5. ______________________________
6. ______________________________

7. ______________________________

8. ______________________________

9. ______________________________

10. ______________________________

PUNCTUATING TO COORDINATE: THE SEMICOLON

If you use no punctuation between independent clauses, you have a sentence error: the run-on sentence. If you use a comma alone (with no coordinating conjunction) between independent clauses, you have another kind of error: the comma splice. A comma by itself simply isn't strong enough to combine independent clauses; it *must* have a coordinating conjunction with it.

wrong (run-on): Most Canadians love hockey most Americans love baseball.

wrong (comma splice): Baseball is a slow and subtle game, some people find it boring.

However, there is a punctuation mark that has the "inner strength," we might say, to combine independent clauses. That mark is the semicolon (;), the comma with a period just above it.

right: Most Canadians love hockey; most Americans love baseball.

right: Baseball is a slow and subtle game; some people find it boring.

PRACTICE 5

Insert a semicolon between the independent clauses in the sentences below. Doing so correctly will eliminate a run-on sentence.

1. Bob ate all the pancakes Roger finished the waffles.
2. Sunny weather improves people's moods rainy weather can cause some of us to get depressed.
3. The new bestseller we bought is very long it has 577 pages.

4. Michael Jordan retired from professional basketball in 1999 he was at the top of his game.
5. My favourite TV shows are comedies I love sitcoms that make me laugh.
6. No one lived at the house anymore they had all moved to a trailer park.
7. A good diet and exercise are essential to a healthy lifestyle they help people maintain a reasonable weight.
8. Having children is a big responsibility young teenagers are often not prepared for the hard work involved in being a parent.
9. Classes for the fall semester begin at the end of August you should register in July through the telephone registration system.
10. Clay hopes to become a forest ranger he wants to get a job in the Canadian Rockies.

PRACTICE 6

Combine these independent clauses, using the strategy suggested. Be careful to capitalize the new sentence correctly. For example:

The police searched the lockers at school.

Their search tactics made the students uneasy.

(comma + *but*) The police searched the lockers at school, but their search tactics made the students uneasy.

1. The windows of the house were dark.

   We assumed no one was home.

   (comma + *so*) ______________________________

   ____

2. Hockey is usually played by young people.

   People of all ages can play golf.

   (comma + *yet*) ______________________________

   ____

3. The homeless man was pale and cold.

   He hadn't eaten all day.

   (comma + *for*) ______________________________

   ____

4. Roch Carrier's "The Hockey Sweater" is a very popular Canadian story.

   Most people read it during their school years.

   (semicolon) ______________________________

   ____

5. He bought a car with a stick shift.

   He didn't know how to drive it.

   (comma + *but*) ______________________________

   ____

6. He doesn't like to skate.

   He doesn't like to ski.

   (comma + *nor*) ______________________________

   ____

7. I don't know how to play tennis.

   I would like to learn.

   (comma + *yet*) ______________________________

   ____

8. A good education will increase your earning potential.

   It will make you a more informed citizen.

   (semicolon) ______________________________

   ____

9. Sherry hates to mow the lawn.

   It's a job that must be done.

   (comma + *but*) ______________________________

   ____

10. Lorne is fascinated by the history of golf.

    He is always searching for books on the subject.

    (comma + *so*) ______________________________

    ____

COORDINATING WITH A SEMICOLON AND TRANSITION WORDS

There are other connecting words that show the ways that writers move from one idea to another. These words are called *transition words*, and they show the relationship between clauses or whole sentences. Here is a list of some of these transition words, along with their meanings and an example:

Showing addition (similar to *and*)

besides	Pete loves hockey; in addition, he loves baseball.
furthermore	
in addition	
moreover	

Showing a contrast (similar to *but*)

however	Pete loves hockey; however, he hates basketball.
instead	
nevertheless	
nonetheless	
on the contrary	
on the other hand	

Showing cause or effect (similar to *so*)

as a result consequently hence still therefore thus	Pete loves hockey; therefore, he spends every Saturday night watching *Hockey Night in Canada*.

Showing time relationships

at the same time finally meanwhile next subsequently then	Pete watches hockey every Saturday night; meanwhile, his wife, Pat, plays bridge with her friends.

Showing more information, examples

as a matter of fact for instance for example indeed in fact	Hockey is a very important game in Pete's life; for example, he watched the Stanley Cup finals on his wedding night.

Look at the punctuation in the examples above. When these transition words are used between independent clauses, a semicolon is also necessary. Using a comma alone is incorrect; in fact, it causes a comma splice. Usually, the connecting word is followed by a comma.

wrong: Most Canadians love hockey, *on the other hand*, most Americans love baseball.

right: Most Canadians love hockey*; on the other hand,* most Americans love baseball.

wrong: Baseball is a slow and subtle game, *therefore*, some people find it boring.

right: Baseball is a slow and subtle game*; therefore,* some people find it boring.

A semicolon can be replaced by a period. The clauses that a semicolon combines are independent; both could be sentences on their own. The semicolon emphasizes the link between them, and the transition word tells the reader exactly what that link is.

PRACTICE 7

Combine these independent clauses using a semicolon and one of the transitions from the list below (use each transition only once). Make sure you punctuate correctly. The first one is done for you.

therefore	however
in fact	thus
meanwhile	consequently
for example	nevertheless
then	furthermore

1. Dana is very good at math and science; therefore, she hopes to become a high school physics teacher.
2. She hoped to be able to finish her degree this year ____________ it is going to take her another year.
3. Mike spent an hour speaking to his boss ____________ I was left sitting in the car.
4. Canada has produced some great racehorses ____________ Northern Dancer was the first Canadian-bred horse to win the Kentucky Derby.
5. John is a fabulous dancer ____________ I refuse to go to a club with him.
6. You must cleanse the wound thoroughly ____________ you must disinfect it and apply a clean bandage.
7. George completed all of the requirements for a diploma ____________ he maintained a very high grade point average.
8. Beatrice studied English for eight years ____________ she did very well on the composition test.

9. Carlos had only studied English for a year ____________________

   he did poorly on the test.

10. Helping the homeless is important to Amy ____________________

    she cooks one night a week at a shelter.

It is important to know when transition words are being used as part of the link between two independent clauses. Occasionally, a writer will use transition words not to join independent clauses, but rather to link ideas at the beginning, middle, or end of a sentence. Then the punctuation is different; commas are used after, around, or in front of the transition words.

> However, most Canadians love hockey.
> Most Canadians, however, love hockey.
> Most Canadians love hockey, however.

In the examples above, the word *however* isn't used to combine independent clauses. It is included in a single independent clause to show a transition in a writer's ideas. (You would need to read the sentences before and after these to understand why the transition has been used.) Now you can see why it is essential to be able to recognize independent clauses.

PRACTICE 8

Punctuate these sentences correctly. Use the semicolon only if the transition word is part of a link between independent clauses.

1. Dierdre hoped to meet the handsome stranger on her cruise

   however he came to dinner with his wife.

2. Dierdre hoped to meet the handsome stranger on her cruise he

   came to dinner with his wife however.

3. Dierdre hoped to meet the handsome stranger on her cruise he

   came to dinner however with his wife.

4. It is hard for me to wake up in the morning therefore I need three

   cups of coffee before class.

5. I've decided nevertheless to give up caffeine for a week.

6. At first, we wanted to take our vacation in Cuba instead we decided to go to Mexico.
7. At first, we wanted to take our vacation in Cuba we decided instead to go to Mexico.
8. Joanna and Rex are excellent dancers for example they know swing, salsa, disco, and merengue.
9. Joanna and Rex are excellent dancers they know for example swing, salsa, disco, and merengue.
10. We usually eat lunch at Flo's Diner on the other hand it would be nice to try a new restaurant.

PRACTICE 9

Below are the independent clauses from Practice 2. Add a different independent clause in Practice 9, and use a semicolon and a transition word instead of a coordinating conjunction. Be careful about the punctuation! The first one is done for you.

1. He was accepted at the University of British Columbia; however, he chose to attend Langara College.
2. I studied math for hours every night ______________________

   ____
3. All of the roads were covered with ice ______________________

   ____
4. Frank had always wanted to be a model ______________________

   ____
5. We could stay home tonight ______________________

   ____

6. Lucy's grandparents came here from China ____________________

____

7. I love to eat pizza ____

____

8. Maria doesn't play golf ____

____

9. ____

______________________ we haven't seen a movie in a long time.

10. ____

____________________________ they became very good friends.

PRACTICE 10

Punctuate these independent clauses, using the strategy suggested. Right now they are run-on sentences.

1. (comma + *but*) We have a beautiful living room guests always gather in the kitchen.
2. (semicolon) Swimming is very good exercise it firms and tones the body.
3. (comma + *or*) Meet me at the corner meet me at the pub.
4. (comma + *for*) The traffic in Vancouver is very slow there are no expressways through town.
5. (semicolon + *in addition*) The Internet is a good way to do research it provides a way to make new friends.
6. (comma + *and*) Adapting to college is difficult for many people they need to be prepared for the challenges.

7. (semicolon + *however*) My mom's birthday is August 1 she won't tell us how old she is.

8. (semicolon + *therefore*) There is no spell-check feature on the computer you'll have to use your dictionary.

9. (comma + *so*) Peter eats all the time and doesn't exercise he is thirty pounds overweight.

10. (semicolon + *meanwhile*) The car ran out of gas on the deserted road it was getting colder and darker all the time.

PRACTICE 11

Add an independent clause to the sentences below. Use the coordinating strategy suggested. The first one is done for you.

1. (comma + *but*) Sunshine is good for us, but it can cause skin damage.

2. (comma + *and*) I saw the new Flaberciser exercise machine on the Shopping Channel ____________________

3. (semicolon + *nevertheless*) Accounting is an important skill for business people ____________________

4. (comma + *so*) There are two sides to every story of divorce ____________________

5. (semicolon + *however*) We tried to rent the movie at the video store ____________________

6. (semicolon) Victoria, B.C., has a mild climate in the winter ____________________

7. (comma + *or*) The man will be found guilty of the murder ____________________

8. (semicolon + *thus*) The final exam was exceedingly difficult

____

9. (semicolon + *therefore*) My brother achieved a 98% average in his high school courses ______________________

10. (comma + coordinating conjunction of your choice) Canadian figure skaters compete at the highest levels of the sport ________

____

To review, here's the complete formula for combining independent clauses:

Independent clause	, and , but , or , nor , for , yet , so	independent clause
	or	
Independent clause	;	independent clause
	or	
Independent clause	; transition word,	independent clause

PRACTICE 12

Now return to Reading 1 on page 176. On a separate sheet of paper, combine independent clauses by coordinating them with one of the strategies you've learned in this unit. After you've coordinated sentences, compare your version with the one below.

Swimming the Lake

In September 1954, sixteen-year-old Marilyn Bell captured most Canadians' imaginations, for she became the first person to swim Lake Ontario. This swim was a grueling 51.5 kilometres from Youngstown, New York, on the south shore of the lake to Toronto on the north shore. Marilyn Bell was a young high-school girl in Toronto; nevertheless, she was also a determined marathon swimmer. She had won a forty-kilometre ocean race in Atlantic City, New Jersey, in July 1954. However, the Canadian National Exhibition offered $10 000 to American marathon swimmer Florence Chadwick to swim Lake Ontario. Bell and her coach, Gus Ryder, thought that a Canadian should be given the chance to become the first person to accomplish this swim. The CNE didn't agree, so on September 9 Marilyn Bell plunged into the twenty-degree water along with Chadwick, the authorized swimmer. Both swimmers had their crews, but Bell's effort wasn't sanctioned by the officials at the CNE.

It was a chilly and rainy night, and the women faced long hours of swimming in the darkness in high waves. By 4:45 in the morning, Florence Chadwick, violently seasick, had to be taken from the water; she was rushed to Toronto for medical care. Bravely, Marilyn Bell continued to fight off lamprey eels that attached themselves to her in the cold, dark lake. She too was sick from the huge rollers and the fumes from oil spills and boats. By mid-morning, heavy winds had driven her off course, but she recovered her direction and kept stroking. Cold and exhausted, Bell scarcely knew what she was doing by evening, yet she swam on supported by the efforts of her coach and team. By this time, thousands of Canadians were cheering for her too as they listened to her progress on the radio. Crowds of people lined the shore, and flotillas of boats came out into the lake as she neared her goal. After twenty-one hours in the dark waters of Lake Ontario, Marilyn Bell touched the north shore and completed her crossing.

The next year Marilyn Bell became the youngest person to swim the English Channel. At eighteen she became the youngest person to cross the treacherous Juan de Fuca Strait between Vancouver Island and the Olympic Peninsula in Washington. The Canadian public was captivated by the strong and courageous young woman, yet she remained a modest, intelligent, and personable hero of Canadian sport.

Fact-Finding

1. How far did Marilyn Bell have to swim in order to cross Lake Ontario?
2. Identify three difficulties that Bell had to overcome in order to complete her lake crossing.

Main Idea

In your own words, write the main idea of each paragraph of "Swimming the Lake."

What Do You Think?

What makes a person undergo a rigorous physical ordeal in order to set or break a record? Can you think of other examples of gruelling physical efforts to accomplish a goal? Do you think such goals are worth the difficulties involved?

SUBORDINATING CONJUNCTIONS

Another very useful method of combining sentences is subordinating one clause to be dependent on an independent clause. *Subordinate* means "not equal" or lower in rank. (If you are the boss of the night staff at the restaurant, the other workers are your subordinates.) When you're writing sentences, using subordinate clauses is an excellent way to show the relationships between your ideas.

At the beginning of the unit, you saw two subordinate clauses that are fragments because they contain a word that makes them dependent on another clause for meaning. (*Subordinate* and *dependent* refer to the same kind of clause.)

> Although most Canadians love hockey.
> While most Americans love baseball.

The words *although* and *while* are subordinating conjunctions; they make the clause that follows dependent on an independent clause to complete the meaning and to make a complete sentence.

> Although most Canadians love hockey, many Americans just don't appreciate the game.
>
> While most Americans love baseball, some people find it slow and boring.

There are far more subordinating conjunctions than there are coordinating conjunctions. (It's easier to memorize the coordinating conjunctions because there are only seven!) In Unit 2 you saw a list of some of the commonly used dependent clause words, also known as subordinating conjunctions. Here, again, are some of the most familiar:

after	even though	when
although	if	whenever
as	since	where
as if	so that	whereas
as though	though	wherever
because	unless	whether
before	until	while

Choosing the appropriate subordinating conjunction is important because it can change meaning in subtle and significant ways. Notice the major difference in meaning that two words, both subordinating conjunctions, can make in the same sentence:

The evening was delightful *because* my boyfriend was with me.
The evening was delightful *although* my boyfriend was with me.

What does the different subordinating conjunction in the sentences tell you about the relationship?

In the sentences above, the independent clause comes first in the sentences. However, the dependent clause can also be first. The order of the independent/dependent clauses makes little difference in the meaning of the sentences.

Because my boyfriend was with me, the evening was delightful.
The evening was delightful because my boyfriend was with me.

Subordinating conjunctions join ideas that are related to each other in a variety of ways. They may tell us *why, when, where*, or *how* the ideas in the clauses are connected to each other. Here is a list that shows some of the relationships expressed by subordinating conjunctions:

Showing why

because	I got a job because I went to college.
since	
so that	

Showing when

after	I got a job after I went to college.
as	
as soon as	
before	
since	
until	
when	
wherever	

Showing where

where	I can get a job wherever I go.
wherever	

Showing how (under what conditions)

although	I can get a job if I go to college.
as	
even though	
if	
though	
unless	

PRACTICE 13

Choose an appropriate subordinating conjunction for each of the sentences below.

1. ____________ the snow stopped, we shovelled the driveway.
2. Please call us ____________ you get to Montreal.
3. You can't get your final marks ____________ you pay your tuition.
4. ____________ we tried to call him all evening, we were not able to get in touch with him.
5. Carmen is taking a computer course ____________ she wants to learn to be a programmer.
6. You are eligible to vote in the election ____________ you are a Canadian citizen.
7. ____________ you go, I will follow.
8. I haven't spoken to him ____________ he insulted me.
9. ____________ Canadians start to exercise more and eat less, their average weight will continue to increase.
10. ____________ we leave for Vancouver, we should book a hotel room.

PUNCTUATING TO SUBORDINATE: THE COMMA

The evening was delightful because my boyfriend was with me.
Because my boyfriend was with me, the evening was delightful.

The difference in the sentences above is punctuation, not meaning. In both sentences, the independent clause is *the evening was delightful*. As Unit 2 points out, when the independent clause is first, there's no punctuation between clauses. When the dependent clause is first, use a comma between clauses. Here's the formula:

Independent clause	**(no comma)**	**dependent clause**
Dependent clause	**(, comma)**	**independent clause**

PRACTICE 14

Combine these clauses, making one of them subordinate to the other. Use the suggested subordinating conjunction and make sure you punctuate your sentence correctly. As they stand, they are run-on sentences. The first one is done for you.

1. (although) We love our dog Fido he is very old and sick.

   We love our dog Fido although he is very old and sick.

2. (because) Mark had never finished high school he was unable to get a well-paying job.

   ____

3. (unless) You'll never finish the project some of the staff help you.

   ____

4. (wherever) Fred and Phyllis have lots of friends they travel.

   ____

5. (while) We were away for the weekend the robbers broke into our house.

   ____

6. (as soon as) We got back and saw the damage we called the police.

   ____

7. (until) The baby gets a bit older we can't take him to the opera.

   ____

8. (whether) I want to know he finishes the cleanup or not.

____

9. (when) The weather turned lovely they arrived in Florida.

____

10. (even though) Jaron's calculus marks were very good he hadn't had to study very hard.

____

PRACTICE 15

Write sentences that include the clauses below, using the subordinating conjunction when specified. Use a comma if it's required. Make sure that the two clauses are logically related. The first one is done for you.

1. Although <u>we invited lots of people,</u> only a few people made it to the party.
2. We will be happy to provide the service after ______________
3. If ______________________________, they can go.
4. It would be a good idea to learn all the details before

   ____
5. Children should get enough calcium in their diets so that

   ____
6. We are going to have a picnic tomorrow whether

   ____
7. Since Tom joined the motorcycle gang ______________
8. I'll do the dishes while ______________
9. Even though he still loves her ______________
10. Whenever Pete calls me ______________

PRACTICE 16

Combine each pair of sentences into a single sentence using an appropriate subordinate conjunction. Use a comma where it's required. The first one is done for you.

1. Hurricane season was over.

   We went to Jamaica.

   When hurricane season was over, we went to Jamaica.

2. The computer industry is thriving.

   Marla enrolled in a programming course at college.

   ____

3. We cleaned the house.

   We heard you were visiting for the weekend.

   ____

4. The professor's class is very demanding.

   Students like his teaching methods.

   ____

5. You intend to study abroad.

   You must get a student visa.

   ____

6. We want to see *Terminator 15*.

   It leaves the movie theatre on Friday.

   ____

7. We all go to the clubs to party.

   The school semester ends.

   ____

8. I cannot skate well enough to play hockey.

   I tried very hard to learn.

   ____

9. I have loved that woman.

   I first met her.

   ____

10. You must make lots of money.

    You want to live in a mansion.

    ____

PRACTICE 17

Combine the clauses below, using the suggested coordination or subordination pattern. Punctuate as required; don't forget the commas. The first one is done for you.

1. (coordinate with *and*) The sky grew very dark a huge storm broke over the lake.

   The sky grew very dark, and a huge storm broke over the lake.

2. (subordinate with *as*) Martha cried her boyfriend boarded the airplane.

   ____

3. (subordinate with *although*) Harold is in excellent shape he is almost fifty.

   ____

4. (coordinate with a semicolon) My son has dark hair my daughter has bright red hair.

   ____

5. (coordinate with *or*) Debra will meet us in Ecuador she will meet us in Chile.

____

6. (coordinate with a semicolon + *nevertheless*) The team had only competed together once they won the tournament.

____

7. (subordinate with *because*) He took the job at the dump he needed the money.

____

8. (coordinate with a semicolon + *however*) Diane wants to be a flight attendant she is afraid of flying.

____

9. (subordinate with *whenever*) People get hungry on the road they want to eat quickly.

____

10. (coordinate with *so*) The copy machine in the office is broken we can't make a duplicate of the contract.

____

PRACTICE 18

Combine the sentences in Practice 17 again, but this time use a different coordination or subordination strategy. Watch the punctuation! The first one is done for you.

1. (coordinate with a semicolon and *then*)

   The sky grew very dark; then a huge storm broke over the lake.

2. (subordinate with *when*)

____

3. (coordinate with *but*)

____

4. (subordinate with *although*)

____

5. (coordinate with *nor*—change the clauses to negatives)

____

6. (coordinate with *yet*)

____

7. (subordinate with *since*)

____

8. (coordinate with *but*)

____

9. (subordinate with *if*)

____

10. (coordinate with a semicolon and *as a result*)

____

PRACTICE 19

Combine these independent clauses by making one of them subordinate to another. Use the subordinating conjunction that best suits your intended meaning. Punctuate and capitalize your sentence correctly. The first one is done for you.

Carl and Debbie had lived apart for three years

call us from the airport

you graduate from college

they filed for divorce

we can go to the game

Betty worked as a prison guard

your plane arrives

they are addicted to alcohol

I have lots of good ideas

it has about one-tenth the population of the United States

people's lives can be destroyed

we manage to buy hockey tickets

he dropped the course

you need a place to stay

her husband stayed home with the kids

you'll be able to get a good job

Canada is a huge country geographically

Roger was failing math

you can use our spare bedroom

I'm afraid to present them in front of a group

1. After Carl and Debbie had lived apart for three years, they filed for divorce.
2. ______________________________
3. ______________________________
4. ______________________________
5. ______________________________
6. ______________________________
7. ______________________________
8. ______________________________
9. ______________________________
10. ______________________________

PRACTICE 20

Practise combining sentences with coordination and subordination by writing your own sentences using the words and patterns below. Be careful about punctuation, especially with words such as *however* and *therefore*. The first one is done for you.

1. Because you are my friend, I'll lend you the fifty dollars.
2. ________________________________ but ________________________________
3. ________________________________ although ________________________________
4. ________________________________ and ________________________________
5. ________________________________ however ________________________________
6. Unless ________________________________ ________________________________
7. ________________________________ so ________________________________
8. ________________________________ if ________________________________
9. ________________________________ therefore ________________________________
10. ________________________________ until ________________________________

PRACTICE 21

Now return to the reading that begins this unit, "Swimming the Lake." On a separate sheet of paper, combine sentences by using subordinating conjunctions to make clauses dependent on others. Punctuate appropriately. After you complete your rewrite, compare it with the version below and with the version in Practice 12. Analyze both versions. Which sentences are combined through coordination and which through subordination? Which version do you prefer?

Swimming the Lake

In September 1954, sixteen-year-old Marilyn Bell captured most Canadians' imaginations when she became the first person to swim Lake Ontario. This swim was a grueling 51.5 kilometres from Youngstown, New York, on the south shore of the lake to Toronto on the north shore. Although Marilyn Bell was a young high-school girl in Toronto, she was also a determined marathon swimmer. She had won a forty-kilometre ocean race in Atlantic City, New Jersey, in July 1954. However, the Canadian National Exhibition offered $10 000 to American marathon swimmer Florence Chadwick to swim Lake Ontario. Bell and her coach, Gus Ryder, thought that a Canadian should be given the chance to become the first person to accomplish this swim. Even though the CNE didn't agree, on September 9 Marilyn Bell plunged into the twenty-degree water along with Chadwick, the authorized swimmer. Both swimmers had their crews although Bell's effort wasn't sanctioned by the officials at the CNE.

It was a chilly and rainy night, and the women faced long hours of swimming in the darkness in high waves. By 4:45 in the morning, Florence Chadwick, violently seasick, had to be taken from the water and rushed to Toronto for medical care. Bravely, Marilyn Bell continued to fight off lamprey eels that attached themselves to her in the cold, dark lake. She too was sick from the huge rollers and the fumes from oil spills and boats. By mid-morning, heavy winds had driven her off course although she recovered her direction and kept stroking. Cold and exhausted, Bell scarcely knew what she was doing by evening, yet she swam on supported by the efforts of her coach and team. By this time, thousands of Canadians were cheering for her too as they listened to her progress on the radio. Crowds of people lined the shore, and flotillas of boats came out into the lake as she neared her goal. After twenty-one hours in the dark waters of Lake Ontario, Marilyn Bell touched the north shore and completed her crossing.

The next year Marilyn Bell became the youngest person to swim the English Channel. At eighteen she became the youngest person to cross the treacherous Juan de Fuca Strait between Vancouver Island and the Olympic Peninsula in Washington. Even though the Canadian public was captivated by the strong and courageous young woman, she remained a modest, intelligent, and personable hero of Canadian sport.

READING WRITING: MORE PRACTICE

Read the three selections below for understanding. As you read, find the phrase or clause from below the passage that fits into each blank space. Include appropriate capitalization and punctuation.

READING 2

Why Canadian Football Is Better than American Football

While NFL football in the United States is a game that seems to become more popular every year, CFL football in Canada often struggles for its existence. This phenomenon is a shame ______________________________ ________________ In Canadian football, the size of the field and the rules of the game can make the action more exciting and the scoring more interesting.

In Canadian football, the field itself is longer (110 yards as opposed to 100 yards), wider, and the end zone is deeper. The additional field of play provides the players with extra space for both the running and the passing game. They have a lot more room to manoeuvre, ______________________________ ____________

The rules of the Canadian game encourage more action. First, Canadian rules allow twelve players on the field as opposed to eleven. The additional player expands the possibilities for a variety of plays. ____________________ ____________________ Hence, the teams tend to pass the ball more in Canadian football in order to advance the ball in fewer downs. Third, Canadian football offers the possibility of a single point in a play other than the conversion after a touchdown (the only time a team can score a single point in American football). The single point adds a scoring dimension to the CFL game ____

It seems odd that NFL football is so popular with sports fans because CFL football is a game with more action, interest, and excitement.

A. and that larger space makes the game more exciting
B. because Canadian football can be a much more exciting game
C. that NFL football lacks
D. second, there are three downs (chances to move the ball) in Canadian football as opposed to four

Fact-Finding

In your own words, explain the three differences between the rules of NFL and CFL football. These differences are given in paragraph 3 of the reading.

Main Idea

What is the main idea of the reading? Write it in your own words. Then rewrite the two reasons that are provided to support the main idea.

Reading 3

Golf vs. Tennis

Imagine that you have been a really good athlete all through your childhood and teenage years. You've played up through the ranks in a demanding team sport such as hockey or soccer. Now you're a bit older, ______________________________ You're also not sure that you'll have the stamina, the "legs," for the game ten years from now. So you are trying to decide on a new sport. The new game should be fun and challenging, and it should be a sport that you can play as you get older. Your friend Moe is trying to talk you into golf. Your friend Curly is giving you the sales pitch for tennis. So what is your new sport going to be?

"Golf," says Moe, "is a terrific game." He goes on to tell you that you can play it by yourself or you can play it with friends. It's both individual and highly social. It also takes a high degree of skill and subtle physical ability. You can spend your life learning the intricacies of a first-rate golf swing. ______________________________ you get plenty of exercise in the seven or eight kilometres that you'll cover in an eighteen-hole round. Moe also tells you that it's a myth that golf is a rich person's game. He says he spends about $40 in green fees for a round of golf: "That's less than $10 an hour for a heck of a lot of fun," he exclaims proudly.

At the same time, Moe tells you, ____________ ____________ there will be trees, lakes, a wonderful variety of settings rather than a boring, clay tennis court. According to Moe, golf is a thoughtful, meditative game where the time you take getting to your ball or setting up a shot will lead to relaxation and peace of mind. In addition, you'll be able to play with a range of players. Because of the handicapping system in golf, you can play with someone who is a much better or a much worse player than you are and still have a game. "How can you play with a really good tennis player if you're just a beginner?" Moe asks. "In golf, you can."

"Whoa," says Curly, "just a minute! Golf is a game for old fat guys." She goes on to claim that tennis demands superb physical conditioning, great reflexes, and a keen competitive edge. Curly tells you that tennis, too, is a good social game; people join clubs and have regular games with partners ____________ "Tennis is far more economical to play. Compare the cost of a tennis racket with that of a set of golf clubs," she exults.

As far as surroundings go, according to Curly, tennis is played all over the world, and it doesn't eat up huge amounts of land to provide people with access to the game. You can play indoors in the winter ____________ ____________ Curly tells you that golf is pathetically slow—that your hair will turn gray while you wait for the group ahead of you to finish their hole. Tennis ____________ is fast-paced and instinctive. A tennis player has to make split-second decisions and adapt to the uninterrupted rhythm of her opponent and the game. Finally, Curly admits that it's best to have a partner whose skills are similar to your own. "But who wouldn't want to play any game with someone who's as good—or as bad—as you are?"

Well, that's the dilemma. Will you join Moe at the golf course or pound the courts with Curly? Will you pick up a club or a racket? It's your choice!

A. on the other hand
B. who become close friends over years of playing together
C. if you walk instead of riding in a cart
D. and you're not sure that you have time for organized team sports
E. you'll play outside in beautiful surroundings
F. when the golf course is covered with snow

Fact-Finding

"Golf vs. Tennis" is a contrast; it shows how the two sports are different from each other. Which paragraphs mainly focus on golf? Which paragraphs focus mainly on tennis?

Main Idea

The comparison and contrast technique is a special kind of writing structure. Comparison shows how two things are similar; contrast shows how two things are different. Comparison and contrast are very useful for a variety of writing tasks.

In your own words, explain the basis of the contrast. Some of the features that Moe and Curly use to emphasize the differences between the two sports are listed below. Can you provide others?

1. physical exercise
2. social opportunities
3. cost
4. ______________________________
5. ______________________________

What Do You Think?

Who do you think has presented the more compelling argument, Moe or Curly? Would you choose golf or tennis? Why?

READING 4

Canadian Becomes World's Fastest Human

When you read the title above, did you think of Ben Johnson, the Canadian sprinter who won the title when he ran the hundred metres in 9.83 seconds in 1988? Johnson, of course, lost the title when he tested positive for a banned substance. Or perhaps you thought of Donovan Bailey, who set a world record of 9.84 seconds at the 1996 Olympics in Atlanta. In fact, the title once belonged to another Canadian, Percy Williams, ______________________________ The year was 1928.

In 1927, Percy Williams was an unknown nineteen-year-old high-school athlete in Vancouver. There was little about him that suggested he would achieve world-class athlete status. He was small physically (59 kg), and ______________________________ His seemingly easy pace as a runner didn't reveal his actual power and speed. In the spring of 1928, Williams ran a 220-yd race on a slow grass track in less than 22 seconds, and if he hadn't slipped, his time would have been even faster. A few track experts were intrigued by what was—in 1928—a singular accomplishment, but Williams was unknown to the general public. After qualifying for Olympic try-outs in British Columbia in June 1928, Percy Williams came east to show the Canadian track establishment what he could do.

In Hamilton, Ontario, on June 30, Williams tied the Olympic record in the 100-m race, breaking the Canadian record by .6 second. Then, two days later, he blasted by the competition in the 200 m. Percy Williams was a double Canadian champ, ____

In 1928, the Olympic Games were held in Amsterdam, Holland. In the track and field events, ninety runners representing thirty-seven countries started in qualifying heats for the 100-m sprint. The finalists would have to run four first-rate races in two days. One poor start, Williams knew, would eliminate him from the event, ____

On day one of competition, Williams won his first round, and in the second he tied the Olympic record of 10.6 seconds. His was the fastest time of the afternoon. Excitement was building in the Canadian contingent. ____ behind an American named McAllister. After resting for a couple of hours, the finalists took the field just after 4 p.m., July 30, 1928. They included two Americans, an Englishman, a German, a South African, and Williams. They all knew that the winner of this premier event would achieve world-wide fame and be accorded the title "world's fastest human."

Two false starts revealed the pitch of the finalists' nerves, but the steely Williams held his mark through both. Then the contestants burst from the starting holes they had carefully dug and ran, legs flying and arms pumping, down the track. They ran as a pack for half the distance. Suddenly, in a dazzling burst of speed, Williams sped up and plunged across the finish line first. ____ Percy Williams mounted the Olympic podium, a gold medallist and world champion.

Remarkably, Williams was also entered in the 200-m race. During the next two days he competed through the gruelling four-round elimination heats for this event. On August 1, he took the field in the final against two Germans, an Englishman, an American, and another Canadian. Williams actually trailed the others around the turn and into the stretch. But with 25 m to go, he moved into fourth; 15 m later he was second. Then in a ferocious release of power, he surged forward and hit the tape a stride ahead of the British runner. ____ and sports immortality within two days.

The formerly unknown B.C. boy came home a full-fledged hero. He was feted in Montreal and given the key to the city of Hamilton. In Toronto, thousands of people jammed Union Station to welcome the runner, and a two-kilometre line of cars, floats, and cheering people followed him ________ ________________________________ Williams would later maintain his domination of the world's top runners in a spectacular series of indoor races in Chicago, Boston, and New York.

Records have certainly been broken since 1928, and Olympic sports have changed dramatically. Yet the achievement of Percy Williams, a Canadian who truly was for a time "the world's fastest human," still makes us proud.

A. on day two, Williams qualified for the final by finishing second in the semifinal race
B. so he had to run flat-out each race
C. childhood rheumatic fever had left him with a damaged heart
D. but the stronger competition of the Olympic Games remained ahead of him
E. who won it long before Johnson and Bailey
F. in a parade through the city
G. to the cheers of the world and the deep emotions of his fellow Canadians
H. Percy Williams had won two Olympic gold medals

Fact-Finding

In your own words, provide a brief summary of details in the narrative of Percy Williams' Olympic triumph.

1. Percy Williams, an unknown teenage athlete in Vancouver, qualifies for Olympic tryouts in June 1928.
2. Williams qualifies for the Olympics by breaking the Canadian record for the hundred metres in Hamilton, Ontario.
3. ______________________________
4. ______________________________
5. ______________________________

Main Idea

Reading 4, "Canadian Becomes World's Fastest Human," tells a true story. A piece of writing that provides a sequence of events is called a *narrative*. Write the main idea of the reading. What does the writer want us to remember about Percy Williams?

What Do You Think?

Do you think that the Olympic Games reflect high or low ideals? Provide examples to support your opinion.

PRACTICE 22

Scan Readings 2, 3, and 4 to answer the following questions.

1. A Canadian football field is ______________________ than an American football field.
2. Canadian football teams have ______________________ players on the team while NFL teams have ______________________ .
3. In Canadian football, a team can score ______________________ point in ways that an American football team can't.
4. Even though ______________________ football may be more exciting than ______________________ football, the NFL game is far more popular.
5. You can play golf by yourself or ______________________ .
6. You can get exercise in golf if you ______________________ instead of ______________________ .
7. The ______________________ system in golf lets players of unequal ability play together.
8. Tennis can be played ______________________ when the weather is bad.
9. Golf equipment is more ______________________ than tennis equipment.
10. Percy Williams was a Canadian who became the "world's fastest human" in the summer of ______________________ .
11. Another Canadian who won the title of "world's fastest human" was ______________________ , but he ______________________ the title for using ______________________ .

12. Williams came from ______________________, and he competed in the Olympic Games in ______________________ .

13. Williams won the ______________________ in the 100-m sprint after two days and ______________________ rounds of races.

14. In the 200-m event, Williams was ______________________ the others for half the race, but he surged forward and ______________________ the race.

15. Williams returned to Canada a ______________________ ; for example, the people of Toronto ______________________ .

Writing Suggestions

1. Write a paragraph that explains why something Canadian is better than its American equivalent. (Suggestions include beer, comedians, city streets, gun laws, a kind of music, or a TV show.)
2. Compare two sports or activities (not golf or tennis) that you are familiar with, and tell your reader which one you recommend.
3. Write a paragraph narrating the accomplishment of a particular athlete. The athlete may be amateur or professional; the accomplishment may be recent or have taken place in the past. But let your reader know why he or she is special.

"Good prose is like a window pane."

(George Orwell)

UNIT SIX

Composing Paragraphs

Unit 6 focuses on an organized approach to reading and writing paragraphs. The fundamental concepts you need to know are listed below. (After you have finished this unit, you can refer back to this box to see whether you have understood the key ideas.)

1. What Is a Paragraph?
2. The Topic Sentence
   - 2.1 Finding the Focus
   - 2.2 Locating a Topic Sentence
   - 2.3 Writing a Topic Sentence
3. Gathering Supporting Details
   - 3.1 Brainstorming
   - 3.2 Questioning
   - 3.3 Discussing
4. Sorting Supporting Details
5. Finishing Your Paragraph
6. Editing and Proofreading Your Paragraph
7. Writing More than One Paragraph
8. Writing a Summary
   - 8.1 The Single-Sentence Summary
   - 8.2 The Selective Summary
   - 8.3 The Point-by-Point Summary

WHAT IS A PARAGRAPH?

All writing is about something. Writing is a means of communication, of sharing facts, information, or ideas. A *paragraph* is an organized unit of writing consisting of a number of sentences that develop a focused topic. Like a sentence, a paragraph is easy to identify on the page. It is a block of print starting with a capital letter, ending with a period, and its first line is usually indented. (The designs of some books, like this one, do not indent certain paragraphs.) A paragraph is also a complete unit of thought, so it can be as short as four or five sentences, or as long as twelve or fifteen. Whatever its length, a paragraph develops one whole idea. When you, as a reader, identify the main idea of a paragraph, you recognize the topic and what the author says about that topic.

THE TOPIC SENTENCE

- **A topic sentence states the single main idea of the paragraph.**

A topic sentence explains to the reader the single main idea of a paragraph. It doesn't simply state a fact; rather it provides a focus for a number of facts and ideas that are contained in the paragraph.

- **A topic sentence provides a focus for the paragraph.**

When something is focused, it has a clear direction or limit. A focused topic sentence directs the writer of the paragraph. It acts as a limit. Only details that relate to the focused topic should be included in the paragraph. Extra details can be separated into a second paragraph. The topic sentence is the writer's outline for the development of the paragraph. It also tells the reader what the writer wants to say about the topic.

The topic is a usually a noun or a noun phrase and it is in a sentence that provides the focus, or limits the scope of the paragraph. See the table below for examples.

Topic (Noun/Noun Phrase)	Topic Sentence (Focus)
Cartoons	Cartoons are a staple of television these days.
Mickey Mouse	The popularity of Mickey Mouse has endured for over seventy years.
Donald Duck	Donald Duck is a bad-tempered, selfish cartoon character.

PRACTICE 1

Look at the paragraph below. It contains a number of interesting facts, but it doesn't have a sentence that clearly states what it is about; in other words, it has no topic sentence. Read the paragraph through and decide which of the topic sentences in the table on page 218 best belongs as its first line.

____

____________________________________. Although he was created by Walt Disney in the early 1920s, he got his big break in 1928 when he starred in *Steamboat Willie*. Actually, this was Mickey's third movie, but it was the one that made him the international star he is today. Back in 1928, Mickey Mouse was not the rounded, childlike character we have come to love; in 1928, he was skinnier and actually more mouselike. He could, of course, sing and dance and already had that high-pitched, squeaky voice we associate with him. After appearing in a series of short cartoons, Mickey starred in *Fantasia*, a full-length feature film. Over the years, subtle changes were made to Mickey's appearance, and to his storylines. Those ears were trademarked in the 1950s when Mickey made the transition from the big screen to television. As his fame and popularity grew, so the fortunes of the Disney studios increased. Mickey is the mouse that created an empire, and through it all Mickey has remained a sweet-natured, generous character. Maybe this is why his popularity has endured, but how do we explain Donald Duck?

Can you give reasons to explain your choice of topic sentence? What is the topic of this paragraph? What is the focus of this paragraph?

PRACTICE 2

Underline the topic in each of the following topic sentences.

1. Fall is always my favourite time of the year.
2. The development of writing was one of the greatest achievements in human history.
3. The Blue Jays have never matched their achievement of 1993.
4. Vancouver's weather dampens the spirit.
5. Learning to ski is not so very difficult.
6. The day I met my girlfriend was the luckiest day of my life.
7. Living on your own can be a challenge.

8. I hate shopping, especially in malls.

9. My part-time job does more than pay my tuition.

10. The first snow of the winter is beautiful.

Finding the Focus

It's important to remember that the topic and the focus are not exactly the same thing, but they are both included in a topic sentence. Look back to the topic sentences in the table on page 218.

The first sentence says it will focus the paragraph on the number of popular cartoon shows currently on TV. The topic is cartoons.

The second sentence says it will focus the paragraph on the longevity of Mickey Mouse's appeal. The topic is Mickey Mouse.

The third sentence says it will focus the paragraph on the grouchy personality of Donald Duck. The topic is Donald Duck.

In each case, the focus statement limits the broad topic, making it possible for you to write just a paragraph on a particular aspect of the topic. A paragraph, after all, is a complete unit of thought that develops one whole idea.

Now look at the topic sentences in Practice 2. What does each one say will be the focus of the paragraph? What are your expectations as the reader of those topic sentences? What would you expect each of those paragraphs to be about? For example, you wouldn't expect sentence 1 to introduce a paragraph on winter, would you? Nor would you expect the paragraph to be about the process by which leaves change colour in fall.

PRACTICE 3

What will be the focus of each of the topic sentences in Practice 2? Explain what you would expect in a paragraph based on each topic sentence. The first one has been done for you.

1. The paragraph will give clear reasons why the writer prefers fall to any other season.

2. ______________________________

3. ______________________________

4. ______________________________

5. ____________________

6. ____________________

7. ____________________

8. ____________________

9. ____________________

10. ____________________

Locating a Topic Sentence

Most of the time, writers place a topic sentence at the beginning of each of their paragraphs, but they don't always build paragraphs this way. Sometimes, a paragraph is part of a longer piece of writing, and an explanatory transition may be needed to join two paragraphs. When that happens, a topic sentence may be placed in the middle of a paragraph. Occasionally, a writer will save the topic sentence for the conclusion of a paragraph where it acts as a summary or provides emphasis.

When you are trying to locate a topic sentence, it makes sense to check the first sentence, but then you will have to think carefully about the topic and the focus of the paragraph itself. Look at the following paragraph. The first sentence is the topic sentence and the rest of the paragraph, as you would expect, gives reasons why the cat is the most popular pet. It's a logical arrangement.

> The cat is the most popular house pet. Its popularity probably arises from the fact that, unlike the dog, a cat makes an ideal indoor pet. If you live in an apartment or next to a major road, it is preferable to keep your pet indoors for safety reasons. It is quite possible to keep a cat indoors permanently. If you plan to do this, you should start with a kitten, not an adult cat that is already familiar with an outdoor life. It doesn't matter how tiny your dwelling happens to be. Any size of dwelling provides sufficient territory for a cat. Cats are small animals, and they can discover space you are unaware of by going up on your furniture. A cat fits in happily, even if there is hardly room to swing a cat.

With a little rewriting, the topic sentence could be moved. For example, the paragraph could begin like this:

> The cat's popularity probably arises from the fact that, unlike a dog, a cat makes an ideal indoor pet.

Now you can place the topic sentence in a number of different places. For example, it could be in the final sentence:

> It's hardly surprising that the cat is the most popular house pet.

In this spot, it acts as a summary of the paragraph and has the effect of reminding the reader that you have shown why the cat is so popular as a pet.

Is there anywhere else you think this topic sentence could appropriately be placed? What would be the effect of its placement?

PRACTICE 4

Read the following paragraphs and underline the topic sentence in each one. Explain why you chose that particular sentence as the topic sentence by discussing the focus of each paragraph.

1. Do you know the story of how Canada got its name? In 1535, Jacques Cartier was travelling the St. Lawrence accompanied by two Iroquois who were acting as his interpreters. When they arrived at the site of a settlement that would later become Quebec City, Cartier asked the name of this place. His interpreters told him it was "Kanata." This noun means a village or a community; the interpreters gave Cartier a generic term, but Cartier misunderstood and thought it was a proper noun naming the area. Canada received its name based on a linguistic mistake.
2. Writing has permanency, leaving its mark while spoken language vanishes in the wind. Although we aren't sure when human beings began to speak to each other, we have a much better idea of when they began to write. There are cave paintings that date back about 22 000 years, but true writing developed much later. Humankind's most amazing invention—writing—made its appearance only about 5000–6000 years ago. Interestingly, it seems to have come into being at approximately the same time in far-removed parts of the world among people who had no contact with each other: in Mesopotamia (modern Iraq) and in China. We have written records for both of these unrelated cultures that date back to 3500–5000 B.C.E.
3. The Earth's ocean water covers seventy-one percent of the planet. We divide this huge connecting body of ocean water into five separate oceans. The five oceans are named (from smallest to largest) the Arctic, the Antarctic, the Indian, the Atlantic, and the Pacific, but we also talk about seas as part of the world's ocean. Some seas, such as the Dead Sea between Israel and Jordan, do not

connect to the ocean, while other seas, such as the Mediterranean, have a narrow channel to the ocean. Other seas share a wide channel with the neighbouring ocean as the Caribbean Sea and the Atlantic Ocean do. Ocean water forms a major part of our Earth. It determines weather patterns and it also contains huge amounts of food. Clearly, the ocean plays a critical role in Earth's habitability.

4. The simple lead in your pencil has a complex origin. The lead in your pencil is composed of two sorts of graphite. The first sort of graphite, which comes from Sri Lanka, is appreciated for its smoothness; the other graphite comes from Mexico and its quality is its blackness. The graphites are first mixed with a clay from Germany; the composition of this mixture determines the hardness of your pencil. This compound of graphite and clay is ground for a week in a revolving drum before it is forced through a hydraulic press. Next the ground mixture is extruded in a continuous string which is allowed to dry before being cut into the appropriate lengths. Finally these leads are fired in a furnace, treated with oil, and then inserted into their wooden holders. Now the lead is part of a pencil.

5. A paragraph elaborates on the topic sentence by providing details that explain or illustrate it. A topic sentence provides a useful way for a hasty reader to grasp the main idea of a paragraph quickly and to decide whether to continue reading further or not. For this reason many professional writers begin their paragraphs with topic sentences. Another advantage to placing the topic sentence at the beginning is that it directs the organization of the rest of the paragraph for the writer. The topic sentence is a vital component of any paragraph.

6. Why is the ocean blue? The colours of the sea show us whether much life exists there. The deep blue colour of the ocean far from land reveals empty seas where little plant or animal life exists. This ocean water looks blue because the sun shines on tiny particles in the water. When more plant life mixes with the water near the coast, the water looks greener. Of course, there is more abundant animal life near abundant plant life. The colour of the water is a clue about the amount of life in it.

7. When you are very interested in a subject, the pupil of your eye will dilate or expand. On the other hand, if you come across something disagreeable, your pupil will contract. These physical changes will occur regardless of the amount of light in a room and the effort you put into trying to control them. Next time you see an ad in which the model seems to be staring straight at you, check for pupil dilation. Almost certainly, the pupil will be

enlarged because ad executives know that a dilated pupil sells more. A dilated pupil, after all, conveys interest and liking for the subject. Psychological studies have demonstrated that the pupil of the eye is a very accurate indicator of a person's response to a situation.

8. A dog is man's best friend, so they say. Archaeological discoveries show the dog beside humans from earliest times. Cave paintings of dogs demonstrate a relationship that began in prehistoric times when our cave-dwelling ancestors recognized the worth of the domesticated dog. Through the ages people valued the dog as a partner on a hunt, a protector of the home, and a companion by the fire. Civilizations around the world tamed and bred dogs, often depending on them for survival. In every culture you will find legends and myths about dogs and their abilities and loyalty. The relationship between humans and dogs may be a cliché, but it has a distinguished past and a vital present. For many people today, the dog is a member of the family.

Writing a Topic Sentence

Now that you can successfully identify topic sentences, let's try composing them. Remember that the topic sentence must state the topic and provide the focus of the paragraph.

PRACTICE 5

Read the following paragraphs carefully, and then write a topic sentence for each that states the topic and focus. You'll probably need several drafts before you write one you're really pleased with.

1. ____

____

For example, we use expository writing to explain something clearly so that a reader can understand the subject easily. In this case we may use examples to show what we mean. We use expository writing to provide information or factual background, so it is the form used when we answer questions. Perhaps we want to outline a process or give our reader directions to follow. In either case, we employ expository writing. When we want to persuade someone to agree with our point of view, we gather our information and write it carefully in order to convince our readers.

We may compare two things to decide which is better for our needs. Expository writing demands thoughtful planning and careful organization to achieve its purpose.

2. ______________________________

____

These days we often place them at the ends of sentences. We do this because it sounds better to us. For example, very few people would say, "To whom am I speaking?" We would say "Who am I speaking to?" However, even fifty years ago it was considered to be bad grammar to place a preposition at the end of a sentence. Winston Churchill, a British prime minister during the Second World War, made fun of such strict grammar rules. He wrote the following sentence to show how awkward and pretentious English can be if we cannot place prepositions at the ends of sentences: "This is the kind of English up with which I cannot put."

3. ______________________________

____

Most of us find it hard to imagine a language without writing, yet for thousands of years this was the case. Even today, there are millions of people in the world who do not write. Some are illiterate, but many speak a language that has no written form. Among such people the oral tradition is very strong. They tell their stories and memorize the history and traditions they want to pass on to the next generation. Recounting culture only in spoken form has obvious problems. For one thing, the human memory is short-term and the brain's capacity to store information is limited.

4. ______________________________

____

It lives in the shallow coastal waters of the Canadian Arctic and the St. Lawrence seaway. It is the chubby white whale with what appears to be an engaging smile. This is what makes the beluga so endearing to humans. Like all whales, the beluga is a social animal, appearing to enjoy the company of other belugas, even engaging in play at times. For example, the beluga likes to toss weed at other belugas and play chase. The beluga communicates through a series of repeated sounds, shrill squeaks, clicks, and chirps. The beluga is the most "talkative" of the whale species.

5. ______________________________

____

Although scientists believe the Milky Way galaxy contains millions of black holes, not one has been reliably identified. A black hole is theorized to have such a strong gravitational force because a great amount of matter has been crushed into such a tiny space. If the Earth could be compressed into a black hole, it would be the size of a marble. The black hole's powerful gravitational force draws everything into it, so that not even light can escape. It is the black hole's ability to trap light that has made it invisible and, so far, undetectable.

6. ______________________________

____

They are the creators of the game called Trivial Pursuit. Canadians Chris Haney and Scott Abbott realized a lot of money could be made if they could only create a game like Scrabble. It took them less than a hour to come up with the idea for their game, which involves answering questions based on common knowledge, but, of course, doing the research to develop the game took considerably more time. They also had to convince their families and friends to invest in the initial test version of the game. It was an investment that paid off. Haney and Abbott and their original investors are now millionaires. Trivial Pursuit is one of the most popular board games in the world, and versions of it are played not only at home, but also in bars and pubs and at charity fundraisers. It's a trivial game that became an important feature of North American play.

7. ______________________________

____

There is a movie called *Arachnophobia* that plays on this widespread fear that people have. In fact, most spiders are completely harmless to humans. While spiders do secrete a poison that can paralyze their prey, most spiders are incapable of piercing the flesh of humans. In fact, the average spider has no interest in attacking a human at all and will only resort to this when it is threatened in some way. Even then, the effects of the spider's bite are rarely serious. Spiders actually pose little threat to people, and could be regarded as beneficial as they help to keep the bug population under control.

8. ____

____

Around 3000 B.C.E., Egyptians kept cats, which they called "miw," as a form of pest control. In addition, they loved the cat as a domestic companion and even worshipped it as a god. The cat's beauty and its ability as a hunter impressed the ancient Egyptians so much that they began to think of it as sacred. Their cat god was Bast, and the Egyptians built a huge temple for its worship. When the cat of a wealthy Egyptian died, it still received special care. The cat's owner embalmed the body, placed it in a wooden coffin, and interred it at the Great Temple of Bast. Archaeologists recovered hundreds of cat mummies from the site. The Egyptians also created many statues and paintings of cats that are on display in museums around the world.

GATHERING SUPPORTING DETAILS

So far in this unit, you have written a topic sentence after having been given the supporting details to focus your sentence. When you write your own paragraphs, you create or receive your topic and then have to focus it for yourself. The focus you give a topic depends on the facts or ideas you have gathered relating to your topic. If you are not required to research your topic, there are a number of methods of generating details. You probably already have your own way of producing the details you need to support your topic, but perhaps an alternative method would produce better results for you.

Brainstorming

This means recording anything that comes to your mind as you think about your topic. Your thoughts can be recorded in a number of different ways, and you should choose the one that most appeals to you. Each activity can be done individually, with a partner, or in a group. Even if you do have to do research at a later stage, this is a good way to begin. Here are three methods of brainstorming: clustering, listing, and freewriting.

Clustering

Write the topic ("cartoons") in the centre of a page, circle it, and then write down and circle any more ideas you have. Connect them with lines to the word they come from.

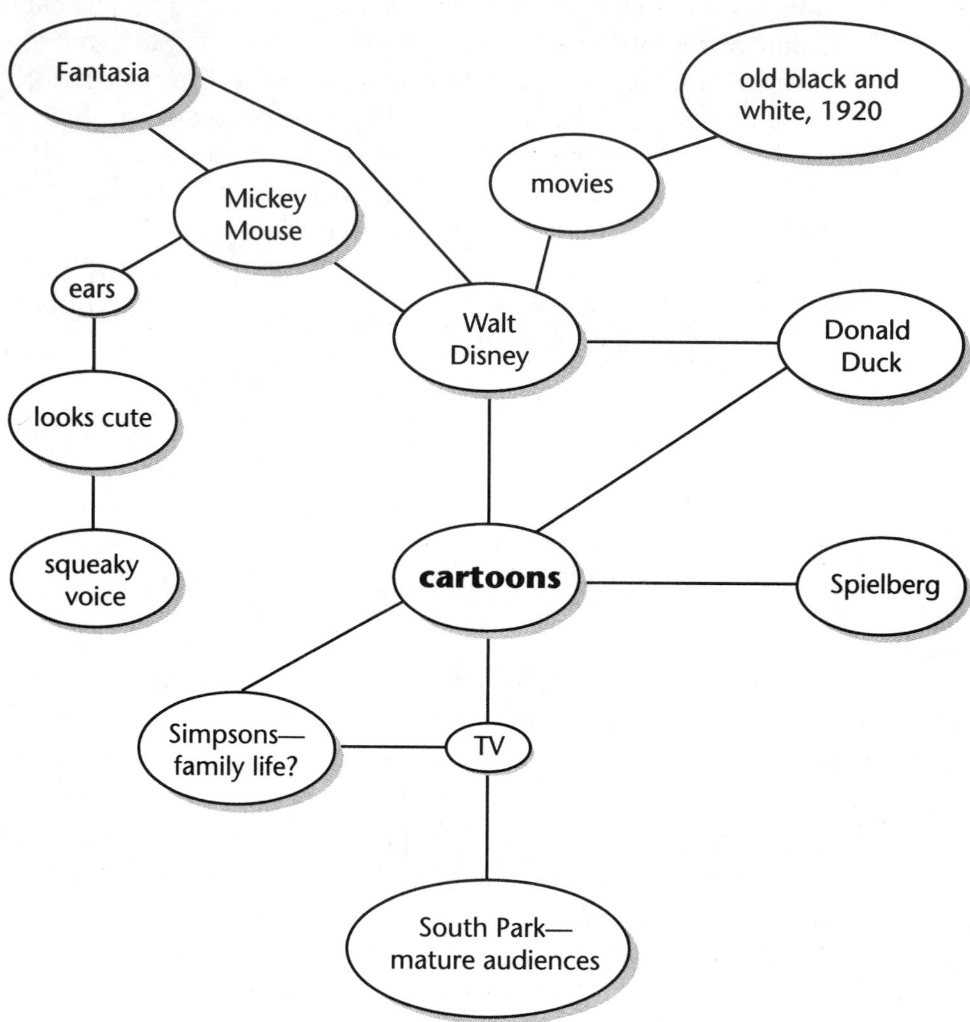

Listing

Just jot down a list of your ideas on the topic ("cartoons"); don't worry about order at this time.

Mickey Mouse around for a long time

Disney

Donald Duck my favourite, grouchy

TV—Saturday mornings for kids

cartoon movies

old black and white Mickey movies—
Steamboat Willie?

adult cartoons — South Park
Simpsons
King of the Hill
Family Guy

Fantasia—I saw that as a kid—Mickey
was in it

Mickey Mouse club—those ears!

squeaky voice, looks cute

Freewriting

Just write about your topic ("cartoons") as the ideas occur to you. Don't worry about the organization right now; just get your ideas down on paper.

Cartoons—I like cartoons even now I'm an adult. On TV there are even adult cartoons. I bet lots of parents don't let their little kids watch South Park. Anyway it's on late. I always liked Donald Duck. I guess Mickey Mouse made Disney really famous. I saw Fantasia when I was a kid and my parents remember it from when they were little. Wait there was an old black and white cartoon about a steamboat that Mickey was in. It looks ancient like maybe 1920s or something. And the Mickey Mouse club on TV, my mom said she watched it.

Questioning

Many writers use the journalism approach of asking questions to help them generate ideas on a topic. The question words are *who, what, when, where, why,* and *how*. This method can be employed individually, with a partner, or in a group. It can also guide you if you have to research information.

Topic—cartoons
Who created Mickey Mouse?
What does Mickey Mouse look like?
When was Mickey Mouse created?
Where did Mickey Mouse get his start?
Why is Mickey Mouse popular?
How did Mickey Mouse change over the years?

Discussing

Talk with your friends or colleagues about a topic. Running your ideas by someone else is always useful as you will receive feedback. Remember to record the details of the discussion.

PRACTICE 6

Choose three of the topics below. Generate ideas on your three chosen topics, using a different method in each case.

1. birthday parties
2. stress
3. making friends
4. summer
5. regular exercise
6. winter driving
7. fishing
8. the last book I enjoyed reading
9. my grandmother
10. last Saturday

SORTING SUPPORTING DETAILS

Once you have a set of ideas or facts to support your topic, however you choose to gather them, the next step is to organize them. You need to go over the details you have in order to decide on your focus. Your details have to be sorted according to *what*, *why*, and *how* you will write.

What You Write

Make sure you have enough separate details to say something worthwhile about your topic. You should be able to write one or two sentences for each separate detail. If you need more information, go through one of the generating processes again.

Be certain that all the facts you provide are correct. Maybe you'll have to check a fact or find additional information in another source. For example, in the paragraph on Mickey Mouse, the date and title of his movie, *Steamboat Willie*, had to be checked in an encyclopedia.

Check that all your details are separate, that you haven't repeated the same detail in different words. If you have a repetition, reject it and don't use it to pad your paragraph.

Make sure that all your ideas relate specifically to your topic. You may find that you've developed another set of ideas that are similar to your topic, but not specifically related. Consider writing a separate paragraph for them with their own topic sentence. In other words, rather than one long paragraph of twelve to fifteen sentences, write two focused paragraphs of six to eight sentences each. Look back to pages 221 and 227 and you will find two different paragraphs on cats. Those two separate paragraphs began life as one long and unfocused paragraph.

Why You Write

Before you begin writing you need to ask yourself, "Why am I writing this?" Determining your purpose for writing will help you decide what and how you will write. One of the following possibilities should be your reason for writing:

- to explore your own feelings or ideas about the topic;
- to understand a topic clearly, which could involve describing, giving examples, giving reasons, comparing, or classifying;
- to understand a process, achieve a result, or solve a problem;
- to persuade your reader to agree with you;
- to tell a story.

How You Write

Once you've determined your purpose for writing, you have to think about how you will write. To do this you first need to consider your audience and your point of view.

Your audience: Your audience consists of the people who will read your writing. Think about them when you are planning what to write. What do you know about your readers? Do you have to explain certain details carefully, or can you assume they will understand the background to your writing? If you can organize your writing to suit their needs and interests, you are more likely to be successful with the purpose of your writing.

Your point of view: Think about how you want to approach your subject. Will it be a personal account or an objective presentation? What person will you write in: first, second, third, and singular or plural? Be consistent in the point of view you choose.

When you have all your facts and have established who your audience will be and the point of view you want to present, you're ready to put your supporting details into an order that will make sense to your readers. When you are initially developing the details, you can record ideas as you come across them. However, a paragraph is an organized unit of writing, so you need to think about the best way to present your information.

Chronological Order: If one event naturally follows another, you should organize according to a time sequence.

Look at the following paragraph (taken from Unit 1). It outlines the life of Joseph Sommers, so it follows a time sequence.

> Mr. Sommers, who died in 1978, grew up in Germany and amused himself as a boy by inventing his own languages. While he was still just a schoolboy, he learned Swedish, Sanskrit, and Persian. He later picked up all the major European languages. By the late 1920s, when he immigrated to the United States, he knew nearly eight dozen languages. What did a man of Mr. Sommers's amazing talent do for a living? He was quite a shy and retiring man who wrote textbooks about learning Russian, Arabic, Chinese, and Japanese. However, he spent his work life as a research librarian at the Cleveland Public Library.

Logical Order: Sometimes a fact or idea has to be explained before the reader can understand another piece of information.

Look at the following paragraph (taken from Unit 1). The writer has to explain that hieroglyphics are a form of writing before discussing how the ancient Egyptians made use of them.

> About 5000 years ago (3000 B.C.E.), the Egyptians developed a complex writing system we have come to know as hieroglyphics. They carved these symbols into metal and stone, but they also revolutionized writing by creating strips of "paper" from the papyrus plant that grows in the Nile delta. The writing of ancient Egypt was used to keep day-to-day records, of course, but it also enabled scribes to record their complex system of history, law, religion, and literature. A parallel development was occurring in India, where the earliest writing also appeared in the third century B.C.E.

Order of Importance: You can sort by order of importance. Decide which of your ideas is the strongest and which the weakest. Many writers choose to "hide" their weakest detail in the middle of the paragraph and save the strongest for a grand finale.

> We all enjoy a well-told joke. A good, hearty laugh makes us feel happier. Quite apart from the psychological benefit of laughter that is easy for us to appreciate, laughter improves our physical well-being. For example, laughter provides us with a physical release from tension. When we laugh we breathe in more deeply, expanding our lungs and increasing our oxygen intake. More oxygen means our circulation is improved, and our brains and hearts benefit from this. Laughter actually energizes us. In fact, a number of studies have been published recently that demonstrate a powerful relationship between our physical health and laughter.

FINISHING YOUR PARAGRAPH

Finally, your paragraph needs a concluding sentence. This wraps up the details and signals to the reader that this part of your discussion is over. If your writing consists of more than one paragraph, your concluding sentence may form a transition to the new topic in the following paragraph.

PRACTICE 7

Go back to the paragraphs in Practices 4 and 5. For each paragraph, identify the purpose, audience, point of view, and organization of details.

PRACTICE 8

1. Go back to the ideas you generated for Practice 6 and sort each set of them into an appropriate order.
2. Write a topic sentence to focus each of your three topics and sets of details from Practice 6.
3. Exchange your topic sentences for Practice 6 with a partner. Explain what you would expect in a paragraph based on each of these three topic sentences your partner has written. Check with your partner to see if you assumed correctly.

PRACTICE 9

Choose one of the topic sentences you wrote for Practice 8. Write a paragraph based on your topic sentences and supporting details. Make sure it has a strong concluding sentence.

EDITING AND PROOFREADING YOUR PARAGRAPH

Once you have finished writing your paragraph, you must edit it. This means a thorough reading of your own work, recognizing both its good and weak points; you may want to change, move, or add sentences. You should also proofread carefully to identify and correct any mistakes in grammar or spelling.

Editing Checklist

- ❒ Are words spelled correctly?
- ❒ Are words used correctly?
- ❒ Is the punctuation correct?
- ❒ Are all the sentences complete?
- ❒ Do subjects and verbs agree?
- ❒ Are pronouns used correctly?
- ❒ Are the correct verb forms used?

- ❒ Are the sentences varied?
- ❒ Is there a topic sentence?
- ❒ Do the details support the topic?
- ❒ Does the paragraph focus on one topic?
- ❒ Is there a concluding sentence?
- ❒ Does the paragraph have unity?
- ❒ Does the paragraph have coherence?

A paragraph that focuses on and develops one topic with a consistent point of view has *unity*. Another feature of good paragraph writing is *coherence*. A paragraph has coherence (it sticks together) when the idea in each sentence clearly relates to the one in the sentence before or after it. You can show this relationship through your choice of transition words or conjunctions; you worked on combining sentences in Unit 5.

WRITING MORE THAN ONE PARAGRAPH

Any extended piece of writing, such an essay, a report, or a letter, is just a combination of paragraphs. In a longer piece of writing you still have one main idea that you are presenting to the reader. While you have more information, you still have to organize the extra details in the same way: you sort your details so that they support a number of focused topic sentences. Extending your writing is simply a repetition of the process of paragraph development.

PRACTICE 10

The following writing suggestions are based on ideas in Unit 4. Write two to three paragraphs (approximately 300 words) on one of the following:

1. Describe an occasion when you had trouble understanding someone because of an accent or your unfamiliarity with the person's language.
2. Discuss your experience of working with a team.
3. Write about your favourite team game, explaining why you enjoy it.

4. Explain how you would classify your friends.

5. Discuss the qualities a best friend should have.

6. Describe your ideal wedding.

7. What do you want in your ideal partner?

8. Contrast the differences between a neighbour and a friend.

9. Describe one of your grandparents.

10. Describe an early experience as a cook.

11. Explain how you think we should treat old people and why.

12. Compare the similarities between yourself and a family member.

13. Parents should decide whom their children date. Agree or disagree with this statement.

14. What is your favourite food? Persuade someone to try your favourite dish.

15. Provide the steps for flirting successfully.

WRITING A SUMMARY

Throughout this text you are asked to identify the main idea of a reading. When you do that you are effectively providing a *summary*. A summary is a shortened version of an original piece of writing. There are a number of other names for a summary: abstract, brief restatement, précis, synopsis.

In a summary you record only information from the original piece of writing; you don't give your own opinion. You save your own ideas for an analysis of, or a commentary on, the passage.

When you summarize, you are taking information or ideas from someone else. You must always acknowledge the source of your information. If you don't state your source, you can be accused of *plagiarism*, which means taking the words and ideas of someone else and presenting them as your own. It's a sort of theft, and the way to avoid it is to always state the name of the original writer and the title of the text at the beginning of a summary.

There are three sorts of summary: the single-sentence summary, the selective summary, and the point-by-point summary.

The Single-Sentence Summary

You'll find this type of summary in textbooks at the beginning or end of a chapter and in formal reports where it is used to introduce a section. It's also used in newspaper articles as a heading although here it's usually a sentence fragment.

Writing a Single-Sentence Summary

Sometimes you can write a single-sentence summary by rewording the topic sentence. However, a combination of the reworded topic sentence and the key supporting details usually offers a more accurate version of the original passage.

> While NFL football in the United States is a game that seems to become more popular every year, CFL football in Canada often struggles for its existence. This phenomenon is a shame because Canadian football can be a much more exciting game. In Canadian football, the size of the field can make the action more exciting. In Canadian football, the field itself is longer (110 yards as opposed to 100 yards) and wider, and the end zone is deeper. The additional field of play provides the players with extra space for both the running and the passing game. They have a lot more space to manoeuvre, and that space makes the game more exciting.

This is the topic sentence:

> In Canadian football, the size of the field can make the action more exciting and the game more interesting.

This a reworded version of the topic sentence:

> The larger field adds to the excitement of Canadian football.

Do you think it's adequate as a summary of the paragraph? Let's try adding the key ideas in the supporting details:

- comparison to American football,
- actual size = 110 yards, and
- more passing and running.

> The Canadian football field, which is ten yards longer than the American field, gives the players more room to run and pass, making the CFL game more exciting.

The second summary is a more accurate representation of the original paragraph, isn't it? Now state the source of the information:

> The writers of *Reading Writing Basics* believe that the Canadian football field, which is ten yards longer than the American field, gives the players more room to run and pass, making the CFL game more exciting.

PRACTICE 11

Go back to Unit 5, page 208, and you'll find the rest of this article comparing the CFL and NFL.

1. Identify the topic sentence of the third paragraph.
2. Reword the topic sentence.
3. Identify the key supporting details.
4. Write a single-sentence summary of the third paragraph combining the topic sentence and the supporting details.
5. Acknowledge your source.

The Selective Summary

You can use this sort of summary in a number of ways: for recording specific information from a text; in gathering relevant details for a research paper or report; and in preparing for an oral presentation.

Writing a Selective Summary

As its name suggests, when you write a selective summary, you only take the information you need for your purpose. You don't summarize the whole article. But the steps you follow when writing a selective summary are the same as those for writing a single-sentence summary.

For example, if you really enjoyed golf and wanted to persuade a friend to play with you, you might choose to summarize the arguments offered in favour of golf in Unit 5 on page 209; however, you would certainly exclude all of the arguments in favour of tennis.

1. Identify and reword the topic sentence in favour of golf.

   Golf is a terrific game.

2. List the key ideas in the supporting details:

   - can play alone or with friends
   - takes skill and physical ability
   - gives exercise

- not too expensive
- beautiful landscape
- relaxing
- beginners enjoy game too

3. Identify the source.

A selective summary can be recorded in note form or written as a paragraph. In this case, it's a good idea to make your first sentence your topic sentence. The identification of the source and the article's main idea are the topic and the focus of the topic sentence because your paragraph will be about the article and its ideas in favour of golf.

PRACTICE 12

Write a selective summary of the reading, "Golf vs. Tennis," on page 209. Write a paragraph in favour of the game of golf. We've done part of the work for you in note form, and you can use the information above. However, you should reread the passage to be sure you are clear about the argument before you write your selective summary.

PRACTICE 13

Write a selective summary using one of the following scenarios.

1. Give advice to a colleague who is going on a business trip to Asia. Using the information in "Moving Meaning," on page 170 at the end of Unit 4, tell your friend how to understand the body language in Asia.
2. Give advice to a friend who wants to make a good impression on a teacher. Select and summarize the information you need on body language from the reading "Moving Meaning" on page 170.

The Point-by-Point Summary

You can use this summary at school or in your workplace, any time a complete, shortened version of a long document is needed.

Writing a Point-by-Point Summary

As you might guess from its name, when you write this sort of summary you shorten an entire piece of writing. You identify the topic sentences and the key supporting details. Then you reword them and record them in a paragraph (or more if the original is very long). Don't forget you need a topic sentence; use the source and main idea for the content of your topic sentence.

PRACTICE 14

1. Reread the article on Terry Fox on page 115. Write a point-by-point summary of this article.
2. Reread the article "Canadian Becomes World's Fastest Human" on page 211. Write a point-by-point summary of this article.

READING WRITING: MORE PRACTICE

READING 1

Superstitions

Are you superstitious? Many people are, and even those who claim not to be perform acts to ward off bad luck or create good luck. How often have you crossed you fingers "for luck," made a detour to avoid walking under a ladder, or said "bless you" or "gesundheit" when someone sneezed? These are all common examples of behaviour based on superstition. Some superstitions seem sensible, like avoiding that ladder, or can be understood culturally, but then there are superstitions that defy rational explanation.

In the past, when medicine was less scientific, colds and flu killed many people. A blessing was therefore an appropriate response to a sneeze. There are some people who believe spilling salt is bad luck. Well, salt used to be a very valuable commodity as it was essential for preserving the quality of meats. Also salt wasn't so easy to obtain as it is today, which added to its worth. In fact, our word *salary* comes from a word meaning salt. Imagine being paid for your work with salt today! Then there is the number thirteen. There is even a word for the fear of the number thirteen: *triskaidekaphobia*. There are many apartment buildings that have a twelfth and a fourteenth floor, but no thirteenth. Many people will admit to feeling uneasy on Friday 13th, but why? The explanation for this superstition lies in the Christian religion. Jesus had twelve apostles, so at his last supper, on a Friday, there were thirteen people in attendance.

Since that time, thirteen and Friday have been linked with suffering and tragedy. Among Chinese speakers, four is the unlucky number. The reason for this is that the word for four is a lot like the word for death. You can see there is a logic associated with many superstitions.

Do you believe a bride and groom should see each other on their wedding day before the ceremony? Lots of people think this is unlucky. A possible explanation for this superstition could lie in the arranged marriages of the past. Some parents might have preferred their child not to see the chosen spouse, and from this preference grew a tradition that today is a superstition. Even gift giving can be a source of bad luck. A purse or a wallet must have money in it when given as a gift. Friends should never give each other a knife or a pair of scissors or their friendship may be cut. While these are superstitions, the symbolism behind them isn't difficult for us to figure out.

You can explain why many superstitions exist or came to be, but there are some that just seem to defy reason. What is it about a rabbit's foot that makes it lucky? Why is opening an umbrella inside a house or putting shoes on a table bad luck? Then there are those people who will do their best to avoid black cats crossing their paths. Why aren't tabbies or Siamese cats unlucky? Could Wiarton Willie really predict the advent of spring on February 2nd? Don't you wonder how a little groundhog knows the exact date? Why does a kiss under the mistletoe bring good luck? Maybe it's just nice to be kissed!

The next time you are carefully selecting your lucky numbers for that winning lottery ticket, stop and think about your superstition. You may have a logical explanation for your choice of numbers. When you put on your jewellery, look at the symbols you may be wearing. Can you explain why people choose to wear a cross, a chai, an ankh, or a cloverleaf on a chain? Superstitions affect even those who don't consider themselves superstitious.

Fact-Finding

Answer each question in complete sentences and support your answers with references to the reading.

1. Why does it seem sensible to avoid walking under a ladder?
2. In your own words, explain why the tradition of saying "bless you" or "gesundheit" developed.
3. Look up *salary* in a dictionary to discover the word from which it is derived. Write a sentence explaining the origins of the word *salary*.
4. What is a phobia? List any other phobias you can think of.
5. Explain what "the symbolism behind them isn't difficult for us to figure out" means.
6. Choose one of the superstitions in paragraph 4 and try to write a reason for its existence.

7. Explain how you choose your lottery ticket numbers. If you never buy lottery tickets, say why.
8. Answer the question asked in the last paragraph.

Main Idea

Sum up this reading in a point-by-point summary.

What Do You Think?

1. Are you superstitious? Why or why not?
2. Are there other superstitions you know about that are not mentioned here?

Writing Suggestion

Write a paragraph of your own about superstition.

The following reading is a story. Like most stories, this one is told in the past tense. The stories we tell or write are usually about events that have already occurred. Most stories are based on memories, even imaginary ones. For this reason, most writers use the past tense when telling or writing a story.

READING 2

The Old Man and His Grandson

by Jakob and Wilhelm Grimm

There was once a very old man, whose eyes had become dim, his ears dull of hearing, and his knees unsteady. When he sat at the table he could hardly hold his spoon, and spilled broth on the tablecloth, or let it run out of his mouth. His son and his daughter-in-law were disgusted by this, so finally they made the old grandfather sit in the corner behind the stove. They gave him food in an earthenware bowl, and not even enough of it. The old man used to look toward the table with his eyes full of tears. Once, his trembling hands could not hold the bowl, and it fell to the ground and broke. His daughter-in-law scolded him, but he said nothing and only sighed. Then for a few pennies they bought him a wooden bowl out of which he had to eat.

Once they were sitting to eat in this manner when his little grandson, who was four years old, began to gather together some pieces of wood on the ground. "What are you doing there?" asked the father. "I am making a little trough," answered the child, "for my father and mother to eat out of when I am big."

The man and his wife looked at each other for a while and presently began to cry. Then they took the old grandfather to the table and from that time on always let him eat with them and likewise said nothing even if he did spill a little of anything.

Fact-Finding

1. Make a list of the physical problems the grandfather suffered from.
2. Why do you think the old man's son and daughter-in-law made him eat behind the stove? Explain the reason in your own words.
3. In a sentence of your own, explain why the woman bought the wooden bowl and say how much it cost.
4. Find the reason the grandson gives for making a trough and explain it in your own words.
5. Write a sentence describing the parents' reaction to their little boy's answer.

Main Idea

Because this is a story, the main idea is not just the information presented. The main idea is the moral or lesson the writers were presenting. This means the main idea is not stated. Instead, you have to figure it out—*infer* it—from the text. As you answer each question, make sure you can find the evidence in the story to support your ideas. Give a clear reason for each of your answers.

1. Is this story set in the present or in the past?
2. Is the family wealthy?
3. What did the little boy learn from his parents' treatment of his grandfather?
4. Why did the man and woman start crying?
5. Does the story have a happy ending?
6. In three to four sentences of your own, explain what this story teaches the reader about human behaviour.

What Do You Think?

1. How should we care for our older family members?
2. How does our society treat old people?
3. How did the story affect you?

Writing Suggestions

1. Imagine you are one of the characters in the story: the son, the wife, the grandson, or the grandfather. Retell the events in this story in your own words from the point of view of the character. You will use the pronoun *I* and write using the past tenses. This could be your first sentence: "I remember how things used to be in my home."
2. Imagine you are a TV reporter recording the scene for your audience. Rewrite "The Old Man and His Grandson" in the present tense. Change any transitions (time words) if you have to. You could begin like this: "Here is a very old man, whose eyes have become dim ..."

Reading 3

What Is It about Sharks?

There is something about sharks that strikes fear into the human mind. Perhaps we can thank Steven Spielberg's 1975 movie, *Jaws*, for a lot of this fear, but it is likely that the movie just intensified a deep human dread of this fascinating animal. In truth, sharks have a lot more to fear from humans than humans do from sharks. While people eat thousands of tonnes of shark meat every year, there are fewer than 100 shark attacks on humans annually worldwide. Only twenty-five to thirty of these attacks are fatal. These figures are quite small given the amount of time people spend in the oceans of the world.

The shark is a very old fish. Remnants of shark-like creatures have been preserved in fossils that are 350 million years old, and sharks have changed very little in the past 70 million years. As an ancient form of sea beast, they differ from other fish (called bony fish) that are more recent on the evolutionary tree. For one thing, sharks' skeletons are made of cartilage, not bone. For another thing, they have a thick durable skin rather than the overlapping scales of most bony fish. A third difference is the gill slits, which lack the gill covers that bony fish have evolved. A final distinction between sharks and bony fish is the way they are able to move in the water. Sharks lack the air-filled organ, known as a swim bladder, that keeps bony fish buoyant and upright in the water. This means that sharks sink when they aren't swimming; therefore, most sharks are constantly moving forward. By keeping their mouths open while they swim, the sharks can feed; they are also able to move water across their mouths to breathe.

The size of sharks varies considerably from species to species, and there are around 350 different species of shark. There is the tiny angel shark that is less than a metre long. At the other end of the spectrum is the enormous fifteen-metre whale shark. In between are such specimens as the three- to five-metre lemon shark and the great hammerhead, which can reach a length of six metres and a weight of seven hundred kilograms. The great hammerhead, by the way, is one of the few sharks actively dangerous to humans. Other kinds of sharks will attack humans only if threatened or if they mistake a hapless swimmer for another mammal, such as a sea lion.

The shark has some remarkable adaptations to its ocean environment that enhance its role as a predator. It can grow, use, and discard tens of thousands of teeth during its lifetime. A shark's eyesight is excellent even in murky water, and it is able to see colours. Similarly, its olfactory sense is superb, so it can smell its prey from a kilometre away. Even more effective than a shark's eyesight or sense of smell is its ability to detect other animals' vibrations in the water. The shark picks up these vibrations by a lateral line of sensitive fluid-filled sacs that extend from its head to its tail. So even if it is totally dark, a shark can feel the movement of its prey. The shark has one more tool for finding its food, a kind of "sixth sense": pores in the skin that are extremely sensitive to the weak electrical charges of other animals, even those buried in the sand. These biological adaptations make the shark a relentless predator.

Sharks are very high on the food chain of the ocean. They mainly prey on fish although larger sharks, such as the great white, will hunt seals, sea lions, and other marine animals. Some sharks are passive feeders that swim with their mouths open, sucking up the plankton and small fish in their path. Other sharks eat crab and other bottom dwellers. As predators, sharks preserve their own energy by tending to consume the slower, weaker fish in a school. By eliminating weaker animals, sharks make an important contribution to the ecological balance of the marine environment.

The shark is a fascinating creature with an important role in the ocean ecosystem. Few other animals can engage—and terrify—our imaginations as does this predator of the deep. Much of the lore that has grown up around the shark is myth. Nevertheless, the fearsome image of the keen-eyed, open-mouthed, sharp-toothed shark ruthlessly prowling the ocean is profoundly rooted in the human psyche.

Fact-Finding

Answer each question with a complete sentence.

1. How often do sharks attack humans in a year?

2. Shark skeleton is made out of cartilage, not bone. (Cartilage is softer and more elastic than true bone.) Find and list three differences between sharks and bony fish, besides their skeletons.
3. Which creature has been on the planet longer, sharks or bony fish?
4. How many different species of shark are there? Give the names of three that are mentioned in this article.
5. Explain the contribution the shark makes to the ocean's ecosystem.
6. Write a selective summary presenting the physical features that make the shark a successful hunter.

Main Idea

Sum up this reading in a point-by-point summary.

What Do You Think?

1. Do you think that sharks deserve their fierce reputation? Why or why not?
2. The article claims the shark is a fascinating creature. Do you agree with this? Why or why not?

Writing Suggestions

1. Have you seen *Jaws*? If so, would you recommend it to a friend? Explain why or why not your friend should rent this video.
2. Is there a creature you are afraid of? Explain your fear using clear reasons, or describe an occasion when you were scared by this creature.

APPENDIX A

Parts of Speech

ADJECTIVE

An adjective is a word that describes or modifies a noun or a pronoun.

Add an appropriate noun to each adjective in the following list.

good	dinner
cranky	____________________
difficult	____________________
artificial	____________________
old	____________________
sweet	____________________
comfortable	____________________
outstanding	____________________
responsible	____________________
successful	____________________

Adjectives can be used to compare things.

When we compare two things, we add *er* to the end of the adjective if it is a short word.

That book is *large*.	That book is *larger* than this one.
The flowers are *pretty*.	These flowers are *prettier* than those are.

Some adjectives, those that are two or more syllables long, use *more* in front of them instead of adding *-er.*

The engagement ring was *expensive.*
That engagement ring was *more expensive.*
Sue is wearing an *elaborate* Halloween costume.
Desmond is wearing a *more elaborate* costume.

When we compare more than two things, we add *est* to the end of the adjective or use *most* before a long adjective.

Mick's Autos is the *nearest* gas station.
Ben is the *most successful* graduate in Robotics this year.

You have to be careful not to make the mistake of using *-er* and *more* or *-est* and *most* together.

wrong: Kathy is more cleverer than her sister.
wrong: Pongo is the most sweetest of the puppies.

There are three common adjectives that have their own forms for comparisons.

good	better	best
bad	worse	worst
little	less	least

ADVERB

An adverb is a word that describes, modifies, or limits the meaning of verbs, adjectives, or other adverbs. Adverbs tell how, where, why, or how much/often.

I *always* go to the movies on the weekend.
I'm feeling *very* tired.
The shoe is *too* small.
You should answer *now.*
Renate walked *away.*
He read the note *quickly.*
My mother *seldom* loses her temper.
Begin work *immediately.*
His drop shot was *perfectly* timed.
David is *quite* small for a seven-year-old.
Jeff reads *well.*
We have *barely* explored space.
Let's go *outside.*
The results can be *clearly* seen.

After each sentence above, indicate whether the adverb tells how, why, where, when, or how much/often.

CONJUNCTION
A conjunction connects words, phrases, or clauses.

Units 2 and 5 provide you with opportunities to recognize and use both coordinating and subordinating conjunctions.

INTERJECTION
An interjection expresses strong feeling. It is often followed by an exclamation mark and should be used sparingly.

> Oh, no!
> Ouch!
> Hurrah! We won!
> Impossible! That can't be true.

NOUN
A noun is the name of a person, place, or thing.

Unit 3 provides you with many opportunities to recognize and use nouns.

PREPOSITION
A preposition shows a relationship between a noun or pronoun and another part of the sentence.

Unit 2 provides you with opportunities to recognize and use prepositions.

PRONOUN
A pronoun is a word that takes the place of, or refers to, a noun.

Unit 3 provides you with many opportunities to recognize and use pronouns.

VERB
A verb is a word, or group of words, that expresses action or a state of being.

Unit 4 provides you with many opportunities to recognize and use verbs.

APPENDIX B

Irregular Verbs and Their Parts

Base Form	Past Tense	Past Participle (use with *have/has/had*)
be (am, is, are)	was, were	been
bear	bore	borne
become	became	become
begin	began	begun
bid	bid	bid
bite	bit	bitten
blow	blew	blown
break	broke	broken
bring	brought	brought
build	built	built
burst	burst	burst
buy	bought	bought
catch	caught	caught

Base Form	Past Tense	Past Participle (use with *have/has/had*)
choose	chose	chosen
come	came	come
cost	cost	cost
deal	dealt	dealt
do	did	done
draw	drew	drawn
drink	drank	drunk
drive	drove	driven
eat	ate	eaten
fall	fell	fallen
feel	felt	felt
fight	fought	fought
find	found	found
fling	flung	flung
fly	flew	flown
forget	forgot	forgotten/forgot
forgive	forgave	forgiven
freeze	froze	frozen
get	got	gotten/got
grow	grew	grown
hang (i.e., suspend)	hung	hung
hang (i.e., put to death)	hanged	hanged

Base Form	Past Tense	Past Participle (use with *have/has/had*)
have (has)	had	had
hear	heard	heard
hide	hid	hidden
hit	hit	hit
hold	held	held
hurt	hurt	hurt
keep	kept	kept
know	knew	known
lay	laid	laid
lead	led	led
leave	left	left
lie (i.e., to be horizontal)	lay	lain
lie (i.e., to be untruthful)	lied	lied
lose	lost	lost
make	made	made
mean	meant	meant
meet	met	met
pay	paid	paid
put	put	put
ride	rode	ridden
ring	rang	rung
rise	rose	risen

Base Form	Past Tense	Past Participle (use with *have/has/had*)
run	ran	run
say	said	said
see	saw	seen
sell	sold	sold
set	set	set
shake	shook	shaken
shine	shone	shone
sing	sang	sung
sit	sat	sat
sleep	slept	slept
slide	slid	slid
speak	spoke	spoken
speed	sped	sped
spend	spent	spent
stand	stood	stood
steal	stole	stolen
strike	struck	struck
swear	swore	sworn
swim	swam	swum
swing	swung	swung
take	took	taken
teach	taught	taught

Base Form	**Past Tense**	**Past Participle** (use with *have/has/had*)
tear	tore	torn
tell	told	told
think	thought	thought
throw	threw	thrown
wear	wore	worn
win	won	won
wind	wound	wound
write	wrote	written

APPENDIX C

The Dictionary

This material originally appeared in *A Canadian Writer's Guide* by Jack Finnbogason and Al Valleau.

CHOOSING A DICTIONARY

Unabridged Dictionaries

Unabridged dictionaries contain the most complete collection of words, meanings, and historical derivations. Their size and bulk, however, make it unlikely you will purchase one. Certainly, they cannot be described as portable. But you need to know how to use them and in what ways they can be helpful.

Your college or university library houses these dictionaries in the reference section. The two you are most likely to consult are *The Oxford English Dictionary* and the *Webster's Third New International Dictionary of the English Language.*

The second edition of *The Oxford English Dictionary*, in twenty volumes, was updated in 1989. It has approximately 620 000 entries and is recognized as the definitive dictionary of the English language. Whenever you need to know what a word meant at a certain historical time, the *OED* is an essential reference; it gives a complete history of each word.

The *Webster's Third New International Dictionary of the English Language* has 470 000 entries, all of them contained in a single volume. It is widely respected, strong in new scientific and technical terms, and organized well for easy access. It caused some controversy on its 1986 publication, however, because it was content to describe rather than prescribe usage. In simply listing variant uses, it did not assist people to distinguish informal from formal usage.

The *Random House Dictionary of the English Language*, second edition, has 315 000 entries and is also a single-volume work. It has useful special features, including atlases and a section on nonsexist language.

Abridged Dictionaries

For daily use, an abridged dictionary is an essential writer's tool. Abridged dictionaries include most commonly used words and often include comments on usage as well. They are affordable and portable, two essential qualities, and offer the practical assistance writers need. Abridged dictionaries that have proved popular include these:

American Heritage Dictionary of the English Language (200 000 entries)
Concise Oxford Dictionary (120 000 entries)
Gage Canadian Dictionary (90 000 entries)
Funk and Wagnall's Canadian College Dictionary (155 000 entries)
Houghton Mifflin Canadian Dictionary of the English Language
ITP Nelson Canadian Dictionary of the English Language (150 000 entries)
Webster's Tenth New Collegiate Dictionary (160 000 entries)
The Penguin Canadian Dictionary (75 000 entries; simplified pronunciation guide ideal for second-language students)

The Canadian abridged dictionaries satisfy most needs. They also provide the correct Canadian spelling, an invaluable aid when the spell checkers provided with word-processing packages give only American spellings. The *Nelson Canadian Dictionary* has the added advantage of including many Canadian words not found in standard college dictionaries.

USING A DICTIONARY

Your dictionary must be sufficient for your purposes. You will need a dictionary that spells common words and has extensive listings. If you look at an entry in your dictionary, it should look similar to this entry from the *Gage Canadian Dictionary:*

spelling and syllabication | **pronunciation** | **parts of speech** | **inflected forms (how a word changes to show singular/plural or verb tense)**

definitions as a noun

pair [pɛr] *n., pl.* **pairs** or (*sometimes after a numeral*) **pair**; *v.*—*n.* **1** a set of two; two that go together: *a pair of shoes, a pair of horses.* **2** a single thing consisting of two parts that cannot be used separately: *a pair of scissors, a pair of pants.* **3** two people who are married or are engaged to be married. **4** two partners in a dance. **5** two animals that are mated. **6** *Card games.* **a** two cards of the same value in different suits, viewed as a unit in one's hand: *a pair of sixes, jacks, etc.* **b** in games using a multiple deck, two identical cards. **7** in a legislative body: **a** two members on opposite sides who arrange not to vote on a certain question. **b** the arrangement thus made.

definitions as a verb

—*v.* **1** arrange or be arranged in pairs. **2** join in marriage. **3** of animals, mate. **4** in a legislative body, form or cause to form a voting pair.

etymology (origin)

pair off or **up**, arrange or form into pairs: *The guests paired off for the first dance.* [F *paire* < L *paria*, neut. pl., equals]

Homonyms (sound-alikes)

☛ *Hom.* PARE, PEAR, PÈRE.

Synonyms (words with similar meanings)

☛ *Syn. n.* **1. Pair,** COUPLE = two of the same kind. **Pair** applies to two things that belong together because they go together to make a set, because they are used together and each is needed to make the other useful, or because they are so well matched they seem to belong together: *I bought a new pair of gloves.* **Couple** applies to any two of the same kind: *I bought a couple of shirts.* **Couple** is also used of people: *the happy couple.*

Usage

☛ *Usage.* **Pair.** In informal usage the plural of **pair** is sometimes **pair** when it comes after a number: *six pair of socks.* Some people now consider this usage nonstandard.

☛ *Usage.* When a **pair** is thought of as a unit, it takes a singular verb: *This pair of shoes is getting old.* When a **pair** is thought of as referring to two individual items, it takes a plural verb: *The pair of vases were both chipped.*

If you compare this entry to one for the same word from *The Concise Oxford Dictionary*, you will see that, although the two dictionaries have a fair amount of similar information, they present information in different formats, and each includes information that the other omits. Choose a dictionary with care. Look to see what it includes and does not include. Here is *The Concise Oxford Dictionary*'s entry for *pair*:

spelling | **pronunciation** | **parts of speech**

definitions as a noun

pair /pɛː/ *n. & v.* •*n.* **1** a set of two persons or things used together or regarded as a unit (*a pair of gloves; a pair of eyes*). **2** an article (e.g. scissors, trousers, or tights) consisting of two joined or corresponding parts not used separately. **3 a** an engaged or married couple. **b** a mated couple of animals. **4** two horses harnessed side by side (*a coach and pair*). **5** the second member of a pair in relation to the first (*cannot find its pair*). **6** two playing cards of the same denomination. **7** *Parl.* either or both of two members of a legislative assembly on opposite sides absenting themselves from voting by

definitions as a verb

mutual arrangement. •*v.tr. & intr.* **1** (often foll. by *off*) arrange or be arranged in couples. **2 a** join or be joined in marriage. **b** (of animals) mate. **3** *Parl.* form a pair (see sense 7 of *n.*). ___**in pairs** in twos.

etymology

[Middle English via Old French *paire* from Latin *paria,* neut. pl. of *par* 'equal']

(Taken from *The Concise Oxford Dictionary*, 9th ed., 1995, by permission of Oxford University Press.)

Canadians have one other reality to deal with: they are caught between the spellings and conventions of British and American English. It is futile to argue which conventions and spellings are preferable. Choose the spellings and conventions you feel comfortable with, but do not switch back and forth between conventions. In fact, to avoid confusion, you might want to stick to a Canadian dictionary, which will use the conventions acceptable in Canada.

APPENDIX D

Answer Key

UNIT 1

PRACTICE 1

Copying lines

PRACTICE 2

Handwriting samples

PRACTICE 3

Answers will vary.

PRACTICE 4

1. College
2. Uncle; Russian
3. summer; ocean
4. Why; English
5. A; grocery store; Carver Street
6. Islamic faith; Ramadan
7. *The X-Files*; television
8. family; summer; Lake Titicaca
9. Chinese; *The Joy Luck Club*
10. Did; singer; Celine Dion; Quebec

PRACTICE 5

1. rise?
2. rise.
3. you!
4. announcement?
5. announcement.
6. stop?
7. dial. *or* dial!
8. limitations?
9. speak?
10. languages. *or* languages!

PRACTICE 6

Corrections of capitalization and punctuation errors are underlined.

Every field of **h**uman endeavour has its stars; for example, **B**abe **R**uth in **b**aseball or **M**ichael **J**ordan in **b**asketball**.** Even an organization known as the Linguistic Society of America has its champion. Its champion is Francis E. Sommer, a man who was fluent in ninety-four languages. (*or* !)

Mr. Sommer grew up in Germany and amused himself as a boy by inventing his own languages. While he was just a schoolboy, he learned Swedish, Sanskrit, and Persian. He later picked up all the major European languages. By the late 1920s, when he emigrated to the United States, he knew nearly eight dozen languages. What did a man of Mr. Sommers' amazing talent do for a living? A shy man, he worked as a research librarian at the Cleveland Public Library. In his spare time he wrote textbooks about learning Russian, Arabic, Chinese, and Japanese.

Toward the end of his life, Mr. Sommer, who died in 1978, said he had given up learning new languages because he was experiencing information overload. He said that he was afraid to cram any more words into his head "or some morning I will wake up speaking Babel."

PRACTICE 7

1. Does; your; know; you're; here
2. Ask; accept
3. We're; our; being
4. It's; buy
5. axe; loose; past
6. chose; fine
7. were; supposed; find; weather
8. They're; no; two; women
9. knew; dose; are; too
10. been; quite

PRACTICE 8

1. used; choose; quit; too
2. hear; passed; your
3. know; whether; than; were
4. Whose; our
5. Their; an
6. We're; to; lose
7. It's; too; ask
8. were; being
9. loose; fine; our
10. You're; supposed; your; new; its

PRACTICE 9

1. threw; through; then
2. Who's; there; quiet
3. new; its
4. Where; their
5. an; woman
6. allot; except; women
7. being; been
8. It's; lose
9. A lot; loose
10. A; here; than

PRACTICE 10

Corrections of spelling errors are underlined.

Have you heard about the woman who ran at the sight of a bear? Goldie was walking in the woods one sunny day hoping to relax and raise her morale. For she had been working very hard all week and needed to take some time off. Goldie found the woods quiet and soon she felt at peace. Suddenly a bear appeared right in front of her. She was really frightened! The bear, of course, growled menacingly when he saw her. Goldie didn't scream for help, but she turned, ran past the bear, and started a sharp descent down the hill she had been climbing. Later she said that she had learned a valuable lesson. Never wander alone in bear country!

PRACTICE 11

you're	they'll
what's	doesn't
I've	you'll
where's	won't
we've	he'd

PRACTICE 12

1. I'll; don't
2. He's; should've
3. Who's; isn't
4. They're
5. We've; they're
6. could've
7. It's; isn't
8. She'd; doesn't
9. Why's; don't
10. It's; won't

PRACTICE 13

1. They've; who's
2. She's; it's
3. There's; doesn't
4. He'll; we've; won't
5. I'm
6. Why's; it's
7. Don't; would've; you'd
8. Who's; whose; wasn't
9. It's; isn't
10. You've; you'd; could've

READING 2: WHEN WAS LANGUAGE INVENTED?

Corrections of spelling errors are capitalized, and those of punctuation and capitalization are underlined.

When did human beings invent language? We really do not KNOW how long ago our human ancestors started talking to each other. THERE are no records that tell us when people began to use organized speech sounds—more THAN grunts and groans—to communicate with other people. Linguists (people who study language) guess that the development of spoken language occurred about 100 000 years ago. They base this estimate on TWO things. One, the earliest signs of civilization at this time suggest that people were talking to one another. Two, the physical remains (skeletons) reveal the brain size necessary to perform the complex tasks of language. Whenever it happened, it is undeniable that OUR ability to USE language—to name things and to extend ourselves in time—is one of the principal things that makes us human.

READING 3: OUR MOST REMARKABLE INVENTION: WRITING

Corrections of spelling errors are capitalized. Capitalization errors are underlined.

If we aren't sure when human beings began to speak to each other, we have a much better idea of when they began to

WRITE. That's because writing has permanency. It leaves ITS mark while spoken language vanishes in the wind. THERE are cave paintings that date back about 22 000 years, but true writing developed much LATER. Humankind's most amazing invention—writing—made its appearance only about 5000 to 6000 years ago. Interestingly, it seems to have come into being at approximately the same time in far-removed parts of the world among **p**eople who had no contact with each other: in Mesopotamia (modern **I**raq) and in China. We have written records from both of these unrelated cultures that date back to 3500–3000 B.C.E.

The Sumerians had a highly developed civilization in Mesopotamia, and their first written symbols were used to keep agricultural records. They carved their symbols (WHICH we call "cuneiform" for their wedge shape) into wet clay with a sharp reed. The clay hardened to become a permanent written record of the world of these vanished people.

At around the same time, people in China developed a writing system that was very similar to the one used to write Chinese today. The earliest Chinese writing was carved into wood, shell, or bone, but later writers learned to use a "new technology," brush and ink. The result was the subtle and beautiful calligraphy of Chinese writing with its thousands of symbols.

About 5000 years ago (3000 **B.C.E.**), the Egyptians developed a complex writing system we have come to know as hieroglyphics. They carved these symbols into metal and stone, but they also revolutionized writing by creating strips of "paper" from the papyrus plant that grows in the Nile delta. The writing of ancient Egypt was used to keep day-to-day records, of course, but it also enabled scribes to record their complex system of history, law, religion, and literature. A parallel development was occurring in India where the earliest writing also appeared in the third millennium B.C.E.

About 3000 years ago, the Phoenicians, sailors and traders in the **M**editerranean, began to use an alphabet that spread with them. Cuneiform writing, Chinese characters, and hieroglyphics are ideographic writing systems. They are made up of thousands of very complicated pictographic symbols. Alphabetic writing doesn't have nearly as many symbols, and the symbols represent not ideas but the sound of the spoken language. For instance, English uses only the twenty-six characters of the Latin alphabet, but those few letters can communicate the million-or-so-word vocabulary of the language.

The Phoenician alphabet led to other Semitic alphabets, such as Hebrew and Aramaic, the languages of the **B**ible, and **A**rabic, the language of the Koran. It also was A forerunner of the Greek and Latin alphabets. Many linguists think that the development of the alphabet is what made reading and learning available to ordinary people who would not have had the time or capacity to learn the multitude of symbols necessary to WRITE cuneiform or Chinese. But there is little doubt that writing, which enables us to preserve the PAST and to communicate with future generations, has BEEN the most remarkable innovation that humans have created. It has led to countless other developments that define human civilization. It's difficult to even imagine a world without writing!

READING 4: GROWTH OF A GLOBAL LANGUAGE

Corrections of spelling errors are capitalized. Capitalization errors are underlined.

The **E**nglish language is a baby compared to Chinese or Hebrew or Hindi or Greek. Two thousand years ago, when the Romans (led by Julius Caesar) arrived in Britain, the English language did not exist. The people on the island spoke Celtic languages. Anglo-Saxon (the earliest version of English) developed about 1500 years ago, but it was spoken by a very small number of people. By 1600, William Shakespeare's time, English was spoken by around six million people, and all of them lived in Britain.

However, in the next 400 years, the English language was to achieve AN astonishing growth. Today it is spoken by at least 750 million people as either a first or second language. Although far more people (about 1.5 billion) speak Chinese, they are mainly concentrated on one continent. English is spoken as a first or as a common second language in North America, Australia, large parts of Africa, and the Indian subcontinent, as well as the British Isles.

The reasons for this growth in the use of English ARE complex. For one thing, people who spoke it WERE very good at colonizing and plundering other places. For another thing, the language itself is flexible and capable of absorbing the vocabulary, syntax, and even culture of other languages. Hybrids (mixtures) of English and other languages have sprung up all over the world; for example, Spanglish in Los Angeles, Russlish in Moscow, and Japlish in Tokyo.

So for BETTER or worse, English has become a truly global language. Millions of people study it as a second language, and it's not an easy ONE to learn. English is BY far the international language of business and technology, the language of sports and Hollywood, the language of air travel and computers, of diplomacy and trade.

Of course, the predominance of English is largely a matter of history and accident. No language is "better" than any other is. But if IT'S your language of birth, or if you've achieved the difficult task of learning it as a second language, you have AN advantage in the globalized world of the twenty-first century. Be sure that YOU'RE able to maximize this advantage by learning to use the language confidently and correctly.

PRACTICE 14

Answers will vary.

1. 100 000
2. linguists
3. physical remains
4. name things or extend ourselves in time
5. 6000; writing
6. hieroglyphics; 3000 B.C.E.
7. alphabet; Mediterranean
8. symbols
9. English language
10. six
11. Spanish, Russian, Japanese
12. entertainment, computers, business, technology

UNIT 2

PRACTICE 1

Answers will vary.

2. swimmer

PRACTICE 2

Answers will vary.

2. will finish

PRACTICE 3

1. swim
2. did (not) notice
3. enjoyed
4. slept
5. looked
6. took
7. went
8. sat
9. will be
10. watched

PRACTICE 4

1. sea
2. I
3. James
4. She
5. Birds
6. *Titanic*
7. They
8. children
9. Daisy
10. we

PRACTICE 5

1. are/were/will be
2. were
3. Were
4. is/was/will be
5. are/were
6. are
7. will be
8. am/will be
9. are/were/will be
10. are/will be

PRACTICE 6

1. S = kids, V = are/were/will be playing
2. S = Fish, V = were swimming
3. S = you, V = Were shopping
4. S = man, V = is/was/will be doing
5. S = friends, V = are/were being
6. S = You, V = are (not) leaving
7. S = moon, V = will be shining
8. S = I, V = am/will be leaving
9. S = children, V = are/were/will be watching
10. S = You, V = are/will be working

PRACTICE 7

S = water, V = covers. S = We, V = divide. S = oceans, V = are named. S = We, V = talk. S = seas, V = do (not) connect. S = seas, V = have. S = seas, V = share. S = Caribbean Sea and the Atlantic Ocean, V = do. S = water, V = forms. S = It, V = determines. S = It, V = contains. S = ocean, V = is. S = life, V = is.

PRACTICE 8

Answers will vary.

2. at

PRACTICE 9

1. S = We, V = went
2. S = woman, V = smiled
3. S = words, V = made
4. not a sentence
5. S = I, V = sent

6. not a sentence
7. S = you, V = will finish
8. S = Sam, V = danced
9. S = name, V = is
10. S = we, V = saw

PRACTICE 10

Answers will vary.

to the ocean/into our minds/of the ocean/in the Mariana Trench/near the Philippines/of the sea/on tiny particles/in the water/near the coast/about the amount/in it

PRACTICE 11

Answers will vary.

2. Steven is a happy man although he never has much money.

PRACTICE 12

Answers will vary.

2. Anne has a difficult time making decisions because her mother makes her nervous.

PRACTICE 13

Answers will vary.

Dependent clauses (from Practice 11):

1. S = we, V = finish
2. S = he, V = (never) has
3. S = man, V = talked
4. S = rain, V = continues
5. S = sun, V = shines
6. S = we, V = tried
7. S = show, V = is
8. S = you, V = have
9. S = you, V = want
10. S = baby, V = smiles
11. S = you, V = go
12. S = he, V = knew
13. S = teacher, V = is
14. S = who, V = spoke

Independent clauses (from Practice 12):

1. S = We, V = will go
2. S = Anne, V = has
3. S = I, V = will buy
4. S = police, V = drove
5. S = party, V = will be
6. S = professor, V = is
7. S = no one, V = knew
8. S = Sharks, V = are found
9. S = it, V = will be
10. S = we, V = stayed

PRACTICE 14

Answers will vary.

Dependent clause/independent clause pattern:

When we hear these words, questions pop into our minds.

S = we, V = hear; S = questions, V = pop

If the highest mountain in the world ... were placed in the Mariana Trench, almost three kilometres of water would still cover it!

S = mountain, V = were placed; S = three kilometres, V = would cover

When plant life mixes with the water near the coast, the water looks greener.

S = plant life, V = mixes; S = water, V = looks

Independent clause/dependent clause pattern:

The deep blue water of the ocean far from land reveals empty seas where little plant or animal life exists.

S = water, V = reveals; S = life, V = exists

This ocean water looks blue because the sun shines on tiny particles in the water.

S = water, V = looks; S = sun, V = shines

PRACTICE 15

Answers will vary.

1. Is Peter doing his homework?
2. There is a good show on television tonight.

PRACTICE 16

Answers will vary.

1. S = Peter, V = is doing
2. S = show, V = is

PRACTICE 17

Answers will vary.

READING 4: THE *TITANIC*

B. carried

E. of extremely wealthy and powerful people

F. even though the crew had been warned about dangerous icebergs in the area.

D. drowned or froze

C. , an oceanographer,

A. . The sinking

READING 5: *TSUNAMI* WAVES

A. , a Japanese word meaning "harbour wave."

D. from the air.

F. its height and destructive potential increase tremendously.

G. of a *tsunami*

C. on nearby islands

H. crashed into Japan and left

B. reached

E. from this Alaskan *tsunami*

I. . Although such waves are relatively rare,

READING 6: AN OCEAN VACATION

D. are the largest creatures on our planet

B. and other wildlife we're likely to see.

E. Many species of whale are threatened or endangered

A. swimming up to forty-eight kilometres per hour

C. popular eco-tourism activity

PRACTICE 18

Answers will vary. (Sample answers are underlined.)

1. The largest ocean <u>in the world is the Pacific</u>.
2. We usually speak of five different <u>oceans</u> even though one continuous body of ocean water actually covers <u>the entire Earth</u>.
3. The world's ocean affects <u>our weather and contains much of the world's food supply</u>.
4. The average depth <u>of the ocean is</u> about three kilometres.
5. In <u>1962 scientists (oceanographers)</u> found out that the Mariana Trench <u>(near the Philippines) is the deepest part of the ocean. It's eleven kilometres deep</u>.

6. Mt. Everest is the mountain that is the highest in the world.
7. Although male sea turtles don't return to land unless they are sick or injured, female sea turtles return to land to lay their eggs.
8. The *Titanic* left Southampton, England, on April 10, 1912, with 2228 passengers on board.
9. About 550 km from Newfoundland, the ship hit an iceberg and sank in less than three hours, taking about 1500 people to the bottom of the Atlantic Ocean.
10. The wreckage was found in 3810 m of water in 1985.

PRACTICE 19

Answers will vary. (Sample answers are underlined.)

Waves

Earthquakes and volcanic eruptions on the ocean bottom cause huge waves known as *tsunamis*. If you were on a boat in the open ocean when a *tsunami* passed under you, you probably would not feel it. However, it could still be traveling at a very high speed. *Tsunamis* become very dangerous when they near the coastline where they increase tremendously in height. *Tsunami* waves as high as thirty metres can hit the shore. They can be incredibly destructive. The *tsunami* waves created by the volcanic eruption of Krakatoa killed more than 36 000 people in 1883. In 1946 an undersea earthquake in the Aleutian Islands near Alaska caused *tsunami* waves that crashed into Hawaii in less than five hours, wiping out hundreds of people. People who live near the ocean must be aware of the danger of *tsunami* waves.

Watching Whales in Maritime Canada

The Bay of Fundy is part of the Atlantic Ocean, and it flows between New Brunswick and Nova Scotia. It has the highest tidal range in the world, as great as twenty-one metres. Whale watching is a favourite eco-tourism activity in the Bay of Fundy. Good whale-watching guides make sure that the boats do not chase or bother the whales. They keep a respectful distance from the animals. A group of whales is known as a pod. Humpback whales like to engage in playful activity. The fastest-swimming whale is the finback whale. The right whale is slow and swims near the surface in shipping lanes; therefore it is an endangered species.

UNIT 3

PRACTICE 1

All nouns are given; proper nouns are underlined.

1. Jack; Jill; hill
2. piggy; market
3. Mary; lamb
4. star
5. wind; snow
6. Jack Sprat; fat
7. Boys; girls; moon; day
8. Lucy Locket; pocket; Kitty Fisher
9. Bo Peep; sheep
10. King Cole; soul

PRACTICE 2

Answers will vary.

1. The sound of the wind woke me up from my nap on the couch.

2. I like anchovies, hot peppers, and double cheese on my pizza.
3. My daughter likes to ride a carousel at the fairground.
4. Whenever the grandmother sees the spring flowers, she is happy.
5. If I win the lottery, I'll get a house and a car right away.
6. We have to leave the house now if we want to catch the train.
7. Michelle wants those fish over there.
8. I want a bike for Christmas.
9. The little dog runs in the yard all the time.
10. A collie is my favourite kind of dog.

PRACTICE 3

1. parties
2. buzzes
3. responsibilities
4. thieves
5. kisses
6. libraries
7. countries
8. dishes
9. knives
10. loaves
11. armies
12. watches
13. scarves
14. strawberries
15. wishes

PRACTICE 4

1. man/woman/child
2. tooth
3. mouse
4. man/woman/child
5. foot
6. ox
7. oasis
8. man/woman/child
9. goose
10. sheep

Sentences using the plural forms:

1. The men/women/children run in the Toronto Rat Race every year.
2. My front teeth look crooked.
3. Those little mice scare most adults.
4. Those men/women/children like to read.
5. Your feet fit the slippers, Cinderella.
6. Oxen work as beasts of burden in many parts of the world.
7. Oases seem a welcome sight in the desert.
8. Those men/women/children want to be members of the legislature.
9. These Canada geese migrate south every year.
10. The sheep graze on grass.

PRACTICE 5

name – common, singular

Valentina Tereshkova – proper, singular

woman – common, singular

program – common, singular

jumper – common, singular

period – common, singular

years – common, plural

blast-off – common, singular

cosmonaut – common, singular

Earth – proper, singular

days – common, plural

June – proper, singular

Andrian Nikolayev – proper, singular

baby – common, singular

interest – common, singular

child – common, singular

parents – common, plural

space – common, singular

ambassador – common, singular

United Nations – proper, singular (This is tricky because it looks plural. Think about what it is, though. It's the name of a *single* organization that is composed of many nations.)

politics – common, singular/plural

PRACTICE 6

The complete subject is given and the simple subject is underlined.

1. James
2. The humidity of the night
3. The uncomfortable and stifling heat
4. James
5. A great, black, hairy, eight-legged tarantula spider
6. The spider and James
7. James
8. the poisonous tarantula
9. One long, hairy leg
10. The trembling, relieved man; the spider

PRACTICE 7

1. cost goes
2. choice is
3. sister enjoys
4. mess needs
5. man likes
6. neighbours want
7. steps have
8. *Titanic* attracts
9. snack ruins
10. offices belong

PRACTICE 8

Answers will vary.

1. My brothers return home every Christmas.
2. These groups perform rap.
3. The bridesmaids look beautiful in those pink dresses.
4. Those Canadians enjoy summer more than winter.
5. Happy children laugh frequently.
6. Snowflakes feel cold.
7. Shapes have a number of sides.
8. Sixteen moons revolve around the planet Jupiter.
9. Rick and Jane come to my cottage every summer.
10. Those cars need gas.

PRACTICE 9

Answers will vary.

1. My brother returns home every Christmas.
2. This group performs rap.

3. The bridesmaid looks beautiful in that pink dress.
4. That Canadian enjoys summer more than winter.
5. A happy child laughs frequently.
6. A snowflake feels cold.
7. A shape has a number of sides.
8. A moon revolves around the planet Jupiter.
9. Rick comes to my cottage every summer.
10. This car needs gas.

PRACTICE 10

Corrected verbs are underlined.

Tony <u>likes</u> ice cream a lot. His favourite flavours include mint chocolate chip and chocolate mousse. These two varieties both <u>involve</u> chocolate. Tony <u>thinks</u> that mint chocolate chip is a refreshing experience, and chocolate mousse <u>tastes</u> rich and creamy to him. His girlfriend, Penny, <u>dislikes</u> all ice cream, so Penny eats fresh fruit instead. Tony and Penny never <u>agree</u> about desserts. However, Penny still <u>believes</u> Tony is a really sweet guy. Maybe all those ice creams <u>make</u> him so sweet.

PRACTICE 11

1. My brother thinks about work all the time.
2. A snake scares little boys more than girls.
3. That girl dislikes spiders.
4. A rolling stone gathers no moss.
5. A holiday provides many opportunities to relax.
6. A massage relieves tension and stress.
7. This woman often attends rock concerts in the summer.
8. The student thinks that grammar is easy,
9. A grammar rule seems hard to grasp at first.
10. A Canadian believes in law, order, and good government.

PRACTICE 12

Answers will vary.

2. Bacon, eggs, and toast make a great breakfast.

PRACTICE 13

1. noun
2. verb
3. noun
4. verb
5. noun
6. noun
7. noun
8. verb
9. verb
10. verb

PRACTICE 14

1. verb
2. verb
3. noun
4. noun
5. noun
6. verb
7. verb

8. noun
9. noun
10. verb

PRACTICE 15

Answers will vary.

1. I love singing in a choir.

PRACTICE 16

1. My favourite sports are swimming, jogging, biking(,) and basketball.
2. The sign told us not to feed the birds, squirrels, raccoons(,) or bears.
3. Math, data processing, accounting(,) and business are the other courses I'm taking this semester.
4. no commas
5. The salad we ordered was made of Boston lettuce, black olives, diced potatoes, crunchy green beans, fresh tuna(,) and hard-boiled eggs.
6. Most of us hope to be able to earn a good salary, live in a comfortable house(,) and raise a happy family.
7. We found lots of interesting things in the back of Ferdinand's car: a Superman cape, a martini shaker, two dumbbells, a Ouija board, a miniature Swiss chalet(,) and a lobster trap.
8. no commas
9. Your house will sell faster if you weed the flower beds, fix the front door, paint the living room(,) and tidy up the basement.
10. The project will be completed quickly whether you choose Lisa, Eric, Bart, Roseanna(,) or me as your partner.

PRACTICE 17

1. a week's time
2. my cat's tail
3. the contract's date
4. the air conditioner's noise
5. the rain's sound

PRACTICE 18

1. the boys' ideas
2. the Jones' dog
3. their guests' voices
4. the twins' cries
5. Charles' wife

PRACTICE 19

1. I don't like my grandmother's cooking.
2. Can I borrow David's book?
3. That is Frank's house.
4. I'll see you in two weeks' time.
5. Linda's car was broken into last night.
6. The flowers' scent was sweet.
7. Your jacket's colour clashes with your pants.
8. The children's noise was too loud to ignore.
9. His dog's bark is worse than its bite.
10. One pizza's toppings were pepperoni, mushroom, onion, and hot peppers.

PRACTICE 20

1. name's
2. world's
3. Helen's

4. no apostrophes
5. father's
6. Helen's
7. husband's
8. Helen's
9. Troy's
10. no apostrophes
11. no apostrophes
12. side's

PRACTICE 21

For centuries it was believed the stories of the Greek and Trojan heroes written about by Homer in *The Iliad* and *The Odyssey* were make-believe. However, a German archaeologist, named Heinrich Schliemann, proved the ancient city of Troy had actually existed. As a child, he had loved the ancient Greek myths and heroic legends, and he desperately wanted to believe they were based in fact, not fantasy. Using clues he found in Homer's writing and in the Greek myths, he spent his adult life searching for the location, and then unearthing the ruins, of the city of Troy. Finding it became a mission he never gave up on, and in 1870 he found the site of the ancient city of Troy. It was near the Dardanelles, part of modern day Turkey. Excavations of the site uncovered a walled city, a great fortress, and a royal palace. Many artifacts were also uncovered, including a magnificent jewelled headdress; Schliemann believed Helen herself might actually have worn it.

PRACTICE 22

1. a. her; b. She
2. a. It; b. it
3. a. She; b. her
4. a. They; b. them
5. a. him; b. He
6. a. it; b. It
7. a. it; b. It
8. a. It; b. it
9. a. She; b. her
10. a. them; b. They

PRACTICE 23

Roberta Bondar has made herself a place in the history books. She is the first Canadian woman to go into space. Bondar was born in Sault Ste. Marie in 1945, and even as a small girl she dreamed of becoming a pilot. She had a distinguished academic career before becoming a member of the Canadian Space Agency. Roberta Bondar earned a B.Sc. in zoology and agriculture, following it with a Masters degree in experimental psychology. Next she gained a Ph.D. and M.D. in neurobiology. During this time, Roberta Bondar also learned to scuba dive and to fly. The pilot's licence, formidable academic credentials, and superb physical conditioning made her a natural candidate for the Canadian Space Agency, which works in partnership with NASA. She was in the first group of Canadian astronauts to be selected, and NASA trained her as an astronaut. It was on January 22, 1992, that Roberta Bondar blasted off into space as a Payload Specialist aboard the shuttle *Discovery*. During the eight days she was in space, Bondar was responsible for the health and well-being of the shuttle crew, as well as for conducting research into the effects of weightlessness on the human nervous system. Now a professor of space medicine at Ryerson Polytechnic University and associate professor of medicine at McMaster University, Dr. Bondar has earned her place among a very select and small group of women who have been in space.

PRACTICE 24

1. him
2. I
3. She and I
4. me
5. me
6. him
7. we
8. they
9. me
10. I

PRACTICE 25

1. I
2. me
3. you
4. You
5. you
6. you/him/her/it/them
7. us
8. I
9. me/us/you/him/her/them
10. I/he/she/they

PRACTICE 26

1. me/you/him/her/us/them
2. me/you/him/her/us/them
3. I
4. I
5. me/you/him/her/us/them
6. you/him/her/them
7. you; me/him/her/us/them
8. I
9. I
10. me/you/him/her

PRACTICE 27

1. makes
2. is
3. say
4. is; want
5. spends; gets
6. learn
7. Are; is; looks
8. pick
9. wags; sees
10. enjoy; makes

PRACTICE 28

Answers will vary.

1. We like watching old movies.

PRACTICE 29

The commuter is a modern day hero whose quest is to get to work on time. Like a knight of old, he battles the elements and overcomes obstacles just to get to work. He is the victim of rush hour. He crawls out of bed around 6 a.m. and grabs quick cups of coffee. Then he rushes off to the station. If he is lucky, he finds a parking spot right away and makes it to the platform before the train pulls out. Of course, if the commuter is on time, the train is late! Next, the commuter struggles to find a place on the train. Often no seat is available, so the commuter finds a standing-room-only spot. Of course, the poor commuter is never able to reach the pole or overhead handle, but since he is unable to move there is no chance for him to fall over. He endures these awful conditions for nearly an hour. When the commuter finally arrives at work, it's no wonder he feels exhausted.

PRACTICE 30

1. our
2. your
3. he
4. you
5. she
6. it
7. him
8. her
9. their
10. your

PRACTICE 31

Answers will vary.

1. Gordon said Sam would probably fail.
2. Jill said Marie should get her hair cut.
3. When Jeff saw the dog, it wagged its tail.
4. Kyle loves watching hockey games on TV and he wants to be a professional sportscaster.
5. Bruce thought of Hamid because he owed Hamid a favour.
6. Marcia finished stirring her coffee, rinsed the spoon, and drank the coffee.
7. At Laurier Academy the students have to wear uniforms.
8. Jackie loves numbers and hopes to be an accountant.
9. no errors
10. My car didn't stop when it hit the van.

PRACTICE 32

1. she
2. you
3. we
4. it
5. you
6. he
7. one
8. herself
9. I
10. us

PRACTICE 33

1. his
2. his; hers
3. their
4. theirs
5. Its
6. her
7. Its
8. theirs
9. Her
10. Its

PRACTICE 34

1. his
2. her
3. our

4. your
5. my
6. its
7. their
8. his
9. her
10. its

PRACTICE 35

1. He and I are going to the concert tomorrow.
2. It's not yours; it's mine.
3. My supervisor and I will attend the meeting.
4. We should know which car is ours.
5. The cat licked its dish clean.
6. no errors
7. Is this book hers?
8. Frank will give Jane and me a ride home.
9. Although it's only been a week since its tuneup, I think this car needs maintenance.
10. You and he are welcome any time.

PRACTICE 36

Simone has a wonderful mother. When I tell you this story you will understand why I admire Mrs. Raduca. When Simone was five years old, she felt that one of the measures of maturity was to walk home from school by herself. For her, the most embarrassing moment each day was when her mother arrived to take her home. She was certain all the bigger children thought she was a baby.

Her family lived quite close to her school. She begged and pleaded with her mother, promising to look carefully before crossing the one road on the way home from school. Finally her mother agreed, and she wrote a letter to Simone's teacher that explained Simone was allowed to come home by herself. After Simone's teacher read the letter, she smiled broadly and told the little girl that she could walk home alone. At that time Simone couldn't read, and she never knew that her mother was following her home each day at a safe distance. Years later, when Simone did discover the truth, she felt grateful that her mother had been sensitive enough to respect her independence.

PRACTICE 37

1. Who's
2. Whose
3. It's
4. whose
5. it's
6. who's
7. Who's
8. Whose
9. its
10. Who's

PRACTICE 38

Answers will vary.

1. Anybody who wants to come to the game can do so.

PRACTICE 39

1. its
2. their
3. him/her

4. his/her
5. his/her
6. him/her
7. his
8. her
9. his/her
10. his

PRACTICE 40

1. her
2. his; it
3. Whose
4. he
5. their; it
6. his; its
7. his/her
8. you; he
9. they; him
10. her

READING 2: A NOBEL PEACE PRIZE WINNER

D. heroic stature in the international arena was Lester B. Pearson.

E. He received this award in 1957

A. helped establish the Food and Agriculture Organization, which works to eliminate world hunger.

C. including Israel, Korea, and the Suez Canal.

B. Canada became the first nation to designate certain battalions of its armed forces to be used as international peacekeepers.

READING 3: THE GREAT ONE

D. his first goal in team play

B. In 1970, he was officially given his first nickname, "The Great Gretzky,"

F. his teammates and opponents were in their late teens and early twenties,

E. its association with his own hockey heroes

A. it has been his number ever since.

C. he was traded to the team where he achieved his first professional success

READING 4: ANANSI AND COMMON SENSE

B. people would turn to him for help

D. but he could charge a lot for his sensible advice and so he would become rich.

C. and then he put it into the biggest calabash he could find.

A. so he couldn't get a firm hold on the tree and he couldn't move his knees above his waist.

E. there was a piece of common sense he did not own

READING 5: TERRY FOX

C. which are named after him,

B. he was in hospital undergoing a long process of radiation and chemotherapy treatment,

F. it was to raise $1 million by running across Canada.

D. he was prepared to run fifty kilometres a day to raise money for his cause.

E. his route followed the course of the St. Lawrence into Montreal;

A. He developed blisters and sores on his stump that bled onto his prosthesis.

G. his arrival in Thunder Bay, Fox was taken to hospital for a check-up.

UNIT 4

PRACTICE 1

1. like (present)
2. experienced (past)
3. will understand (future)
4. seem (present)
5. make (present)
6. need (present)
7. will finish (future)
8. proofread (present)
9. worked (past)
10. did enjoy (past)

PRACTICE 2

Answers will vary.

1. The children love to play in the park.
2. My dog seems to growl at strangers.
3. The teacher wants us to complete the assignment.
4. Deciding whom to invite to a party is not easy.
5. The manager asked me to work overtime on Saturday.
6. I enjoy the weekends when I get the chance to garden.
7. To go or not to go, that is the question.
8. She plans to visit next year.
9. You always try to be polite to your parents.
10. We want you to be happy.

PRACTICE 3

1. is
2. has
3. did
4. was
5. is
6. had
7. will do
8. will be
9. has; does/will do
10. has

PRACTICE 4

1. is
2. were
3. were
4. are
5. was
6. was
7. is
8. was; was
9. are
10. is

PRACTICE 5

1. is
2. is
3. is
4. is

5. are
6. am
7. is
8. are
9. is
10. are

PRACTICE 6

My favourite teacher is Mr. Desmond. Even now after all these years, I have very strong memories of him. He was my teacher in grade five. Every morning, before the announcements and "O Canada," he did stretches with the class. He used to say that the physical exercises were our wake-up call, and that we had to get the blood moving to our brains. He also had a great sense of humour and did strange things in class. I have never forgotten about projectiles and velocity because he threw chalk or balls of paper at us when we were noisy. Then he did an impromptu lesson on the science of throwing. He was six feet four inches tall, so he was a powerful presence in a class of ten-year-olds. He never had to shout or even raise his voice to get our attention; every kid in his class wanted to pay attention to him. He was a great teacher.

PRACTICE 7

Coaching a little league soccer team is a big responsibility. Yvonne and Terry are the coaches of a team of five- to six-year-olds, and they have eighteen children on their team. Because a soccer team has only eleven players on the field at a time, the coaches have to make a lot of substitutions to ensure that every child has an opportunity to play. This is not as easy as it sounds because the team also wants to win its games. Yvonne is the one with experience as she was a coach last year, and she did such a great job the league asked her to come back again. Terry still has a lot of doubts about her ability as a coach, but with Yvonne's encouragement and help she has a lot of fun on game night. The team has a game once a week. Because the children on the team are so young, each game is only one hour long. The game has two twenty-minute halves and a break of about ten minutes for the children to have drinks and snacks. Before each game, Yvonne and Terry do warm-up exercises with the children for half an hour. First Terry does stretches with the team, and when she has the children's attention, she and Yvonne do a lap around the field with them. Then Yvonne is in charge of ball-control activities. The three activities are dribbling, passing, and shooting. The team and the coaches have a lot of fun each week. They hope the team will be champions next month.

PRACTICE 8

1. It isn't time to go now.
2. He wasn't late for his appointment yesterday.
3. You can't give me a hand with the laundry.
4. They weren't watching TV last night.
5. The Leafs didn't play well in their last game.
6. She doesn't like reading mystery novels.
7. We didn't go for a meal at that new Indian restaurant.
8. The VCR isn't working now.

9. You won't be late for your practice.
10. Denton doesn't enjoy journal writing.

PRACTICE 9

Answers will vary.

1. He isn't lost.

PRACTICE 10

Sentences will vary.

1. impossible
2. irregular
3. illogical
4. disrespect
5. unreliable
6. illegal
7. unable
8. unlock
9. imperfect
10. illegible
11. disappear
12. incapable

PRACTICE 11

1. seems
2. consists
3. believe; makes; go
4. choose; inherit
5. possess
6. enjoy
7. call
8. rely
9. get
10. call
11. know; chat
12. consider
13. come
14. like; consider
15. shares; trust

PRACTICE 12

1. rushes
2. lunches
3. uses
4. fusses
5. crushes
6. misses
7. loses
8. chases
9. patches
10. passes
11. expresses
12. asks
13. punches
14. pushes
15. catches

PRACTICE 13

Answers will vary.

2. I find the vegetables are fresher at Vega's fruit stall.

PRACTICE 14

1. fries
2. plays
3. says

4. cries
5. tries
6. stays
7. tries
8. lies
9. delays
10. applies

PRACTICE 15

1. thought
2. began
3. chose
4. slept
5. sped
6. threw
7. taught
8. ate
9. felt
10. wore

PRACTICE 16

Answers will vary.

1. We thought we heard a strange noise.

PRACTICE 17

1. They walked to the pool every day.
2. He usually played second base.
3. We hurried to school on Mondays.
4. You worried too much about the future.
5. Carlene sang with the choir.
6. The dogs ran in the park.
7. I drank diet cola.
8. The sun rose in the east.
9. I wrote a letter to my girlfriend every day.
10. The premier threw the first pitch at the game.

PRACTICE 18

1. heard
2. said
3. took
4. thought
5. felt
6. drew
7. chose
8. had
9. wore
10. bought
11. were
12. cost
13. drank
14. made
15. ate
16. bit
17. got
18. went
19. came
20. brought

PRACTICE 19

Answers will vary.

1. We studied for over two hours.

PRACTICE 20

Answers will vary.

1. I will go shopping with you later.

PRACTICE 21

Answers will vary.

1. After I go shopping, I'll take the car to the garage. *or* After I go shopping, I am going to take the car to the garage.

PRACTICE 22

Answers will vary.

1. Ben is playing drums in the garage at the moment.

PRACTICE 23

Answers will vary.

1. When I see you, I'll give you my decision.

PRACTICE 24

1. been
2. being
3. been
4. being
5. been
6. been
7. been
8. been
9. being
10. being
11. been
12. been
13. being
14. been
15. been

PRACTICE 25

1. is
2. was
3. has been
4. been
5. is
6. will be
7. will be
8. were/are; was
9. is; am
10. been

PRACTICE 26

Answers will vary.

PRACTICE 27

1. become
2. chosen
3. told
4. said
5. heard
6. given
7. thought
8. taken
9. spoken
10. written
11. given
12. said

PRACTICE 28

1. I saw Diane last night.
2. No one did/has done a better job than Jason on the assignment.
3. correct
4. Paul came to the party alone last night.
5. He has grown a lot since I last saw him.
6. Mary and Joanna have gone to the library to study.
7. correct
8. Mike began college before Labour Day.
9. They ate/have eaten all the chocolate cake I was saving for dessert tonight.
10. correct

PRACTICE 29

1. correct
2. You have broken your arm.
3. She should have given him a piece of her mind.
4. Peter has gone to Las Vegas on the four o'clock flight.
5. Madison has chosen her clothes carefully.
6. They could have taken the last bus home.
7. correct
8. The sun must have risen, but there are too many clouds to be sure.
9. I have done my best work for you.
10. He would have written the answers carefully if he had enough time.

PRACTICE 30

Angela was helping her mother to tidy the closet in the spare room. She came across a box of old photographs that she hadn't seen before. Most of the photographs weren't in colour. They were in black and white. Angela thought these photos hadn't been taken recently. However, when she looked at the photos more closely, she felt a certain young woman in many of them looked just like her. Angela didn't have the same hairstyle or wear such unfashionable clothes. Apart from these facts, the young woman could have been Angela, but that was impossible. Angela had no idea who the woman was, so she asked her mother. Angela's mother went through a couple of the photos and laughed. She told Angela that they weren't pictures of Angela, but of her grandmother.

PRACTICE 31

Angela is helping her mother to tidy the closet in the spare room. She comes across a box of old photographs that she hasn't seen before. Most of the photographs aren't in colour. They are in black and white. Angela thinks these photos haven't been taken recently. However, when she looks at the photos more closely, she feels a certain young woman in many of them looks just like her. Angela doesn't have the same hairstyle or wear such unfashionable clothes. Apart from these facts, the young woman could be Angela, but that is impossible. Angela has no idea who the woman is, so she asks her mother. Angela's mother goes through a couple of the photos and laughs. She tells Angela that they aren't pictures of Angela, but of her grandmother.

PRACTICE 32

Ever since he was a little boy, Frank has loved to read. Back then books opened new worlds for him. He identified with the heroes in novels, so he solved mysteries or he had adventures in his imagination. Nowadays, he always reads on the subway, but last night when he was reading a book, he became very engrossed in it. He was concentrating so hard that he missed his stop. By the time he realized this, he had gone five stops beyond his destination. Of course he hurried to get off the train at the next station. He was angry and embarrassed. He felt that everyone noticed his mistake. That wasn't true. No one paid any attention to him. When he got off the train, he was lucky. A train that was going in the other direction arrived at the platform only a minute later. Frank was able to board it and to return to his station. He didn't read on his return journey.

PRACTICE 33

The subject–verb agreement corrections are capitalized.

My great-grandmother, who is still as lively as a cricket, LOVES to tell stories of when she was young. She was born in 1918, so society HAS undergone a lot of changes in her lifetime. For example, when she was a young woman, dating WAS a completely different experience. After all, who was a suitable date? Of course, my mother and I still DISAGREE about this issue, but for my great-grandmother the rules WERE rigorous. My great-grandmother was not permitted to date anyone whom her parents considered unsuitable. Suitable young men came from the same social class; that is, they WERE working in a job similar to her father's. If a young man wanted to date my great-grandmother, he HAD to be introduced to and approved by her parents. Finally, if any man was capable of meeting her parents' requirements of family background, education, and employment, he was permitted to "walk out with" her. Even this HAD a catch to it. A chaperone always accompanied the couple on the date. My great-grandmother TELLS wonderful stories about how she and her dates WERE able to avoid the chaperone and actually get to know each other. After all, my great-grandmother didn't want to marry a stranger.

PRACTICE 34

Answers will vary.

Yesterday morning, my clock radio came on at 6:30.

By 6:33 I managed to open my eyes.

It wasn't until 6:34 when a soprano hit a high note that I realized my radio was tuned to the wrong station. Who needs opera, especially first thing in the morning?

It took me a couple of minutes to re-tune the radio, but by 6:36 I had my favourite station on the air.

The weather forecast at 6:40 promised heavy rain.

That depressed me, so it took me five more minutes to crawl out of bed.

By seven o'clock I finished in the shower and started to get dressed.

At 7:10 I was still looking for a clean shirt.

When I got downstairs at 7:15, I discovered I was out of coffee, juice, and milk.

I managed to have a quick drink of water before leaving at 7:20.

It wasn't my day! My car wouldn't start, so at 7:30 I gave up and went to catch the bus.

It took a while to get to the bus stop, and in fifteen minutes I was soaked to the skin.

Of course the bus was late, so at ten past eight I gave up. I went to the donut store for an intake of calories and caffeine.

PRACTICE 35

Answers will vary.

PRACTICE 36

Answers will vary.

1. Yesterday he went home early, but tomorrow he'll stay late.
2. They will see you later today if they finish their work.
3. She hates chocolate now, but when she was a child she loved it.
4. The moon revolves around the Earth. It takes the moon twenty-eight days to complete its cycle.
5. Before we met her, we believed blondes had more fun.
6. When he was seven, he began to study karate. Now he is a black belt.
7. Next year I will go to Mexico. I love hot weather and the beach.
8. The dog barked when it saw me. It always does that.
9. You are the first person to visit our new home since we moved in last week.
10. Jennifer wants to see *Hunks from Outer Space*, but I heard that movie is boring.

PRACTICE 37

2. get
3. do; have
4. am
5. moved; came
6. cuts
7. shovels
8. wonder; do
9. share; keep; is
10. will be

PRACTICE 38

Even today, Luke vividly remembers his very first day in school when he was five years old. His memory of that day is so clear even now because he had such an embarrassing experience back then. On his first day, he arrived at school at 9 a.m., and by 9:30 he was desperate to go to the washroom. He knew that he had to ask permission. Of course, the teacher said yes and Luke went to the washroom. That was the start of his embarrassment. At the age of five, Luke knew how to go to the bathroom by himself, but he went to the girls' washroom. Luke didn't know boys and girls have/had their own washrooms in school. When he came back into the classroom, some of the children began to tease him. This made Luke unhappy and he cried so much that the teacher sent him home at recess.

PRACTICE 39

Corrected verbs are underlined.

My favourite childhood memories relate to my grandma and the way she taught me to cook. With my grandma, I've studied baking since I was a little boy. When I was too small to see over the top of the counter, I loved to stand by my grandma when she was cooking. If she was baking a sponge cake, I heard the eggs as she cracked their shells and whisked them up. Then she bent down with the bowl and showed me the golden egg froth. She put aside the frothy eggs and beat butter and sugar together. When she added the flour, I saw she worked hard to blend the mixture. As soon as she had mixed the eggs and some vanilla into her mixture, it was my turn. Grandma carefully placed the bowl on my lap and I held it tight. My grandma convinced me that without my effort the cake wouldn't rise. While my grandma greased the cake pans and checked the oven temperature, I stirred that batter with all my strength. Once the cake was in the oven, my favourite part came: cleaning the bowl.

PRACTICE 40

1. All of the chocolate chip ice cream was eaten by Roger.
2. The ball was caught by that boy.
3. That huge bone was buried by the dog last week.
4. My beautiful red rose bush was destroyed by the storm.
5. The terrified rabbit was mesmerized by the snake.

PRACTICE 41

1. City council reached consensus on the new subway line late last night.
2. My uncle is renovating that dilapidated, old house on the corner.
3. His own dog bit Mark yesterday.
4. My cat mauled that poor little bird.
5. Drillco has donated the award for Student Achievement in Engineering this year.

PRACTICE 42

1. Someone built my house in 1890.
2. Someone started a fire in the West End this morning.
3. Someone will mail this letter as soon as possible.
4. Someone has forbidden people to walk on the grass.
5. Someone has discovered the *Titanic* deep in the Atlantic.
6. At this moment, someone is giving Bob a tetanus shot.

PRACTICE 43

1. The stop sign was hit last night.
2. The directions to the camp have been lost.
3. The last piece of chocolate cake has been eaten.
4. Your account is being closed.
5. The restless students were bored.

PRACTICE 44

Answers will vary; no answers are suggested for this practice as they depend on careful reading as well as recognition of grammar.

UNIT 5

PRACTICE 1

Answers will vary.

2. , and/but
3. , but/yet
4. , so
5. , but/yet
6. , for
7. , nor
8. , so
9. , or
10. , but/yet

PRACTICE 2

Answers will vary.

2. I studied math for hours every night, but I still failed the test.

PRACTICE 3

Answers will vary.

2. We vacationed in Jamaica last winter, and we visited Prince Edward Island in the summer.
3. Minh's mother speaks English, but his father speaks Vietnamese.
4. In 1954, sixteen-year-old Marilyn Bell became the first person to swim Lake Ontario, and she later swam the English Channel and Juan de Fuca Strait.
5. Pat started college to study nursing, but she finished with a degree in engineering.
6. The family worked day and night in their store, for they wanted to achieve a higher standard of living.
7. I don't have any interest in hockey, nor do I have any interest in baseball.
8. Carolyn wanted to meet a new man, so she put a personal ad in the newspaper.
9. Carolyn got a lot of phone calls, but the men all sounded a little weird.
10. Sarah earned the highest marks in her program, so she got free tuition for next year.

PRACTICE 4

Answers will vary.

2. Gary applied for a job at Burger King, and he got it.
3. I don't like spicy foods, nor do I like sweet foods.
4. David may go to Red Deer College, or he may attend the University of Manitoba.
5. The snow fell all night, so the roads were impassable in the morning.
6. I love to read mystery novels, for the plot twists always keep me interested.
7. Linda knows how to ski, for she grew up in Whistler, B.C.
8. Jack bought a fancy sports car, but he never drives it.
9. Ron visited Niagara Falls for the first time, but he was too scared to look into the gorge.
10. Our peacekeeping forces are respected in the world, and most Canadians are proud of them.

PRACTICE 5

1. pancakes; Roger
2. moods; rainy
3. long; it
4. 1999; he
5. comedies; I
6. anymore; they
7. lifestyle; they
8. responsibility; young
9. August; you
10. ranger; he

PRACTICE 6

1. The windows of the house were dark, so we assumed no one was home.
2. Hockey is usually played by young people, yet people of all ages can play golf.
3. The homeless man was pale and cold, for he hadn't eaten all day.
4. Roch Carrier's "The Hockey Sweater" is a very popular Canadian story; most people read it during their school years.
5. He bought a car with a stick shift, but he didn't know how to drive it.
6. He doesn't like to skate, nor does he like to ski.
7. I don't know how to play tennis, yet I would like to learn.
8. A good education will increase your earning potential; it will make you a more informed citizen.
9. Sherry hated to mow the lawn, but it's a job that must be done.
10. Lorne is fascinated by the history of golf, so he is always searching for books on the subject.

PRACTICE 7

Answers will vary.

2. year; however, it
3. boss; meanwhile, I
4. racehorses; for example, Northern
5. dancer; nevertheless, I
6. thoroughly; then you
7. diploma; furthermore, he
8. years; consequently, she
9. year; thus, he
10. Amy; in fact, she

PRACTICE 8

1. Dierdre hoped to meet the handsome stranger on her cruise; however, he came to dinner with his wife.
2. Dierdre hoped to meet the handsome stranger on her cruise; he came to dinner with his wife, however.
3. Dierdre hoped to meet the handsome stranger on her cruise; he came to dinner, however, with his wife.
4. It is hard for me to wake up in the morning; therefore, I need three cups of coffee before class.
5. I've decided, nevertheless, to give up caffeine for a week.
6. At first, we wanted to take our vacation in Cuba; instead, we decided to go to Mexico.

7. At first, we wanted to take our vacation in Cuba; we decided, instead, to go to Mexico.
8. Joanna and Rex are excellent dancers; for example, they know swing, salsa, disco, and merengue.
9. Joanna and Rex are excellent dancers; they know, for example, swing, salsa, disco, and merengue.
10. We usually eat lunch at Flo's Diner; on the other hand, it would be nice to try a new restaurant.

PRACTICE 9

Answers will vary.

2. I studied math for hours every night; therefore, I got an A on the final exam.

PRACTICE 10

1. We have a beautiful living room, but guests always gather in the kitchen.
2. Swimming is very good exercise; it firms and tones the body.
3. Meet me at the corner, or meet me at the pub.
4. The traffic in Vancouver is very slow, for there are no expressways through town.
5. The Internet is a good way to do research; in addition, it provides a way to make new friends.
6. Adapting to college is difficult for many people, and they need to be prepared for the challenges.
7. My mom's birthday is August 1; however, she won't tell us how old she is.
8. There is no spell-check feature on the computer; therefore, you'll have to use your dictionary.
9. Peter eats all the time and doesn't exercise, so he is thirty pounds overweight.
10. The car ran out of gas on the deserted road; meanwhile, it was getting colder and darker all the time.

PRACTICE 11

Answers will vary.

2. I saw the new Flaberciser exercise machine on the Shopping Channel, and I had to buy it.

PRACTICE 12

Answers will vary.

PRACTICE 13

Answers will vary.

1. As soon as
2. when
3. unless
4. Although
5. because
6. if
7. Wherever
8. since
9. Unless
10. Before

PRACTICE 14

2. Because Mark had never finished high school, he was unable to get a well-paying job.
3. You'll never finish the project unless some of the staff help you.
4. Fred and Phyllis have lots of friends wherever they travel.

5. While we were away for the weekend, the robbers broke into our house.
6. As soon as we got back and saw the damage, we called the police.
7. Until the baby gets a bit older, we can't take him to the opera.
8. I want to know whether he finishes the cleanup or not.
9. The weather turned lovely when they arrived in Florida.
10. Jaron's calculus marks were very good even though he hadn't had to study very hard.

PRACTICE 15

Answers will vary.

2. We will be happy to provide the service after you pay your bill.

PRACTICE 16

Answers will vary.

2. Because the computer industry is thriving, Marla enrolled in a programming course at college.
3. We cleaned the house when we heard you were visiting for the weekend.
4. Although the professor's class is very demanding, students like his teaching methods.
5. If you intend to study abroad, you must get a student visa.
6. We want to see *Terminator 15* before it leaves the movie theatre on Friday.
7. We all go to the clubs to party when the school semester ends.
8. I can't skate well enough to play hockey although I tried very hard to learn.
9. I have loved that woman since I first met her.
10. You must make lots of money if you want to live in a mansion.

PRACTICE 17

2. Martha cried as her boyfriend boarded the airplane.
3. Harold is in excellent shape although he is almost fifty.
4. My son has dark hair; my daughter has bright red hair.
5. Debra will meet us in Ecuador, or she will meet us in Chile.
6. The team had only competed together once; nevertheless, they won the tournament.
7. He took the job at the dump because he needed the money.
8. Diane wants to be a flight attendant; however, she is afraid of flying.
9. Whenever people get hungry on the road, they want to eat quickly.
10. The copy machine in the office is broken, so we can't make a duplicate of the contract.

PRACTICE 18

2. Martha cried when her boyfriend boarded the airplane.
3. Harold is in excellent shape, but he is almost fifty.
4. My son has dark hair although my daughter has bright red hair.
5. Debra will not meet us in Ecuador, nor will she meet us in Chile.
6. The team had only competed together once, yet they won the tournament.

7. He took the job at the dump since he needed the money.
8. Diane wants to be a flight attendant, but she is afraid of flying.
9. If people get hungry on the road, they want to eat quickly.
10. The copy machine in the office is broken; as a result, we can't make a duplicate of the contract.

PRACTICE 19

2. Call us from the airport when your plane arrives.
3. You'll be able to get a good job if you graduate from college.
4. Because Roger was failing math, he dropped the course.
5. We can go to the game if we manage to buy hockey tickets.
6. While Betty worked as a prison guard, her husband stayed home with the kids.
7. People's lives can be destroyed because they are addicted to alcohol.
8. Although I have lots of good ideas, I'm afraid to present them in front of a group.
9. Even though Canada is a huge country geographically, it has about one-tenth the population of the United States.
10. When you need a place to stay, you can use our spare bedroom.

PRACTICE 20

Answers will vary.

2. Alligators can run very quickly, but they can't run very far.

PRACTICE 21

Answers will vary.

READING 2: WHY CANADIAN FOOTBALL IS BETTER THAN AMERICAN FOOTBALL

B. because Canadian football can be a much more exciting game.

A. and that larger space makes the game more exciting.

D. Second, there are three downs (chances to move the ball) in Canadian football as opposed to four.

C. that NFL football lacks.

READING 3: GOLF VS. TENNIS

D. and you're not sure that you have time for organized team sports.

C. If you walk instead of riding in a cart,

E. you'll play outside in beautiful surroundings;

B. who become close friends over years of playing together.

F. when the golf course is covered with snow.

A. on the other hand,

READING 4: CANADIAN BECOMES WORLD'S FASTEST HUMAN

E. who won it long before Johnson and Bailey.

C. childhood rheumatic fever had left him with a damaged heart.

D. but the stronger competition of the Olympic Games remained ahead of him.

B. so he had to run flat-out each race.

A. On day two, Williams qualified for the final by finishing second in the semifinal race

G. To the cheers of the world and the deep emotions of his fellow Canadians,

H. Percy Williams had won two Olympic gold medals

F. in a parade through the city.

PRACTICE 22

Answers will vary.

1. larger
2. twelve players; eleven
3. a single
4. Canadian; American
5. with other people
6. walk the course; riding in a cart
7. handicapping
8. indoors
9. expensive
10. 1928
11. Ben Johnson; lost; a banned substance
12. Vancouver, British Columbia; Amsterdam, Holland
13. gold medal; four
14. behind; won
15. hero; gave him a huge parade

UNIT 6

The content of this unit engages the learners in looking at a whole paragraph rather than discrete grammatical items. The practices for the most part require learners to generate their own writing. Answers are not supplied for all of the practices in this unit.

PRACTICE 1

The popularity of Mickey Mouse has endured for over seventy years.

PRACTICE 2

1. <u>Fall</u> is always my favourite time of the year.
2. The <u>development of writing</u> was one of the greatest achievements in human history.
3. The <u>Blue Jays</u> have never matched their achievement in 1993.
4. <u>Vancouver's weather</u> dampens the spirit.
5. <u>Learning to ski</u> is not so very difficult.
6. The day I met my girlfriend was <u>the luckiest day of my life</u>.
7. <u>Living on your own</u> can be a challenge.
8. I hate <u>shopping</u>, especially in malls.
9. My <u>part-time job</u> does more than pay my tuition.
10. The <u>first snow</u> of the winter is beautiful.

PRACTICE 4

The topic sentences are identified, but your reasons for selecting them will vary.

1. Do you know the story of how Canada got its name?
2. Although we aren't sure when human beings began to speak to each other, we have a much better idea of when they began to write.

3. Clearly, the ocean plays a critical role in Earth's habitability.
4. The simple lead in your pencil has a complex origin.
5. The topic sentence is a vital component of any paragraph.
6. Why is the ocean blue?
7. Psychological studies have demonstrated that the pupil of the eye is a very accurate indicator of a person's response to a situation.
8. A dog is man's best friend, so they say.

Index

To the owner of this book

We hope that you have enjoyed Dasgupta and Waldman's *Reading Writing Basics* (ISBN 0-17-616716-1), and we would like to know as much about your experiences with this text as you would care to offer. Only through your comments and those of others can we learn how to make this a better text for future readers.

School ________________ Your instructor's name ________________________

Course ___________ Was the text required? _______ Recommended? _____

1. What did you like the most about *Reading Writing Basics?*

____

____

____

2. How useful was this text for your course?

____

____

____

3. Do you have any recommendations for ways to improve the next edition of this text?

____

____

____

4. In the space below or in a separate letter, please write any other comments you have about the book. (For example, please feel free to comment on reading level, writing style, terminology, design features, and learning aids.)

____

____

____

____

Optional

Your name ______________________________ Date __________________

May Nelson Thomson Learning quote you, either in promotion for *Reading Writing Basics* or in future publishing ventures?

Yes _______ No _______

Thanks!

You can also send your comments to us via e-mail at **college@nelson.com**

PLEASE TAPE SHUT. DO NOT STAPLE.

TAPE SHUT

TAPE SHUT

FOLD HERE

Nelson

Canada Post Corporation
Société canadienne des postes

Postage paid
if mailed in Canada
Business Reply

Port payé
si posté au Canada
Réponse d'affaires

0066102399 01

0066102399-M1K5G4-BR01

NELSON THOMSON LEARNING
MARKET AND PRODUCT DEVELOPMENT
PO BOX 60225 STN BRM B
TORONTO ON M7Y 2H1

TAPE SHUT

TAPE SHUT